Scottish Philosophy in America

Edited and Introduced
by James J.S. Foster

IMPRINT ACADEMIC

Copyright © James J.S. Foster, 2012

The moral rights of the author have been asserted.
No part of this publication may be reproduced in any form
without permission, except for the quotation of brief passages
in criticism and discussion.

Published in the UK by Imprint Academic
PO Box 200, Exeter EX5 5YX, UK

Published in the USA by Imprint Academic
Philosophy Documentation Center
PO Box 7147, Charlottesville, VA 22906-7147, USA

ISBN 9781845401610

A CIP catalogue record for this book is available from the
British Library and US Library of Congress

Full series details:

www.imprint-academic.com/losp

Contents

Series Editor Note   v

Introduction   1

1. William Smith (1727–1803)   11
   Reading I: Religion and Science   12

2. Benjamin Rush (1746–1813)   27
   Reading II: Thoughts on Common Sense   29

3. John Witherspoon (1723–1794)   34
   Reading III: Introduction to Moral Philosophy   35
   Reading IV: Internal Sensation   41
   Reading V: The Nature, Foundation, and Obligation of Virtue   46

4. James Wilson (1742–1798)   55
   Reading VI: Sensation, Consciousness, and Memory   57
   Reading VII: Judgment, Reason, and Common Sense   71

5. Samuel Stanhope Smith (1751–1819)   93
   Reading VIII: The Active Powers of Human Nature   94
   Reading IX: Volition   110

6. Archibald Alexander (1772–1851)   125
   Reading X: Miracles   126

7. William Ellery Channing (1780–1842)   138
   Reading XI: Slavery   140
   Reading XII: Conscience and Prejudice   149

8. Alexander Campbell (1788–1866)	155
Reading XIII: On the Limits of Philosophy	157
9. James McCosh (1811–1894)	184
Reading XIV: What an American Philosophy Should Be	186
10. Charles Sanders Peirce (1839–1914)	205
Reading XV: Pragmat(ic)ism and Common Sense	206
Index of Names	215

Series Editor's Note

The principal purpose of volumes in this series is not to provide scholars with accurate editions, but to make the writings of Scottish philosophers accessible to a new generation of modern readers in an attractively produced and competitively priced format. In accordance with this purpose, certain changes have been made to the original texts:
- Spelling and punctuation have been modernized.
- In some cases the selections have been given new titles.
- Some original footnotes and references have not been included.
- Some extracts have been shortened from their original length.
- Quotations from Greek have been transliterated, and passages in languages other than English translated, or omitted altogether.

Care has been taken to ensure that in no instance do these amendments truncate the argument or alter the meaning intended by the original author. For readers who want to consult the original texts, full bibliographical details are provided for each extract.

The Library of Scottish Philosophy was originally an initiative of the Centre for the Study of Scottish Philosophy at the University of Aberdeen. The first six volumes, published in 2004, were commissioned with financial support from the Carnegie Trust for the Universities of Scotland. In 2006 the CSSP moved to Princeton where it became one of three research centers within the Special Collections of Princeton Theological Seminary, and with the Seminary's financial support more volumes have been published. *Scottish Philosophy in America* is the thirteenth volume in the series and has been prepared for publication by James Foster.

Acknowledgements

The CSSP gratefully acknowledges financial support from the Carnegie Trust and Princeton Theological Seminary, the enthusiasm and excellent service of the publisher Imprint Academic, and the permission of the University of Aberdeen Special Collections and Libraries to use the engraving of the Faculty of Advocates (1829) as the logo for the series.

Gordon Graham,
Princeton, January 2012

James J.S. Foster

Introduction

I. Pre-Revolutionary America

The one hundred years between the first half of the eighteenth century and the second half of the nineteenth mark out a period of remarkable intellectual achievement in Scotland. On account of the lasting and significant impact that the work of Scottish thinkers had during this time on the fields of science, philosophy, economics, and politics, this period has often been labelled 'the Scottish Enlightenment'. In the pre-Revolutionary era in America, the philosophy of the Scottish Enlightenment influenced the intellectual climate of the British colonies in chiefly two ways. The first was straightforwardly academic and literary. Volumes by Scottish philosophers such as Henry Home (Lord Kames), Francis Hutcheson, and Adam Ferguson were frequently found alongside those of their English and French peers in the libraries of educated colonials. Accordingly, the writers of the Scottish Enlightenment were part of the general European influence on the intellectual climate of America. In this capacity, Scottish philosophy had a measurable impact on academic work in the colonies: as the influence of Thomas Reid and David Hume on Benjamin Rush's writings on epistemology (see Reading II) and on the future Supreme Court Justice James Wilson's *Lectures on Law* (see Reading VI and VII) attest. Discounting regional and confessional differences, however, the Scots were at this time no more or less influential than their British and Continental contemporaries; all of whom stood beneath the long shadow of the great English triumvirate of Bacon, Newton and Locke.

More significantly, the Scottish Enlightenment was also pedagogically influential in pre-Revolutionary America. Although the British colonists were, overall, by no means as culturally advanced as their European cousins, several colleges — including Harvard, Yale, Princeton, and Penn — were established during this era. In both the structure and the staffing of these institutions, Scottish Enlightenment thinking played an important role. In contrast to the more theoretically oriented dons of Oxford and Cambridge, educators in the colonies saw higher education as a method for training capable and responsible citizens. They therefore found themselves in much agreement with the ancient but similarly practical universities of Scotland. Thus, for example, when William Smith set out to write his *A General Idea of the College of Mirania* (see Reading I), which would later serve as the blueprint for the College of Philadelphia (now University of Pennsylvania), he looked first to integrated pedagogy of Marischal and King's College in Aberdeen for inspiration. Further, in constant need of English-speaking professors to fill their faculties, newly founded American colleges frequently sought graduates of Scottish institutions. Although often initially reluctant to relocate to what was then the western edge of civilization, upon arriving in the New World, Scottish educators frequently played formative roles in the education of the Revolutionary generation.

II. The Early Days of the Republic

Due to the personal contact between leaders in the Revolutionary generation and educators steeped in Scottish Enlightenment thinking, the influence of Scottish philosophy increased during the time surrounding the war. Thomas Jefferson, for example, who was mentored by the Scottish William Small at The College of William and Mary, frequently attested to his life-long admiration for the moral philosophy of Francis Hutcheson and political writings of Henry Home (Lord Kames). Similarly, there is good reason to believe that James Madison, who attended the College of New Jersey (now Princeton University) during the presidency of Rev. John Witherspoon (see Readings III–V) drew heavily on the writings of Kames, Smith, and Hume during the composition of his immensely influential pamphlet 'Federalist Number 10'. Further increasing the stature of Scottish philosophy in America, the years of the Revolution and the founding of the United States also coincided with what may be considered the high-water mark of the Enlightenment in Scotland. Famously, Adam Smith published *The Wealth of Nations* in the momentous year of 1776; while Reid published the *Essays on the Intellectual Powers of Man* in 1785, drawing further attention to Hume's previously under-appreciated *Treatise* (1739) and *Enquiries* (1748 and 1751). Yet, for all this, the philosophy of the Scottish Enlightenment during this period is still better seen as part of the pan-European intellectual influence on America than as a single tradition. For, even as the stature of English writers withered in the United States under the heat of revolutionary fervour, the popularity of France's *philosophes* flourished on account of the close political ties between the two young republics. Further, although the Scottish luminaries of the day, like the great majority of intellectuals in the late eighteenth century, were near-unanimous in their admiration of Baconianism, there was as yet too much diversity in their methods and considered opinions to warrant the now-common, if misleading, identification of Scottish Enlightenment philosophy with Common-Sense Realism.

In the final years of the eighteenth century, as the optimism of the early stages of the French Revolution rapidly devolved into the horror for which it is remembered today, however, a conservative reaction precipitated both a narrowing of the Scottish Enlightenment tradition and a dramatic increase in its influence in the United States. During the American Revolution, Voltaire and Rousseau were widely read and admired on account of their disdain for monarchy and the Roman Catholic church. Following the execution of Louis XVI, the terror, and, most especially, the French invasion of the Calvinist heartlands of Switzerland and Holland, though, French irreligion could no longer be ignored. Indeed, in a stark departure from their previous attitude of indifference, American religious leaders turned sharply against the fledgling French Republic and—despite the tenuous connection between even Rousseau's most immodest comments regarding the General Will and the tyranny of Robespierre—the previously lauded works of its intellectual forebears. Thus, by the advent of the nineteenth century, the previously tolerated philosophical and religious scepticism of the French *philosophes* was widely portrayed in America not only as heretical and blasphemous, but as part of an insidious international conspiracy bent on undermining traditional religion and morality.

Somewhat unfairly, several non-French writers were also implicated in the general anti-sceptical reaction. Foremost among these newly condemned was David Hume, whose scepticism and thinly-veiled criticism of Christianity had until then been largely neglected in the United States on account of the popularity of his six-volume *History of England* (1754–62). No doubt aided by the posthumous publication of his *Dialogues Concerning Natural Religion* (1779), Hume's popular image quickly shifted from that of a genial if irreverent Scot to that of an intellectual bomb-thrower who sought to undermine both religious belief and ethical judgment through philosophical deconstruction. In order to combat the supposedly malign influence of Hume's scepticism, Americans found a convenient weapon in the philosophy of Scottish Common-Sense Realism.

Although he sought more to reappropriate than coin the philosophical term 'common sense', the origin of the school of Scottish Common-Sense Realism is commonly traced to the publication of Thomas Reid's *Inquiry into the Human Mind on the Principles of Common Sense* (1764). In the first chapter of this work, Reid famously proclaims 'I despise Philosophy, and renounce its guidance: let my soul dwell with Common Sense'.[1] Since, in the *Inquiry*, Reid's chief goal is to expose the illicit Cartesian assumptions inherent in Locke's philosophy and the Humean scepticism to which they lead, it is best to read this rather dramatic proclamation ironically. In his own life at least, as the later publication of his subtle and measured *Essays* (1785 and 1788) proves, Reid did not renounce philosophy as such, so much as the then-canonical belief that mental images and ideas must stand between the physical world and human perception.

Although Reid and his fellow Common-Sense Realists James Beattie and Dugald Stewart had long been influential in Presbyterian circles—and especially at Princeton, where president Samuel Stanhope Smith (see Readings VIII and IX) followed in Witherspoon's philosophical footsteps—their

---

[1] Reid (1764) *Inquiry* I.iii.

popularity and influence grew precipitously during the early years of the nineteenth century. In the aftermath of the French Revolution and the conservative American reaction to it, however, the distinction between Reid's rejection of undefended epistemological assumptions and the rejection of philosophy more broadly construed was dulled. Already somewhat debased by Reid's immediate Scottish inheritors and its transmission from the university culture of Scotland to the more rough and tumble intellectual climate of the United States, the sophistication of Reid's reply to scepticism was further obscured by the polemical use to which it was put by religious educators such as Archibald Alexander (see Reading X), who retained little of the Glasgow professor's playfulness and subtlety in their engagements with Hume's criticisms of revealed religion. Both the popularity and simplification of Common-Sense Realism were also increased through its adoption by the spiritual leaders of the Second Great Awakening. Seeing unchecked philosophical enquiry as corrosive to Christian doctrine and devotion, evangelical educators such as Alexander Campbell (see Reading XIII) used appeals to common sense as a bulwark against religious scepticism.

This is not to say that such American adaptations of Common-Sense Realism were without merit. Indeed, despite the coarsening of Reid and Stewart's more considered opinions at the hands of their American adopters, the confidence in a shared moral sense and reasoning faculty engendered by the Common Sense tradition served as a powerful platform for attacks on America's most monstrous institution: chattel slavery. William Ellery Channing (see Readings XI and XII), for example, whose education at the moderate and deistic Harvard included a thorough introduction to the works of the Scottish Enlightenment, felt that the shared rationality of humankind simultaneously proved the illogic of slavery and secured the intelligibility of his arguments in the minds of even its most hardened proponents. Tragically, although the great force of his moral argument for the fundamental equality of all humankind on account of common rationality is still fresh today, his belief that an appeal to this rationality was enough to secure the eventual end of slavery was much mistaken.

III. Post-Civil War America

The failure of rational argument to secure a peaceful end to slavery and the protracted bloodiness of the American Civil War has often been credited with the destruction of Common-Sense Realism in the United States. Certainly, the war had shown that, whatever our shared mental faculties and capabilities, human beings are not, on the whole, nearly as reasonable nor sagacious as many like Channing had hoped. And, just as certainly, this loss of confidence led to a decline in the stature of Scottish Enlightenment philosophy in the United States. Yet, given that the works of the Scottish Enlightenment, and especially those which promoted the Common-Sense Realist position, were still widely read and assigned in its colleges and seminaries in the late nineteenth century, it is far too hasty to credit the Civil War with the near vanishing of its influence in the early twentieth. Rather, the decline of the Scottish Enlightenment tradition in the United States is better explained by appeal to the same forces that led to its rise a century earlier: a change in the intellectual climate of Europe and pedagogical reforms in American higher education.

Although interrupted in its intellectual development by the upheavals of the Napoleonic wars, by the latter half of the nineteenth century, the centre of Enlightenment gravity in Europe had shifted to Germany. There, the relative peace and prosperity brought about by the industrial revolution and the savvy diplomacy of Otto von Bismarck enabled a flourishing university system to promote and develop the idealist philosophy of seminal German thinkers such as Immanuel Kant, Johan Gottlieb Fichte, G.W.F. Hegel, and Arthur Schopenhauer. Partly on account of the language barrier between the two countries and the United States' own political troubles, the full effect of this German Enlightenment on America was delayed until the end of the 1800s. By the turn of the century, however, bolstered by the increasing availability of new English translations, interest in German philosophy and science surged in the New World. Further, much as the Scottish model of higher education aided the promulgation of Scottish philosophy in the eighteenth century, the spread of the German university model in America increased the influence of German philosophy in the late nineteenth and early twentieth century.

The tenure of James McCosh, who served as president of the College of New Jersey between 1868 and 1888 illustrates this transition well. When McCosh assumed the presidency of the college, the academic culture of Princeton was already divided. Having established a Presbyterian seminary across the street in 1812, religious conservatives found themselves in a running battle with academic liberals over control of the college. In the opinion of the conservative trustees, the college, like the seminary, ought to be a bastion of explicitly Christian scholarship. As the liberals on both the board and the faculty saw it, on the other hand, having been relieved of the duty of educating Christian ministers, the college was better served by taking advantage of is freedom from religious institutions to pursue rigorous scientific investigation. Though religiously conservative himself, and a fierce proponent of Scottish Common-Sense Realism, McCosh ultimately sided with the latter faction, and devoted a significant amount of the college's resources toward scientific education. According to McCosh, this emphasis on science was, in fact, required by the principles of Scottish Common Sense, and fully consonant with Christian devotion (see Reading XIV). This was, however, the minority opinion among European and American intellectuals. Having been so long associated with anti-philosophical defences of Christian doctrine, Scottish Common-Sense Realism looked ill-equipped to accommodate the rapid scientific and technological development of the new century; especially when compared to the more modern German idealism.

IV. The Twentieth Century

Contrary to his intent, McCosh's devotion to scientific enquiry while president of the College of New Jersey helped lead to the retrenchment and eventual retreat of the college's conservative trustees. Within fifteen years of McCosh's resignation, the College of New Jersey was renamed Princeton University, and its faculty were rearranged under the now-familiar German model of academic departments: a change many of Princeton's peer institutions had already made. No longer undergirded by the structural holism of Scottish pedagogy, the influence of Scottish Enlightenment philosophy continued to diminish. Before disappearing almost entirely from the scene of American intellectual life, however, the insights of the Scottish Enlightenment were taken up by the founders of the Untied States' singular contribution to philosophy: American Pragmatism. This influence is especially pronounced in the 'pragmaticism' of C.S. Peirce; who self-consciously combined Reid's rejection of Cartesian representationalism with the insights of Kant's idealism. Unfortunately, for both the legacy of American Pragmatism and the tradition of the Scottish Enlightenment, Peirce's philosophical influence was hindered by his baroque prose and the greater popularity of William James's more pluralistic pragmatism.

With the exception of Hume—whose star has never completely faded on account of his impact on Kant—and Smith—who was remembered nigh exclusively for his economic work—Scottish Enlightenment philosophy thus almost completely disappeared from American philosophical consciousness for the majority of the twentieth century. Happily, thanks to recent work by recent philosophers such as Nicholas Wolterstorff, Samuel Fleishacker, Alexander Broadie, and David Fate Norton, who have done much to expose the intellectual rigour of this maligned tradition, interest in Scottish philosophy has been rekindled. Yet, despite this resurgence of interest, the contributions of American thinkers who stood within the Scottish Enlightenment tradition still carry the stigma of unsophistication. As we have seen in this introduction, this characterization is not without cause. By and large, American appropriators of Scottish Enlightenment philosophy in the eighteenth, nineteenth, and early twentieth centuries were less interested in the subtleties of philosophical enquiry and more loosely connected to the broader philosophical debates of Europe than their Scottish cousins. Still, notwithstanding their more or less occasional avoidance of philosophical problems, as the selections collected here prove, there is much of value in the American branch of the Scottish Enlightenment tradition. For in the United States we find not only the extension of Scottish Enlightenment thinking—often toward surprising conclusions—but also, as well befits a tradition founded on the Baconian principle of experiment and observation, its practical application.

Historical Information

Samuel Fleishacker (2006) 'The Impact on America: Scottish Philosophy and the American Founding', in *Cambridge Companion to Scottish Philosophy*, edited by A. Broadie, Cambridge: Cambridge University Press.

Bruce Kuklick (2002) *A History of Philosophy in America 1720–2000*, Oxford: Clarendon Press.

Henry F. May (1976) *The Enlightenment in America*, Oxford: Oxford University Press.

Mark A. Noll (1989) *Princeton and the Republic 1786–1822: The Search for a Christian Enlightenment in the Era of Samuel Stanhope Smith*, Princeton, NJ: Princeton University Press.

Douglas Sloan (1971) *The Scottish Enlightenment and the American College Ideal*, New York: Teacher's College Press.

A Note on the Text

In these selections I have used the following notation for demarcating which footnotes were written by the original author, by the selected text's editor, and by me. Footnotes by the author appear without brackets. Footnotes by the selected text's editors appear in angle brackets. And footnotes by me appear in square brackets. Any changes made by me to either footnotes or main text also appear in square brackets.

A Note on Translations

In accordance with the aims of this series, translations have been provided for all Greek and Latin quotations. Full bibliographic information for the translations used in this volume is provided below.

Cicero (1923) *On Old Age. On Friendship. On Divination*, translated by W.A. Falconer, Cicero Volume XX, Loeb Classical Library 154, Cambridge, MA: Harvard University Press.

Columella (1941) *On Agriculture, Volume I, Books 1–4*, translated by H.B. Ash, Loeb Classical Library 361, Cambridge, MA: Harvard University Press.

Ovid (1921) *Metamorphoses, Volume I*, 2nd edition, translated by Frank Justus Miller, Loeb Classical Library 585:1, Cambridge MA: Harvard University Press.

Tacitus (2004) *The Annals*, translated by A.J. Woodman, Indianapolis, IN: Hackett Publishing.
Virgil (1916) *Eclogues, Georgics, Aneid 1-6*, translated by H.R. Fairclough, revised by G.P. Goold, Cambridge, MA: Harvard University Press.

One

William Smith (1727–1803)

William Smith was born to Anglican parents in 1727 in Aber, Scotland. In 1743, he entered Aberdeen University, but left in 1747 without completing a degree. In 1751, Smith moved to the colonies in order to become a tutor in the home of Josiah Martin, one of the founders of King's College (now Columbia University) on Long Island, New York. There, as the protégé of the college's first president—the Reverend Samuel Johnson—Smith became deeply involved in the tumultuous political and intellectual climate of the colonies.

Drawing on these experiences, in 1753 Smith wrote an influential essay, from which the following passages have been excerpted, entitled *A General Idea of the College of Mirania*. In this essay Smith vividly describes a fictional college in the New World; explaining in detail the school's academic coursework, administration, and even architecture. This essay so impressed Benjamin Franklin that Franklin arranged for Smith to first become a tutor at the Academy of Philadelphia, and then provost of the institution following its reorganization into the College of Philadelphia (now University of Pennsylvania). Feeling that he needed greater qualifications for this latter role, Smith became an Anglican priest in 1754. In the years that followed, Smith would also be awarded several honorary Doctorates of Divinity, including one from the University of Aberdeen in 1759, which was signed by Thomas Reid.

Although Smith's relationship with Franklin began on friendly terms, Smith quickly fell out of favour with Franklin and his circle. Several matters of colonial politics were involved in the falling-out, but one of the main sources of contention was Smith's perceived sympathy with the British ruling powers. Although he ultimately supported the revolution, Smith took a much more cautious approach to independence than many other statesmen of the time. For example, in response to Thomas Paine's famous and incendiary pamphlet *Common Sense*, Smith called for moderation. Further, from the pulpit he repeatedly assailed those who sought to secure independence through violent means.

Despite ordination to the Anglican priesthood, as an educator Smith was one of the most ardent supporters of non-sectarian college education in the New World. As can be seen in the selection below, Smith thought that a curriculum lacking in explicit religious instruction was the best way to inculcate proper religious affections and opinions among students. This approach informed both his teaching and his administrative work. As a teacher Smith frequently assigned works by authors of various Christian denominations and various faiths; and as an administrator, both welcomed students of diverse backgrounds and founded the non-denominational Washington College of Maryland in 1780.

Biographical Information: Robert M. Calhoon, *American National Biography Online*.

READING I

Religion & Science[1]

Supposed to have been Spoken at the Opening of the College of Mirania

It comes! it comes! the *promis'd* æra comes!
Now Gospel Truth shall dissipate the glooms
Of Pagan Error—and, with cheerful ray
O'er long benighted realms shed heavenly day.
Hark! the glad Muses strike the warbling string,

---

[1] [Extracted from William Smith (1803) {1753} 'A General Idea of the College of Mirania', in *The Works of William Smith, D.D.*, Volume II, editor unattributed, Philadelphia, PA: Hugh Maxwell & William Ery, pp. 169-227.]

And in melodious accents, thus they sing—
'Woods, Brooks, Gales, Fountains, long unknown to Fame
At length, as conscious of your future claim,
Prepare to nurse the *philosophic thought,*
To prompt the *serious* or the *sportive* note!
Prepare, ye *Woods,* to yield the Sage your shade,
And wave ambrosial verdures o'er his head!
Ye *Brooks* prepare to swell the Poet's strain,
Or gently murmur back his am'rous pain!
Haste, O ye *Gales,* your spicy sweets impart,
In music breathe them to the exulting heart!
Ye *Fountains,* haste the inspiring wave to roll,
And bid *Castalian* draughts refresh the soul!'

'Tis done—woods, brooks, gales, fountains, all obey;
And say, with general voice, or seem to say—
'Hail Heaven-descended, holy Science hail!
Thrice welcome to these shores; here ever dwell
With shade and silence, far from dire alarms,
The trumpet's horrid clang and din of arms:
To thee we offer every softer seat,
Each sunny lawn and sylvan sweet retreat,
Each flower verg'd stream, each amber-dropping grove,
Each vale of pleasure and each bower of love,
Where youthful nature with stupendous scenes,
Lifts all the powers, and all the frame serenes—
Oh! then, here fix—earth, water, air invite,
And bid a new Britannia spring to light.

Smit deep, I antedate the golden days,
And strive to paint them in sublimer lays.
Behold! on periods, periods brightening rise,
On worthies, worthies croud before mine eyes!
See other Bacons, Newtons, Lockes appear,
And to the skies their laureat honours rear!
Amidst undying greens they lie inspir'd,
On mossy beds, by heavenly visions fir'd;
Aloft they soar on Contemplation's wing
O'er worlds and worlds, and reach th' eternal King!
Awak'd by other suns, and kindling strong
With purest ardour for celestial song,

Hark! other Homers, Virgils touch the string,
And other Popes and Miltons, joyous, sing;
Find other Twit'nams in each bowery wood,
And other Tibers in each sylvan flood!

Lo! the wild Indian, soften'd by their song,
Emerging from his arbours, bounds along
The green Savannah, patient of the lore
Of dove-ey'd Wisdom, and is rude no more.
Hark! even his babes Messiah's praise proclaim,
And fondly learn to lisp Jehovah's name!

Oh! Science! onward thus thy reign extend
O'er realms yet unexplor'd till time shall end;
Till death-like ignorance forsake the ball,
And life endearing knowledge cover all;
Till wounded slavery seek her native hell,
With kindred fiends eternally to dwell!
Not trackless deserts shall thy progress stay,
Rocks, mountains, floods, before thee shall give way;
Sequester'd vales at thy approach shall sing,
And with the sound of happy labour ring;
Where wolves now howl shall polish'd villas rise,
And towery cities grow into the skies!
'Earth's farthest ends our glory shall behold,
And the new world launch forth, to meet the old.'

[...]

Here Evander paused, as if in expectation of some remarks from me upon the excellency of the institution he had given me an account of.[2] I told him, that as far as he had yet proceeded, I greatly approved of it: but that I thought the study of religion, without which no scheme of education could be of advantage to the state, or private persons, did not sufficiently enter into his account; and that if the Miranians did nothing more this way than he had spoken of, I judged their scheme deficient in the most interesting article.

---

[2] [The preceding account is given in the form of a dialogue between Evander, an alumnus of the College of Mirania, and the author, concerning the course of study for each of the college's five classes.]

He resumed, that my observation was just; and that it was for this very reason he had left the account of their method of inculcating religion and morals to a separate article; as well, because of their importance, as because they are the chief object of the studies of every class, and consequently could not be brought into the account of any particular one.

My countrymen, proceeded he, are fully persuaded that those, who are entrusted with the education of youth, can do more lasting service to the interests of religion and virtue, at a time when the heart is susceptible of every impression, than all the good men, armed with all the power of a country, can do; if, for want of education, the heart is suffered to become callous, as it were, and obstinate in the habits of vice. They were therefore extremely careful to look for something still better than learning in all the masters they chose into this seminary, admitting none but men of irreproachable characters; men whose lives should be a daily comment on their precepts, and their genuine goodness of heart a constant pledge for the morals of the youth committed to their care; men indefatigable in the discharge of their duty, from a consciousness of the weighty trust reposed in them, and an unfeigned zeal for the present and future interests of their pupils; men, in a word, formed to command love and reverence, and, from their sweetness of temper, disposed to strew the path to science with roses. They prudently foresaw, that upon their meeting with men of this character at first, not only depended the reputation of the college, but, in a great measure, the morals and genius of their country to the latest generations.

Such men it was their happiness to meet with; and it will prove a pleasing speculation to take a more particular view of the method of inculcating virtue, which is practiced by them, and may be practiced by every good master, in the course of these studies. Some may be ready to imagine that they bestow a great deal of labour this way; but, on the contrary, though religion and goodness be a subject always in their eye, it is not always in their mouth. They know well enough that youth are apt to give but a cool attention to whatever has the appearance of set lectures, and formal discourses on morality; while a word dropped, as it were casually, by a skillful master, in a proper season, shall strike so much the deeper as it was not expected, and make an impression perhaps never to be erased.

His great business then, who would train up youth to the love of religion, seems to consist, in the first place, in getting the entire possession of their hearts, in keeping a watchful eye over them, in preventing the approach of everything that is of a noxious quality, in making all around them breathe innocence, purity and truth; and, lastly, while the heart is in this sound state, in watching the proper opportunities of dropping into it the seeds of goodness, which will not fail to bring forth an hundred fold; provided he adds to the whole his own example, and seems fully persuaded of the truths he would impress upon them, never mentioning religion and virtue, but with the utmost devotion and fervor of soul.

Opportunities of this kind will never be wanting to the master, who has himself a good heart. I shall take notice of a few of them; and though every classic author may be made to furnish them, I shall confine myself to the five learned classes last mentioned, because I would be brief. I shall take care to ascribe nothing more to the scholar than I myself have felt, nor can I ascribe half so much to the master, as I have known the good Aratus [the headmaster] to put in practice; for under him I had the happiness to pass through these five classes, being one of the youth with whom he opened the college, and which he could not open higher than the first or Greek-Class aforesaid.

Now, in this class, the reading of Homer under such a master, was like traveling through some delightful country, richly variegated with everything that could please the fancy or exalt the genius. Numerous were the opportunities which the good man took, from the writings even of this heathen author, to press home upon us respect for kings, magistrates, parents, and all superiors. Beautifully would he mark for us the *Decorum* and *Honestum*[3] of life, painted in the characters, and everything ignoble and unworthy exposed. Often would he dwell with rapture on the poet's noble images of ancient hospitality, generosity, benevolence, justice, honor, piety, integrity, friendship, fidelity, sincerity, intrepidity, patience,

---

[3] ['Propriety' and 'Honor']

resignation, and the like. At the same time, while he taught us to gather the roses of such an author, he not only made us shun the thorns; but, as bees from poisonous herbs extract healing liquids, he taught us even to reap advantages from those absurdities, which were more the fault of the age than of the poet. Such are the monstrous fictions about the nature of the Gods, their jars, thefts, robberies, rapes, incests, drunkenness and the like; from which Aratus would take occasion to teach us the just value of those sacred volumes, which have rescued us from such superstition and blindness.

In the second class, what fresh opportunities did he find of leading us from wonder to wonder, and bringing the Deity as it were before our eyes, in the study of his stupendous works! How were our minds dilated and exalted when he led us to consider the heavenly bodies, and put them in competition with what we usually called great! Even the terraqueous globe on which we dwell, with all its kingdoms and boasted grandeur, seemed in our eye but a point in the solar-system! The solar-system itself dwindled into a narrow spot, when compared with the numerous systems of those stars that in a clear night stud the Cerulean! All these systems again were lost in the vast expanse, when compared with that infinity of systems, which philosophy's purer view can descry beyond the reach of all optics.

Thus, having raised us from system to system, beyond all definite space, till he perceived us lost in the imagination, and, as it were, laboring under the weight of our own conceptions; the good Aratus, knowing his opportunity and exulting in his success, would turn his address immediately to us in words like these.

'My dear youths! I think it not strange that such speculations should fill your minds with wonder and amazement. Yet be assured, (if we may use the inadequate language of men) that so far are we from having even in thought reached the limits, that we are still but on the frontiers, of the Creator's kingdom. How much, then, ought we to be astonished at our own littleness, and his grandeur, whose[4] hand framed all

---

[4] Whose arm almighty put these wheeling globes
In motion, and wound up the vast machine!
Who rounded in his palm those spacious orbs;
Who bowl'd them flaming thro' the vast profound,

those clusters of systems, kindled all their Suns, and feeds their immense fires from age to age! How daring is it for us, the atom-lords of this atom-world, to exalt ourselves against the great Sovereign of such an incomprehensible domain! How ridiculous to strut about in pride, and boast that all these systems were made for us! — Certain I am, that very different sensations must now actuate your bosoms. Doubtless, you have already, in your own imaginations, peopled all these various systems with ten thousand various orders of being, rising rank above rank in the scale of intelligence. Nay, if I deceive myself not, your very souls are now ardently affecting that period when, shaking off this cumbrous vehicle of flesh, you shall soar perhaps through the wide realms of nature, see all things as they are, and be indulged in a correspondence with all those systems, and all their inhabitants. — Such affections as these, my dear youths, are from above; — They are divinely inspired; — O check them not! They speak the worth and immortality of your Souls! If a God, that does nothing in vain, has endowed you with desires so incommensurate to all terrestrial objects, and a capacity of soaring so far beyond them; if he has given you such a restless curiosity of prying farther and farther into the boundless scheme of nature; be assured that this curiosity will not be frustrated. There are in reserve for you future periods of existence, when all these noble desires will be fully satisfied, and superior displays be eternally opened upon you, as your powers are forever enlarging.'

But it was not alone, by ascending in the scale of nature, that our amiable tutor taught us to admire the Creator's goodness. We were forced to acknowledge him still greater, if possible, in the smallest than in the greatest things, when in the third class we descended in the study of nature towards its other extreme.

To speak only of that single branch of physics called micrography, how did it surprise us to discover living creatures, thousands of which would be imperceptible to the unassisted sense, swarming by legions in each leaf and grain; animating our choicest viands, mantling our purest liquors, and crowding even the transparent atmosphere? But when

---

And set the bosom of old Night on fire.
            Dr. Young [(1742) *Night Thoughts*].

we were convinced that these animalcules are so far from being the last degree of smallness, that there are others as much smaller than them as they are smaller than us, we were then as much lost in the divisibility of matter, as formerly in its multiplicity. As in the one case, we could conceive no end of the magnitude and addition of heavenly bodies, so in the other we could conceive no end of division and smallness. On either side of us, the gradation exceeds all our conceptions; and, astonished at ourselves, we now saw man in a different light. He that but a little before seemed only an atom of an atom world, almost imperceptible in the bosom of the universe, seemed now distended into a world, even into an universe, when compared but with the last degree of perceptible smallness. Taking the view, therefore, on both sides, we were naturally led to assign him his proper place as the — *nexus utriusque mundi*.[5]

But, to proceed. How greatly was our astonishment increased, when we were convinced that the minutest of these animals is formed with as exact proportion, nicety and design as man himself! That they have their distinct joints, limbs and vessels, all disposed in number, weight and measure; and that—

> Each within this little bulk contains,
> An heart to drive the torrent thro' its veins;
> Muscles to move its limbs aright; a brain,
> And nerves disposed for pleasure and for pain;
> Eyes to distinguish; sense, whereby to know
> What's good or bad, is, or is not, its foe!
> They too are pain'd with love address the fair,
> And, with their rivals, wage destructive war.
> UNIVERSE.[6]

Such speculations, conducted by the pious and fervent Aratus, did not fail to impress us with grand and elevated conceptions of the Deity!

'Think, my dear youths (he would say to us) Oh! think how wonderful, how incomprehensible must that God be, whose works are so amazingly various! Who performed all these minute operations, who made the small heart, and

---

[5] ['the middle link of creation'.]
[6] [Henry Baker (1727) 'The Universe: A Poem Intended to Restrain the Pride of Man'.]

poured the exceedingly subtile liquids into the small vessels, of these diminutive animalcules—all with the very same right hand, wherewith he rounded those immense orbs, and launched forth all those systems of worlds through immeasurable space, whose magnitude and numbers so lately confounded us!'

Forgive me, my friend, said Evander, if in this part of my narrative, I should seem tedious, or discover any unbecoming raptures. The time spent in these studies was the happiest period of my life; a period which I can never reflect upon, without having before me the idea of the good Aratus, pouring forth important truths to us, and leading us imperceptibly from the visible to the invisible things of God.

It is impossible to express what a foundation in piety may be made, on such occasions, by a good and fervent man, whose person and character we love, and whom we suspect of no design upon us but our own welfare; and he who fails to make a due improvement of such opportunities of instilling goodness into youth, doth indeed neglect one of the most essential designs of education. He neglects to form that relish for the devout contemplation of God's works, which is not only capable to give us joy and satisfaction in all conditions of life; but will, no doubt, constitute a part of our pleasure, and be the subject of our contemplation and wonder, forever and ever! On the contrary, he who embraces such opportunities, with judgment and discretion, will have no reason to complain that youth are unsusceptible of serious impressions; or that true philosophy is unfriendly to religion. Perhaps, it may be true of philosophy, as the poet beautifully expresses it from Bacon,—

> That shallow draughts intoxicate the brain;
> But drinking largely sobers us again.[7]

So far in respect to the third class. As to the fourth, I have already hinted how far the studies of rhetoric, poetry, and what is commonly called the *belles lettres*, tend to soften the heart, and serene the temper. I pass on, therefore, to the fifth, or highest class.

And here, what need I speak of agriculture; which is only a capital part of natural knowledge reduced to practice?

---

[7] [Alexander Pope (1711) 'An Essay on Criticism'.]

Indeed Tully[8] and Columella[9] have expressly honored this study with the name of Wisdom and the life of a wise man; — a study that hath given that happiness to the most renowned names in story, which the world could not give, and afforded them solid pleasures in their declining years, after being cloyed with all that mankind call great! Indeed, it would be endless to enumerate all the opportunities which Aratus here found of improving our religious sentiments. He could not explain the theory of vegetation, without exhibiting whole worlds of wonders. He could not examine the structure of the most indifferent plant, without making us perceive in it the same wisdom and design that appear in the structure of the most perfect animal. He could not examine the fossil and mineral kingdoms, without pointing out to us the same agreement, fitness and design in the disposition of things, even amid the dark recesses and secret bowels of the earth, as on her beautiful surface. And her beautiful surface he could not survey without filling our hearts with wonder, love, and gratitude.

In this class, having now arrived to the last stage of our studies, and just entering into manhood, Aratus treated us more as his bosom-friends and companions, than as his pupils or scholars; and often, when the season permitted, would lead us to the adjoining fields, to make the proper remarks on the different plants, trees, &c.

Early, one morning, he appointed us to meet him in the public garden, where, being convened, he told us, that the plant which he proposed to show us was not there, but that it grew wild near the top of a mountain, at about a mile and a half distance to the northward of Mirania. To this place, therefore, he invited us to walk, expressing his hopes that he might be able to furnish amusement for us, sufficient to compensate the toil. Having reached the summit, and found

---

[8] *Venio nunc ad voluptates Agricolarum, quibus ego incredibiliter delector; quæ nec ulla impediuntur senectute, et mihi ad sapientis vitam proxime accedere videntur.* ['I come now to the pleasures of agriculture in which I find incredible delight; they are not one whit checked by old age, and are, it seems to me, in the highest degree suited to the life of the wise man.' Cicero, *On Old Age*, XV.]

[9] *Res rustica, sine dubitatione, proxima et quasi consanguinea sapientiæ est.* ['Agriculture alone, is without doubt most closely related and, as it were, own sister to wisdom.' Columella, *On Agriculture*, I.i.]

what he was in search of, he seated himself beneath the shade of an ancient oak, and began his remarks on the curiosity of the plant he had mentioned to us.

The morning was serene, and the prospect around us enchanting. The city lay open to the view, and the sun was just darting his first beams to gild its various turrets and spires. Two mighty rivers, whose sources are among nations and regions yet unexplored, embracing each other before us, rolled their united flood in silent majesty to the main. On each bank vast woods and forests, planted by Nature's own hand, time immemorial, waved their graceful verdure to every gale; while, between these woods, at different distances, vales and savannas, opening interminable, gave a beautiful diversity to the scene—Here gentle brooks meandering along their pebbly channels, to pour their tributary urns into these larger rivers; and there a rich profusion of hillocks, tufted with various trees, among which groups of tame animals fed in mingled peace and happiness with their wild brothers of the woods, as yet undisturbed by the barbarous huntsman's toils. The whole rural prospect was closed by vast mountains, piled into the clouds, whose enormous height even ache the beholder's eye, and charm the soul with delightful grandeur.

Turning to this landscape, and dropping the small plant that he held in his hand, 'Look round you, my dear friends! look round you', said Aratus! 'Who can confine his attention to a single production of nature, when such immense scenes lie before him? How inseparably connected are beauty and utility, magnificence and frugality, in all the works of God! These inequalities and varieties, on the surface of the earth, not only serve to form those prospects, which now enchant us, but also to fructify and enrich the soil! These hillocks and lesser valleys form rivulets, and drain off the supervacaneous moisture. These rivulets form rivers; and these rivers supply the expense of evaporations from the ocean. These evaporations form magazines of dews and rains; and, lastly, these magazines of dews and rains are condensed, and brought down upon the earth, by the help of the high mountains. Thus the globe is ever supplied with fresh recruits of moisture, and saline juices. And thus, though all things differ, all agree to promote the same wise ends. Order walks hand in hand with variety. The mountains but stand the lofty ministers of the vales. Unless they thus reared their gelid crests into the sky, to arrest and condense the fluctuating vapors, the hotter countries would probably be left destitute of rain, and the whole moisture of the globe might, by degrees, evavagate towards the colder regions, and be at length congealed round the poles; not to mention that the mountains also produce many curious minerals and vegetables of sovereign use, which are not to be found elsewhere. Such, for instance, is this plant, which we ascended hither in search of, and which I shall afterwards give you a further account of. But let us, in the meanwhile, return homewards, to avoid the increasing heat of the day.'

Aratus having finished, and taken a few of the plants with him, which he might readily have procured with less labour to himself, we were at no loss to guess what had been his principal motive in leading us to this delightful place.

But you will excuse this digression, if you should esteem it such. The last study to be spoken of is history, which, as Aratus managed it, is nothing else but religion and philosophy taught by examples.

When the mirror of ages was held up to us, and all the celebrated names of antiquity made to pass in bright review before us; when we beheld the glorious effects of virtue, with the train of private and public miseries, which have always been the consequence of vice; when we saw the public villain branded with eternal infamy, and delivered down as a malefactor to all posterity, while the patriot's name is embalmed, and rendered forever illustrious, by the concurring plaudits of the world; could we, do you think, forbear, in our own imaginations and resolutions, to enlist ourselves for life, under the banner of virtue? Could we forbear to glow with a generous desire of earning the fair esteem of good men, and partaking some share of fame with those venerable worthies we read of? Or could we once think of committing a base and dishonest action, without shrinking from it with horror, at the apprehension of the lasting reproaches of mankind?

The study of history, and a view of the greatness, illustrious achievements, and manners of other nations, may, in some degree, supply the place of traveling, and make youth shake off that narrowness of mind, which is apt to substitute the customs, manners, and actions of the small spot wherein they were born, as the standard of right and wrong, the model of everything great and good. It begets in them a more noble and generous turn of thought, extends their views, and teaches them, as citizens of the world, to do impartial justice to the virtues of every people and nation.

Indeed there is some danger, that history, with all its advantages, should go too far in this respect, and beget a love of false magnificence and external show. The partiality of historians to their own great men, the pompous accounts of victories and triumphs, with the colorings often employed to heighten actions that have little or no intrinsic greatness, are apt to dazzle the eyes of unwary readers. But here it was, that Aratus, ever watchful and sagacious, took particular care to make the proper distinctions, and to cultivate in us the taste of solid glory.

He would ask us, whether, in our own private judgment, Timoleon, when he declined all the dignities offered him by a grateful people, and retired to practice in silence the virtues of a private life, only saving to himself the pleasure of seeing thousands happy by his means, did not appear as venerably great, as when he came at the head of an army, resolved either to die, or rescue that people from slavery and oppression? Whether Curius, when he rejected the vast sums offered him by the Samnite ambassadors, though they found him so poor as to be cooking his own supper, did not show as much magnanimity, as when in the front of dreadful war he conquered wherever he came? Whether Fabius hath not been as much applauded for saving from destruction his rival and adversary, Minucius, who had endeavored to supplant him in the esteem of the people, as for defeating the great Hannibal, and saving the Republic? Whether Cincinnatus deserved more praises for his triumph over the Æqui, or his immediate abdication of the dictatorship (when he could be of no farther public service), and stealing away from the acclamations of his fellow-citizens, to manure his little farm, and cheer his lovely Racilia, to whom in his absence he had committed the care of it? Whether he might not appear as great, when seated on an humble turf he decided a difference among his neighbor-peasants, and restored peace to a poor family, as when seated on the high tribunal of Rome, and vested with uncontrollable authority, he gave law and peace to half the world.

These renowned worthies (Aratus would observe) when they conquered nations, saved their country, and triumphed over its enemies, did that which was great indeed! Nevertheless many others have equalled them in this. But when they conquered themselves; when they saved their bitterest enemies; when they triumphed over poverty, and would not stoop to gather gold, diadems and kingdoms, for their own private emolument; — they did that in which they have had but few equals.

By contrasts like these, and questions frequently asked, I have known Aratus' labour to form and improve our notions of true greatness. By laying before us those bright examples of public virtue, who managed the treasures and filled the most eminent posts of their country with unsullied integrity; who conquered the most opulent kingdoms without adding a single drachm to their private fortune; and, whenever their country's service did not require their immediate presence, descended voluntarily from the command of mankind to manure a few private acres, and trace the divine wisdom in the works of nature; — I say by laying such bright examples as these before us, he led us naturally to this conclusion.

That nothing can be honorable but integrity and the approbation of good men; nothing shameful but vice and communion with the bad; nothing necessary but our duty; nothing great and comfortable but the conscientious discharge of it; and that true glory does not consist in breathing the fiery spirit of war, and thirsting eagerly after dominion; but in delighting to see the world happy and unalarmed, in fervently striving to promote this happiness, in cultivating the arts of peace, encouraging agriculture and manufactures, educating children aright as the rising hopes of the state, and serving God in tranquillity of mind and purity of heart. History shows that none but those who acted thus, have either been happy in their life, or esteemed after their death.

[...]

And now, my friend, continued Evander, by this time I hope you are fully satisfied, that the study of religion, both natural and revealed, enters sufficiently into the plan of this seminary. For surely, when such care, as is above mentioned, is taken through the week, to embrace every opportunity of laying a foundation of natural religion and goodness, the great truths of Christianity cannot fail of a favorable reception on the Sundays, whether they come from the masters in the evening classes, or from the pulpit in the time of divine service.

Easy and delightful must the task of the clergy be, when, by the regulations of society, the whole instructors of youth go thus hand in hand with them in advancing the interests of virtue and piety! Happy, continued Evander, (his face brightening with a laudable fondness for his country) happy are the people that are in such a case! What can we figure to ourselves more noble than the whole wisdom of a community, thus using every human effort to train up and secure to the state a succession of good citizens to the latest generations? What can we conceive more lovely than the youth of a country thus collected into one great school of virtue, and striving, in the sight of the public, with a noble emulation to excel each other in every thing that does honor to their nature? Can anything be more praiseworthy than to contrive and execute proper means for exciting and encouraging this noble contest among youth? Considered in this light, well might Tully call education a divine work! Well might Plato call it a godlike one!

Here Evander concluded his account of this seminary; and how far it may be imitated or improved by you, gentlemen, in this province, is entirely submitted to your wisdom.

Two

Benjamin Rush (1746–1813)

Benjamin Rush was born in Byberry Township, Pennsylvania in 1746. A child prodigy, Rush entered the College of New Jersey (now Princeton University) at the age of thirteen, and completed his degree only a year later in 1760. Following graduation, Rush moved to Philadelphia in order to study medicine. After six years of apprenticeship under some of the finest doctors in the colonies, Rush then travelled to Scotland in order to further his medical education at the University of Edinburgh.

In 1768, Rush left Edinburgh and moved first to London and then to France in order to complete his training. During this time he also met Benjamin Franklin, who became a financial supporter of his studies. In the summer of 1769, follOwing nine years of medical training, Rush returned to Philadelphia and set up his practice. Shortly thereafter he was offered a professorship in chemistry at the College of Philadelphia (now University of Pennsylvania).

In the years between his return to America and the revolution, Rush's prosperity and reputation grew. In early 1776, he married Julia Stockton, the daughter of the prominent judge and revolutionary Richard Stockton. Soon thereafter, in July of 1776, Rush joined his father-in-law at the Second Continental Congress, and became with him a signer of the Declaration of Independence. On account of his medical competence and political connections, Rush was initially named as surgeon general to Washington's army. In 1778, however, after writing a letter complaining bitterly of disorganization and corruption in army hospitals, Rush was dismissed by Washington for disloyalty.

Distraught over both the state of the army's medical operations and his dismissal, Rush again returned Philadelphia, determined to leave politics behind. In 1787, however, Rush was elected to the Pennsylvania ratifying committee, where he joined James Wilson in pushing for the Constitution's swift adoption. Following the ratification of the Constitution, Rush devoted himself to his professorship and medical practice, distinguishing himself in both fields. In academics, Rush gained fame for his meticulous and voluminous writings on medical science. In 1793, Rush was given occasion to test his theories when a particularly virulent yellow fever epidemic hit Philadelphia. Although Rush's methods of rigorous purging and bloodletting likely did little to help his patients, and drew criticism from contemporaneous medical professionals, his devotion to his patients was widely acclaimed.

Today, Rush's medical theories and methods of treatment are of little to no scientific value. At the time, however, he was one of the few Americans doing theoretical work in medicine, and provided one of the first first-hand accounts of a yellow fever epidemic by a trained medical professional. In addition to writing on medical matters, Rush also wrote essays and lectures on contemporary politics, literature, and philosophy. The short passage below has been selected from one of these. Although Rush presents more extended thoughts about Scottish Philosophy in his *Lectures on the Mind*,[1] this essay is of particular interest because it reveals the malleability of the term 'Common Sense' in the American context.

Biographical Information: Robert B. Sullivan, *American National Biography Online*.

---

[1] Benjamin Rush (1981) *Lectures on the Mind*, edited by E.T. Carlson, J.L. Wollock and P.S. Noel, Memoirs of the American Philosophical Society, Number 44, Philadelphia, PA: American Philosophical Society.

READING II

Thoughts on Common Sense[2]

The human mind, in common with other branches of philosophy, has become the subject of attention in the present age of free and general enquiry. While new faculties are discover[ed] in it, it will conduce equal to our acquiring a perfect knowledge of its powers, to detect and remove such *supposed* faculties as do not belong to it.

I have long suspected the term *common sense* to be applied improperly to designate a faculty of the mind. I shall not repeat the accounts which have been given of it by Cicero—Burner—Berkeley—Shaftesbury—Bentley—Fenelon—Locke—Hume—Hobbes—Priestley and others, all of whom agree in describing it as a *faculty* or *part* of a faculty, possessing a quick and universal perception *of right* and *wrong, truth* and *error,* and of *propriety* and *impropriety* in human affairs.

I shall copy, as the substance of all that those authors have said upon this subject, Dr. Reid's account of common sense, published in the 2d. chapter of the sixth number of his *Essays on the Intellectual Powers of Man.* —

> It is absurd to conceive (says the Doctor) that there can be any opposition between reason and common sense. It is the first born of reason, and, as they are commonly joined together in speech and writing, they are inseparable in their nature.
>
> We ascribe to reason two offices or two degrees. The first is to judge of things self-evident; the second is to draw conclusions that are not self-evident from things that are. The first of these is the province, and the sole province, of common sense, and therefore it *coincides* with reason in its *whole* extent, and is only *another* name for one *branch* or one *degree* of reason.
>
> There is an obvious reason why this degree of reason should have a name appropriated to it, and that is, that in the greatest part of mankind no other degree of reason is to be found. It is this degree of reason that entitles them to the denomination of reasonable creatures.
>
> These two degrees of reason differ in other respects which would be sufficient to entitle them to distinct names.

---

[2] [Extracted from Benjamin Rush (1806) {1791} 'Thoughts on Common Sense', in *Essays Literary, Moral, and Philosophical,* 2nd Edition, Philadelphia, PA: Thomas and William Bradford, pp. 249-55.]

The first is the gift of heaven—the second is learned by practice and rules, when the first is not wanting.

—Thus far Dr. Reid.

It is with great diffidence that I object to anything that comes from a gentleman from whose writings I have derived so much entertainment and instruction, and who has done so much towards removing the rubbish that has for many ages obscured the science of metaphysics. This diffidence to offer a single objection to Dr. Reid's opinion upon the subject under consideration, is increased by the group of popular and respectable names under which he has supported it.

The idea which I have adopted of common sense is plain and simple. I consider it as the perception of things as they appear to the *greatest* part of mankind. It has no relation to their being *true* or *false*, *right* or *wrong*, *proper* or *improper*. For the sake of perspicuity, I shall define it to be, *opinions and feelings in unison with the opinions and feelings of the bulk of mankind*.

From this definition it is evident that common sense must necessarily differ in different ages and countries and, in both, must vary with the progress of taste, science, and religion. In the uncultivated state of reason, the opinions and feelings of a majority of mankind will be *wrong*, and, of course, their common or universal sense will partake of their errors. In the cultivated state of reason, *just* opinions and feelings will become general, and the common sense of the majority will be in unison with truth. I beg leave to illustrate what I mean by a few examples.

1. There are many things which were contrary to common sense in former ages, both in philosophy and religion, which are now universally believed, insomuch that to call them in question is to discover a want of judgment, or a defective education.

2. It is contrary to common sense to speak or write in favor of republicanism, in several European countries; and it is equally contrary to it to speak or write in favor of monarchy, in the United States of America.

3. The common sense of the planters in Jamaica, is in favor of the commerce and slavery of the Africans. —In Pennsylvania, reason, humanity, and common sense, have universally declared against them.

4. In Turkey, it is contrary to the common sense of delicacy which prevails in that country for a gentleman to dance with a lady. No such common sense prevails in any of the western countries of Europe, or in the States of America.

5. It is contrary to the common sense of many numerous sects to believe that it is possible for men to go to heaven, who do not embrace their principles, or mode of worship. — Among rational men, this common sense is contrary to truth and Christian religion.

6. The common sense of mankind has generally been in favor of established modes and habits of practice, in medicine. Opium, bark, mercury and the lancet have all forced their way into general use, contrary to this common sense. Their utility is a proof how little common sense accords with the decisions of reason, and how improperly it is supposed to be a part of that noble power of the mind.

7. It is agreeable to the common sense of a great part of mankind, to revenge public and private injuries by wars and duels, and yet no wise or just reason has ever been given to justify the practice of either of them.

8. The common sense of the bulk of the inhabitants of the British Dominions, and of the United States, is in favor of boys spending four or five years in learning the Latin and Greek languages, in order to qualify them to understand the English language. Those persons who recollect that the most perfect language in the world, *viz.* the Greek, was learned without the medium or aid of a dead or foreign language, consider the above practice (founded in common sense) as contrary to right reason and productive of many evils in education. But further, under this head. The common sense of the same immense proportion of people, is in favor of teaching boys *words*, before they are taught *ideas*. Now nature and right reason both revolt at this absurd practice.

9. The common sense of nearly all nations, is in favor of preventing crimes by the punishment of death, but right reason, policy, and the experience of a wise and enlightened prince,[3] all concur in proving that the best means of preventing crimes, is by *living* and not by *dead* examples.

---

[3] Leopold, Emperor of Germany.

In the perfection of knowledge, common sense and truth will be in unison with each other. It is *now more* related to error than to truth, and in the sense in which I have described it, it implies more praise than censure to want it.

To say that a man has common sense, is to say that he thinks with his age or country, in their *false*, as well as their *true* opinions; and the greater the proportion of people, he acts and thinks with, the greater share he possesses of this common sense.—After all that has been said in its favor, I cannot help thinking that it is the characteristic only of common minds.

To think and act with the majority of mankind, when they are *right*, and differently from them, when they are *wrong*, constitutes in my opinion, the perfection of human wisdom and conduct.

The *feelings* and *opinions* of mankind are often confounded; but they are widely different from each other. There may be *just* feelings connected with *erroneous* opinions and conduct. This is often the case in religion and government — But, in general, opinions and feelings are just and unjust in equal degrees, according to the circumstance of age, country, and the progress of knowledge before mentioned.

Had this common sense depended upon the information of any one of the *five external* senses, I should have had no difficulty in admitting Dr. Reid's account of it, inasmuch as the perceptions they afford are the *same*, in their nature, in all healthy men, and in all ages and countries. But to suppose it to be an inferior degree, or the *first* act of reason, and afterwards to suppose it to be *universal*, is to contradict every thing that history and observation teach us of human nature.

In matters addressed to our reason, the principal business of reason is to correct the evidence of our *senses*. Indeed, the perception of truth, in philosophy, seems to consist in little else than in the refutation of the ideas acquired from the testimony of our senses. In the progress of knowledge, when the exact connection between the senses and reason is perfectly understood, it is probable that the senses and reason will be in unison with each other, and that mankind will as suddenly connect the evidence of all the senses with the decisions of reason, as they now connect, with certainty, the distance of objects with the evidence of the eyes. This general unison between the senses and reason, as in the case of vision, must be the result only of experience and habit.

I cannot dismiss this subject without adding the following remark.

Mankind are governed, says Mr. Bayle, by their prejudices, and not by their principles. To do them good, we must, in some measure, conform to those prejudices;—hence we find the most acceptable men in practical society, have been those who have never shocked their contemporaries, by opposing popular or common opinions. Men of opposite characters, like objects placed too near the eye, are seldom seen distinctly by the age in which they live. They must content themselves with the prospect of being useful to the distant and more enlightened generations which are to follow them. Galileo, who asked pardon of the Pope, on his knees, for contradicting the *common sense* of the church, respecting the revolution of the earth, and Dr. Harvey, who lost all his business by refuting the *common sense* of former ages, respecting the circulation of the blood, now enjoy a reputation for their opinions and discoveries, which has in no instance ever been given to the cold blood of common sense.

Three

John Witherspoon (1723-1794)

John Witherspoon was born on 5th February, 1723 in Gifford, Scotland, just outside of Edinburgh. The son of a Church of Scotland minister, Witherspoon began his preparation for ministry at an early age, entering the University of Edinburgh to study theology when only thirteen years old. He received his first call to the parish of Beith, Ayrshire in 1745. The next year, on account of his participation in the resistance against the Roman Catholic 'Bonnie Prince Charlie' Stuart's rebellion, Witherspoon was captured by rebel forces and briefly imprisoned at the Castle Doune.

Following the failure of the Stuart rebellion, Witherspoon became a renowned orator and polemicist for the conservative Popular Party within the Church of Scotland. In 1753 he anonymously published the *Ecclesiastical Characteristics* — a viciously satirical attack on the philosophy of Francis Hutcheson (1694-1746) and its influence on Church of Scotland's other faction, the Moderate Party. In accordance with his rising prominence, in 1757 Witherspoon was called to the prosperous town of Paisley, just outside of Glasgow, where he stayed until his move to America nine years later.

Witherspoon's relocation to the New World was precipitated by the need to find a new president for the College of New Jersey (now Princeton University) who was acceptable to both the conservative Old Side and liberal New Side Presbyterians of the British Colonies. Well known in the colonies through his writings as a person of wit, intelligence, and fervour, Witherspoon was elected in absentia by the trustees.

Although initially unwilling to accept the position on account of his wife's preference to stay in Scotland, Witherspoon was persuaded to make the move to Princeton by the American physician Benjamin Rush, who was then studying medicine in Edinburgh.

Beginning his presidency in 1768, Witherspoon worked quickly and tirelessly to improve the college by expanding its curriculum and placing it on firm financial footing. By the time of the revolution, Witherspoon had transformed the College of New Jersey from a small regional seminary into a prestigious institution of higher education. In addition to his work at the college, Witherspoon also became well known for his fervent promotion of liberty and independence, and was therefore elected as a representative of New Jersey to the 1776 Continental Congress in Philadelphia. There, he became the only clergyman to sign the Declaration of Independence.

Following the war, Witherspoon remained active in politics, but also continued his work at the College of New Jersey. In addition to his administrative duties, Witherspoon taught a yearly course in Moral Philosophy from which the following selections have been extracted. In these lectures, Witherspoon drew the intellectual climate of the College of New Jersey, and by extension the United States, away from the idealist epistemology of George Berkeley and the theocentric ethics of Jonathan Edwards and toward the more realist, scientific, and classically inspired philosophy of Scottish Enlightenment thinkers like Thomas Reid, Adam Smith, and, ironically, Francis Hutcheson.

Biographical Information: Mark A. Noll, *American National Biography Online*.

READING III

Introduction to Moral Philosophy[1]

Moral philosophy is that branch of science which treats of the principles and laws of duty or morals. It is called phil-

---

[1] [Extracted from John Witherspoon (1912) {1800} 'Lecture I', in *Lectures on Moral Philosophy*, edited by Varnum Lansing Collins, Princeton, NJ: Princeton University Press, pp. 1–8.]

osophy, because it is an inquiry into the nature and grounds of moral obligation by reason, as distinct from revelation.

Hence arises a question, is it lawful, and is it safe or useful to separate moral philosophy from religion? It will be said, it is either the same or different from revealed truth; if the same, unnecessary—if different, false and dangerous.

An author of New England,[2] says, moral philosophy is just reducing infidelity to a system. But however specious the objections, they will be found at bottom not solid.—If the Scripture is true, the discoveries of reason cannot be contrary to it; and therefore, it has nothing to fear from that quarter. And as we are certain it can do no evil, so there is a probability that it may do much good. There may be an illustration and confirmation of the inspired writings, from reason and observation, which will greatly add to their beauty and force.

The noble and eminent improvements in natural philosophy, which have been made since the end of the last century, have been far from hurting the interest of religion; on the contrary, they have greatly promoted it. Why should it not be the same with moral philosophy, which is indeed nothing else but the knowledge of human nature? It is true, that infidels do commonly proceed upon pretended principles of reason. But as it is impossible to hinder them from reasoning on this subject, the best way is to meet them upon their own ground, and to show from reason itself, the fallacy of their principles. I do not know anything that serves more for the support of religion than to see from the different and opposite systems of philosophers, that there is nothing certain in their schemes, but what is coincident with the word of God.

Some there are, and perhaps more in the present than any former age, who deny the law of nature, and say, that all such sentiments as have been usually ascribed to the law of nature, are from revelation and tradition.

We must distinguish here between the light of nature and the law of nature: by the first is to be understood what we can or do discover by our own powers, without revelation or

---

[2] <MS. C adds footnote: *President Edwards*. See his dissertation on Virtue. The reference presumably is to 'The nature of true virtue', the second of the elder Edwards' 'Two dissertations', published in one volume at Boston in 1765.>

tradition: by the second, that which, when discovered, can be made [to] appear to be agreeable to reason and nature.

There have been some very shrewd and able writers of late, *viz.* Dr. Wilson, of New Castle, and Mr. Ricalton of Scotland, who have written against the light of nature, showing that the first principles of knowledge are taken from information. That nothing can be supposed more rude and ignorant, than man without instruction. That when men have been brought up so, they have scarcely been superior to brutes. It is very difficult to be precise upon this subject, and to distinguish the discoveries of reason from the exercise of it. Yet I think, admitting all, or the greatest part, of what such contend for, we may, notwithstanding, consider how far anything is consonant to reason, or may be proven by reason; though perhaps reason, if left to itself, would never have discovered it.

Dr. Clarke was one of the greatest champions for the law of nature; but it is only since his time that the shrewd opposers of it have appeared. The Hutchinsonians (so called from [John] Hutchinson of England) insist that not only all moral, but also all natural knowledge comes from revelation, the true system of the world, true chronology, all human arts, &c. In this, as is usual with most other classes of men, they carry their nostrum to extravagance. I am of opinion that the whole Scripture is perfectly agreeable to sound philosophy; yet certainly it was never intended to teach us everything. The political law of the Jews contains many noble principles of equity, and excellent examples to future lawgivers; yet it was so local and peculiar, that certainly it was never intended to be immutable and universal.

It would be more just and useful to say that all simple and original discoveries have been the production of providence, and not the invention of man. On the whole, it seems reasonable to make moral philosophy, in the sense above explained, a subject of study. And indeed let men think what they will of it, they ought to acquaint themselves with it. They must know what it is, if they mean ever to show that it is false.

The Division of the Subject

Moral philosophy is divided into two great branches, Ethics and Politics, to this some add Jurisprudence, though this may be considered as a part of politics. Ethics relate to personal duties, Politics to the constitution, government, and rights of societies, and Jurisprudence, to the administration of justice in constituted states.

It seems a point agreed upon, that the principles of duty and obligation must be drawn from the nature of man. That is to say, if we can discover how his Maker formed him, or for what he intended him, that certainly is what it ought to be.[3]

The knowledge of human nature, however, is either perplexed and difficult of itself, or hath been made so, by the manner in which writers in all ages have treated it. Perhaps this circumstance itself, is a strong presumption of the truth of the Scripture doctrine of the depravity and corruption of our nature. Supposing this depravity, it must be one great cause of difficulty and confusion in giving an account of human nature as the work of God.

This I take to be indeed the case with the greatest part of our moral and theological knowledge.

Those who deny this depravity, will be apt to plead for everything, or for many things as dictates of nature, which are in reality propensities of nature in its present state, but at the same time the fruit and evidence of its departure from its original purity. It is by the remaining power of natural conscience that we must endeavor to detect and oppose these errors.

(1) We may consider man very generally in his species as distinct from and superior to the other creatures, and what it is, in which the difference truly consists. (2) As an individual, what are the parts which constitute his nature.

1. Philosophers have generally attempted to assign the precise distinction between men and the other animals; but when endeavoring to bring it to one peculiar incommunic-

---

[3] <MS. A adds Dr. Clarke; *Puffendorf de Officiis hominum, & Civium; Cicero de Officiis;* Hutcheson; Shaftesbury's *Characteristics;* Mandeville's *Fable of the Bees;* Wollaston's *Religion of Nature delineated:* and Kames' *Essay of the Principles of Morality,* are the Authors to be consulted in these lectures.>

able characteristic, they have generally contradicted one another and sometimes disputed with violence and rendered the thing more uncertain.

The difficulty of fixing upon a precise criterion only serves to show that in man we have an example of what we see also everywhere else, *viz.* a beautiful and insensible gradation from one thing to another, so that the highest of the inferior is, as it were, connected and blended with the lowest of the superior class. Birds and beasts are connected by some species so that you will find it hard to say whether they belong to the one or the other—So indeed it is in the whole vegetable as well as animal kingdom. (1) Some say men are distinguished from brutes by reason, and certainly this, either in kind or degree, is the most honorable of our distinctions. (2) Others say that many brutes give strong signs of reason, as dogs, horses and elephants. But that man is distinguished by memory and foresight: but I apprehend that these are upon the same footing with reason, if there are some glimmerings of reason in the brute creation, there are also manifest proofs of memory and some of foresight. (3) Some have thought it proper to distinguish man from the inferior creatures by the use of speech, no other creatures having an articulate language. Here again we are obliged to acknowledge that our distinction is chiefly the excellence and fullness of articulate discourse; for brutes have certainly the art of making one another understand many things by sound. (4) Some have said that man is not completely distinguished by any of these, but by a sense of religion. And I think it must be admitted that of piety or a sense of a Supreme Being, there is not any trace to be seen in the inferior creatures. The stories handed about by weak-minded persons, or retailed by credulous authors, of respect in them to churches, or sacred persons, are to be disdained as wholly fabulous and visionary. (5) There have been some who have said that man is distinguished from the brutes by a sense of *ridicule.*

The whole creation (says a certain author)[4] is grave except man, no one laughs but himself. There is something whimsical in fixing upon this as the criterion, and it does not seem

---

[4] \<MS. C adds footnote *Shaftesbury.*\>

to set us in a very respectable light. Perhaps it is not improper to smile upon the occasion, and to say, that if this sentiment is embraced, we shall be obliged to confess kindred with the apes, who are certainly themselves possessed of a risible faculty, as well as qualified to excite laughter in us. On the whole there seems no necessity of fixing upon some one criterion to the exclusion of others.

There is a great and apparent distinction between man and the inferior animals, not only in the beauty of his form, which the poet takes notice of. *Os homini sublime dedit, &c.*[5] but also in reason, memory, reflection, and the knowledge of God and a future state.

A general distinction, which deserves particularly to be taken notice of in moral disquisitions, is that man is evidently made to be guided, and protected from dangers, and supplied with what is useful more by reason, and brutes more by instinct.

It is not very easy and perhaps not necessary to explain instinct. It is something previous to reason and choice. When we say the birds build their nests by instinct, and man builds his habitation by reflection, experience or instruction, we understand the thing well enough, but if we attempt to give a logical definition of either the one or the other, it will immediately be assaulted by a thousand arguments.

Though man is evidently governed by something else than instinct, he also has several instinctive propensities, some of them independent of, and some of them intermixed with his moral dispositions. Of the first kind are hunger, thirst, and some others; of the last is *storgi* or parental tenderness towards offspring.

On instinct we shall only say farther, that it leads more immediately to the appointment of the Creator, and whether in man, or in other creatures, operates more early and more uniformly than reason.

---

5 <MS. C adds footnote *Ovid* and makes an attempt to complete the quotation (Metamorphoses I. 85-86).> [*os homini sublime dedit caelumque videre iussit et erectos ad sidera tollere vultus,* 'he gave to man an uplifted face and bade him stand erect and turn his eyes to heaven'.]

READING IV

Internal Sensation[6]

Internal sensation is what Mr. Hutcheson calls the finer powers of perception. It takes its rise from external objects, but by abstraction, considers something farther than merely the sensible qualities —

1. Thus with respect to many objects there is a sense of beauty in the appearance, structure or composition, which is altogether distinct from mere color, shape and extension. How then is this beauty perceived? It enters by the eye, but it is perceived and relished by what may be well enough called an internal sense, quality or capacity of the mind.

2. There is a sense of pleasure in imitation, whence the arts of painting, sculpture, poetry, are often called the imitative arts. It is easy to see that the imitation itself gives the pleasure, for we receive much pleasure from a lively description of what would be painful to behold.

3. A sense of harmony.

4. A sense of order or proportion.

Perhaps after all, the whole of these senses may be considered as belonging to one class, and to be the particulars which either singly, or by the union of several of them, or of the whole, produce what is called the pleasures of the imagination. If so, we may extend these senses to everything that enters into the principles of beauty and gracefulness — order, proportion, simplicity, intricacy, uniformity, variety — especially as these principles have anything in common that is equally applicable to all the fine arts, painting, statuary, architecture, music, poetry, [or] oratory.

The various theories upon the principles of beauty, or what it is that properly constitutes it, are of much importance on the subject of taste and criticism, but of very little in point of morals. Whether it be a simple perception that cannot be analyzed, or a *Je ne sais quoi*, as the French call it, that cannot be discovered, it is the same thing to our present purpose, since it cannot be denied, that there is a perception of beauty, and that this is very different from the mere color or dimen-

---

[6] [Extracted from John Witherspoon (1912) {1800} 'Lecture III', in *Lectures on Moral Philosophy*, edited by Varnum Lansing Collins, Princeton, NJ: Princeton University Press, pp. 16–22.]

sions of the object. This beauty extends to the form and shape of visible, or to the grace and motion of living objects; indeed, to all works of art, and productions of genius.

These are called the reflex senses sometimes, and it is of moment to observe both that they really belong to our nature, and that they are very different from the grosser perceptions of external sense.

It must also be observed, that several distinguished writers have added as an internal sense, that of morality, a sense and perception of moral excellence, and our obligation to conform ourselves to it in our conduct.

Though there is no occasion to join Mr. Hutcheson or any other, in their opposition to such as make reason the principle of virtuous conduct, yet I think it must be admitted, that a sense of moral good and evil, is as really a principle of our nature, as either the gross external or reflex senses, and as truly distinct from both, as they are from each other.

This moral sense is precisely the same thing with what, in scripture and common language, we call conscience. It is the law which our Maker has written upon our hearts, and both intimates and enforces duty, previous to all reasoning. The opposers of innate ideas, and of the law of nature, are unwilling to admit the reality of a moral sense, yet their objections are wholly frivolous. The necessity of education and information to the production and exercise of the reflex senses or powers of the imagination, is every whit as great as to the application of the moral sense. If therefore anyone should say, as is often done by Mr. Locke, if there are any innate principles, what are they? enumerate them to me, if they are essential to man they must be in every man; let me take any artless clown and examine him, and see if he can tell me what they are. — I would say, if the principles of taste are natural they must be universal. Let me try the clown then, and see whether he will agree with us, either in discovering the beauty of a poem or picture, or being able to assign the reasons of his approbation.

There are two senses which are not easily reducible to any of the two kinds of internal senses, and yet certainly belong to our nature. They are allied to one another.— A sense of ridicule, and a sense of honor and shame. A sense of the ridiculous is something peculiar; for though it be admitted that everything that is ridiculous is at the same time unreasonable and absurd; yet it is as certain the terms are not convertible, or anything that is absurd is not ridiculous. There are an hundred falsehoods in mathematics and other sciences, that do not tempt anybody to laugh.

Shaftesbury has through his whole writings, endeavored to establish this principle that ridicule is the test of truth: but the falsehood of that opinion appears from the above remark, for there is something really distinct from reasoning in ridicule. It seems to be putting imagination in the place of reason. —See Brown's Essays on the Characteristics.[7]

A sense of honor and shame seems, in a certain view, to subject us to the opinions of others, as they depend upon the sentiments of our fellow-creatures. Yet, perhaps we may consider this sentiment as intended to be an assistant or guard to virtue, by making us apprehend reproach from others for what is in itself worthy of blame. This sense is very strong and powerful in its effects, whether it be guided by true or false principles.

After this survey of human nature, let us consider how we derive either the nature or obligation of duty from it.

One way is to consider what indications we have from our nature of the way that leads to the truest happiness. This must be done by a careful attention to the several classes of perceptions and affections, to see which of them are most excellent, delightful, or desirable.

They will then soon appear to be of three great classes, as mentioned above, easily distinguishable from one another, and gradually rising above one another.

1. The gratification of the external senses. This affords some pleasure. We are led to desire what is pleasing and to avoid what is disgustful to them.

2. The finer powers of perception give a delight which is evidently more excellent, and which we must necessarily pronounce more noble. Poetry, painting, music, &c. the exertion of genius, and exercise of the mental powers in general, give a pleasure, though not so tumultuous, much more refined, and which does not so soon satiate.

---

[7] <John Brown, 'Essays on the Characteristics of the Earl of Shaftesbury', London, 1751. Dr. Witherspoon's copy is in the Library of Princeton University.>

3. Superior to both these, is a sense of moral excellence, and a pleasure arising from doing what is dictated by the moral sense.

It must doubtless be admitted that this representation is agreeable to truth, and that to those who would calmly and fairly weigh the delight of moral action, it must appear superior to any other gratification, being most *noble, pure* and *durable*. Therefore we might conclude that it is to be preferred before all other sources of pleasure—that they are to give way to it when opposite, and to be no otherwise embraced than in subserviency to it.

But though we cannot say there is anything false in this theory, there are certainly very essential defects.—As for example, it wholly confounds, or leaves entirely undistinguished, acting virtuously from seeking happiness: so that promoting our own happiness will in that case be the essence or definition of virtue, and a view to our own interest will be the sole and complete obligation to virtue. Now there is good ground to believe not only that reason teaches us, but that the moral sense dictates to us, something more on both heads, *viz.* that there are disinterested affections that point directly at the good of others, and that these are so far from meriting to be excluded from the notion of virtue altogether, that they rather seem to claim a preference to the selfish affections. I know the friends of the scheme of self-interest have a way of coloring or solving this. They say, men only approve and delight in benevolent affections, as pleasing and delightful to themselves. But this is not satisfying, for it seems to weaken the force of public affection very much, to refer it all to self-interest, and when nature seems to be carrying you out of yourself, by strong instinctive propensities or implanted affections, to turn the current and direction of these into the stream of self-interest in which experience tells us we are most apt to run to a vicious excess.

Besides it is affirmed, and I think with good reason, that the moral sense carries a good deal more in it than merely an approbation of a certain class of actions as beautiful, praiseworthy or delightful, and therefore finding our interest in them as the most noble gratification. The moral sense implies also a sense of obligation, that such and such things are right and others wrong; that we are bound in duty to do the one, and that our conduct is hateful, blamable, and deserving of punishment, if we do the contrary; and there is also in the moral sense or conscience, an apprehension or belief that reward and punishment will follow, according as we shall act in the one way, or in the other.

It is so far from being true, that there is no more in virtuous action than a superior degree of beauty, or a more noble pleasure, that indeed the beauty and sweetness of virtuous action arises from this very circumstance—that it is a compliance with duty or supposed obligation. Take away this, and the beauty vanishes, as well as the pleasure. Why is it more pleasant to do a just or charitable action than to satisfy my palate with delightful meat, or to walk in a beautiful garden, or read an exquisite poem? Only because I feel myself under an obligation to do it, as a thing useful and important in itself. It is not duty because pleasing, but pleasing because duty.—The same thing may be said of beauty and approbation. I do not approve of the conduct of a plain, honest, industrious, pious man, because it is more beautiful than that of an idle profligate, but I say it is more beautiful and amiable, because he keeps within the bounds of duty. I see a higher species of beauty in moral action: but it arises from a sense of obligation. It may be said, that my interest and duty are the same, because they are inseparable, and the one arises from the other; but there is a real distinction and priority of order. A thing is not my duty, because it is my interest, but it is a wise appointment of nature, that I shall forfeit my interest, if I neglect my duty.

Several other remarks might be made to confirm this. When any person has by experience found that in seeking pleasure he embraced a less pleasing enjoyment, in place of one more delightful, he may be sensible of mistake or misfortune, but he has nothing at all of the feeling of blame or self-condemnation; but when he hath done an immoral action, he has an inward remorse, and feels that he has broken a law, and that he ought to have done otherwise.

READING V

The Nature, Foundation, and Obligation of Virtue[8]

This therefore lays us under the necessity of searching a little further for the principle of moral action. In order to do this with the greater accuracy, and give you a view of the chief controversies on this subject, observe, that there are really three questions upon it, which must be inquired into, and distinguished. I am sensible, they are so intimately connected, that they are sometimes necessarily intermixed; but at others, not distinguishing, leads into error. The questions relate to

I. The nature of virtue.
II. The foundation of virtue.
III. The obligation of virtue.

When we inquire into the nature of virtue, we do enough, when we point out what it is, or show how we may come to the knowledge of every particular duty, and be able to distinguish it from the opposite vice. When we speak of the foundation of virtue, we ask or answer the question. Why is it so? Why is this course of action preferable to the contrary? What is its excellence? When we speak of the obligation of virtue, we ask by what law we are bound, or from what principles we ought to be obedient to the precepts which it contains or prescribes.

After speaking something to each of these—to the controversies that have been raised upon them—and the propriety or importance of entering far into these controversies, or a particular decision of them I shall proceed to a detail of the moral laws or the several branches of duty according to the division first laid down.

I. As to the nature of virtue, or what it is; or, in other words, what is the rule by which I must try every disputed practice—that I may keep clear of the next question, you may observe, that upon all the systems they must have recourse to one or more of the following, *viz.* conscience, reason, experience. All who found virtue upon affection, particularly

---

[8] [Extracted from John Witherspoon (1912) {1800} 'Lecture IV' & 'Lecture V', in *Lectures on Moral Philosophy*, edited by Varnum Lansing Collins, Princeton, NJ: Princeton University Press, pp. 23-35.]

Hutcheson, Shaftesbury and their followers, make the moral sense the rule of duty, and very often attempt to exclude the use of reason on this subject. These authors seem also to make benevolence and public affection the standard of virtue, in distinction from all private and selfish passions.

Doctor Clarke and most English writers of the last age, make reason the standard of virtue, particularly as opposed to inward sentiment or affection. They have this to say particularly in support of their opinion, that reason does in fact often control and alter sentiment; whereas sentiment cannot alter the clear decisions of reason. Suppose my heart dictates to me anything to be my duty, as for example, to have compassion on a person detected in the commission of crimes; yet if, upon cool reflection, I perceive that suffering him to go unpunished will be hurtful to the community, I counteract the sentiment from the deductions of reason.

Again: Some take in the air of experience, and chiefly act upon it. All particularly who are upon the selfish scheme, find it necessary to make experience the guide, to show them what things are really conducive to happiness and what not.

We shall proceed to consider the opinions upon the nature of virtue, the chief of which are as follows:

1. Some say that virtue consists in acting agreeably to the nature and reason of things. And that we are to abstract from all affection, public and private, in determining any question upon it. Clarke.

2. Some say that benevolence or public affection is virtue, and that a regard to the good of the whole is the standard of virtue.[9] What is most remarkable in this scheme is, that it makes the sense of obligation in particular instances give way to a supposed greater good. Hutcheson.

3. One author (Wollaston Rel. of Nat. delineated[10]) makes truth the foundation of virtue, and he reduces the good or evil of any action to the truth or falsehood of a proposition. This opinion differs not in substance, but in words only from Dr. Clarke's.

---

[9] <MS. C adds footnote *Hutcheson*.>
[10] <William Wollaston, 'The religion of nature delineated', London 1722.>

4. Others place virtue in self love, and make a well regulated self love the standard and foundation of it. This scheme is best defended by Dr. Campbell, of St. Andrews.[11]

5. Some of late have made sympathy the standard of virtue, particularly Smith in his *Theory of Moral Sentiments*. He says we have a certain feeling, by which we sympathize, and as he calls it, go along with what appears to be right. This is but a new phraseology for the moral sense.

6. David Hume has a scheme of morals that is peculiar to himself. He makes everything that is *agreeable* and *useful* virtuous, and vice versa, by which he entirely annihilates the difference between natural and moral qualities, making health, strength, cleanliness, as really virtues as integrity and truth.

7. We have an opinion published in this country, that virtue consists in the love of being as such.[12]

Several of these authors do easily and naturally incorporate piety with their system, particularly Clarke, Hutcheson, Campbell and Edwards.

And there are some who begin by establishing natural religion, and then found virtue upon piety. This amounts to the same thing in substance; for reasoners upon the nature of virtue only mean to show what the Author of nature has pointed out as duty. And after natural religion is established on general proofs, it will remain to point out what are its laws, which, not taking in revelation, must bring us back to consider our own nature, and the rational deductions from it.

II. The opinions on the foundation of virtue may be summed up in the four following:

1. The will of God. 2. The reason and nature of things. 3. The public interest. 4. Private interest.

1. The will of God. By this is not meant what was mentioned above, that the intimations of the divine will point out what is our duty; but that the reason of the difference between virtue and vice is to be sought no where else than in the good pleasure of God. That there is no intrinsic excellence in any thing but as he commands or forbids it. They pretend that if it were otherwise there would be something

---

[11] <Archibald Campbell, 'An inquiry into the original of moral virtue', London 1733.>

[12] <MS. A adds *Mr. Edwards*.>

above the Supreme Being, something in the nature of things that would lay him under the law of necessity or fate. But notwithstanding the difficulty of our forming clear conceptions on this subject, it seems very harsh and unreasonable to say that the difference between virtue and vice is no other than the divine will. This would be taking away the moral character even of God himself. It would not have any meaning then to say he is infinitely holy and infinitely perfect. But probably those who have asserted this did not mean any more than that the divine will is so perfect and excellent that all virtue is reduced to conformity to it—and that we ought not to judge of good and evil by any other rule. This is as true as that the divine conduct is the standard of wisdom.

2. Some found it in the reason and nature of things. This may be said to be true, but not sufficiently precise and explicit. Those who embrace this principle succeed best in their reasoning when endeavoring to show that there is an essential difference between virtue and vice. But when they attempt to show wherein this difference doth or can consist, other than public or private happiness, they speak with very little meaning.

3. Public happiness. This opinion is that the foundation of virtue, or that which makes the distinction between it and vice, is its tendency to promote the general good; so that utility at bottom is the principle of virtue, even with the great patrons of disinterested affection.

4. Private happiness. Those who choose to place the foundation of virtue here, would have us to consider no other excellence in it than what immediately conduces to our own gratification.

Upon these opinions I would observe, that there is something true in every one of them, but that they may be easily pushed to an error by excess.

The nature and will of God is so perfect as to be the true standard of all excellence, natural and moral: and if we are sure of what he is or commands, it would be presumption and folly to reason against it, or put our views of fitness in the room of his pleasure; but to say that God, by his will, might have made the same temper and conduct virtuous and excellent, which we now call vicious, seems to unhinge all our notions of the supreme excellence even of God himself.

Again, there seems to be in the nature of things an intrinsic excellence in moral worth, and an indelible impression of it upon the conscience, distinct from producing or receiving happiness, and yet we cannot easily illustrate its excellence but by comparing one kind of happiness with another.

Again, promoting the public or general good seems to be so nearly connected with virtue, that we must necessarily suppose that universal virtue could be of universal utility. Yet there are two excesses to which this has sometimes led. — One the fatalist and necessitarian schemes to which there are so many objections, and the other, the making the general good the ultimate practical rule to every particular person, so that he may violate particular obligations with a view to a more general benefit.

Once more, it is certain that virtue is as really connected with private as with public happiness, and yet to make the interest of the agent the only foundation of it, seems so to narrow the mind, and to be so destructive to the public and generous affections as to produce the most hurtful effects.

If I were to lay down a few propositions on the foundation of virtue, as a philosopher, they should be the following:

1. From reason, contemplation, sentiment and tradition, the being and infinite perfection and excellence of God may be deduced; and therefore what he is, and commands, is virtue and duty. Whatever he has implanted in uncorrupted nature as a principle, is to be received as his will. Propensities resisted and contradicted by the inward principle of conscience, are to be considered as inherent or contracted vice.

2. True virtue certainly promotes the general good, and this may be made use of as an argument in doubtful cases, to determine whether a particular principle is right or wrong, but to make the good of the whole our immediate principle of action, is putting ourselves in God's place, and actually superseding the necessity and use of the particular principles of duty which he hath impressed upon the conscience. As to the whole I believe the universe is faultless and perfect, but I am unwilling to say it is the *best* possible system, because I am not able to understand such an argument, and because it

seems to me absurd that infinite perfection should exhaust or limit itself by a created production.

3. There is in the nature of things a difference between virtue and vice, and however much virtue and happiness are connected by the divine law, and in the event of things, we are made so as to feel towards them, and conceive of them, as distinct. We have the simple perceptions of duty and interest.

4. Private and public interest may be promoted by the same means, but they are distinct views; they should be made to assist, and not destroy each other.

The result of the whole is, that we ought to take the rule of duty from conscience enlightened by reason, experience, and every way by which we can be supposed to learn the will of our Maker, and his intention in creating us such as we are. And we ought to believe that it is as deeply founded as the nature of God himself, being a transcript of his moral excellence, and that it is productive of the greatest good.

III. It remains only that we speak of the obligation of virtue, or what is the law that binds us to the performance, and from what motives or principles we ought to follow its dictates.

The sentiments upon the subject differ, as men have different views of the nature and foundation of virtue, yet they may be reduced within narrower bounds.

The obligation of virtue may be easily reduced to two general kinds, duty and interest. The first, if real, implies that we are under some law, or subject to some superior, to whom we are accountable. The other only implies that nature points it out to us as our own greatest happiness, and that there is no other reason why we ought to obey.

Now I think it is very plain that there is more in the obligation of virtue, than merely our greatest happiness. The moral sentiment itself implies that it is duty independent of happiness. This produces remorse and disapprobation as having done what is blamable and of ill desert. We have two ideas very distinct, when we see a man mistaking his own interest and not obtaining so much happiness as he might, and when we see him breaking through every moral obligation. In the first case we consider him as only accountable to himself, in the second we consider him as accountable to some superior, and to the public. This sense of duty is the primary notion of law and of rights taken in their most extensive signification as including everything we think we are entitled to expect from others, and the neglect or violation of which we consider as wrong, unjust, vicious, and therefore blamable. It is also affirmed with great apparent reason by many, particularly Butler in his *Analogy* and his sermons, that we have a natural feeling of ill desert, and merited punishment in vice. The patrons of the selfish ideas alone, are those who confine the obligation of virtue to happiness.

But of those who are, or would be thought of the opposite sentiment, there are some who differ very considerably from others. Some who profess great opposition to the selfish scheme, declare also great aversion to founding the obligation of virtue in any degree on the will of a superior, or looking for any sanction of punishment, to corroborate the moral laws. This they especially treat with contempt, when it is supposed to be from the deity. Shaftesbury speaks with great bitterness against taking into view a future state of what he calls more extended self-interest. He says men should love virtue for its own sake, without regard to reward or punishment. In this he has been followed by many reasoners, as far as their regard to religion would permit them.

If however, we attend to the dictates of conscience, we shall find evidently, a sense of duty, of self-approbation and remorse, which plainly show us to be under a law, and that law to have a sanction: what else is the meaning of the fear and terror, and apprehension of guilty persons? *Quorum mentes se recludantur, &c*, says Cicero.[13]

Nor is this all, but we have all certainly a natural sense of dependence. The belief of a divine being is certainly either innate and necessary, or has been handed down from the first man, and can now be well supported by the clearest

---

[13] <The quotation is not from Cicero, but is a misprinted adaptation from Tacitus (Annals VI. 6). Each MS. attempts the quotation in full and garbles it.> [*si recludantur tyrannorum mentes, posse aspici laniatus et ictus, quando ut corpora verberibus, ita saevitia, libidine, malis consultis animus dilaceretur*, 'if the minds of tyrants could be opened up, mutilations and blows would be visible, since, just as bodies were mauled by lashings, so was the spirit by savagery, lust, and evil decisions'.]

reason. And our relation to him not only lays the foundation of many moral sentiments and duties, but completes the idea of morality and law, by subjecting us to him, and teaching us to conceive of him, not only as our Maker, preserver and benefactor, but as our righteous governor and supreme judge. As the being and perfections of God are irrefragably established, the obligation of duty must ultimately rest here.

It ought not to be forgotten that the belief or apprehension of a future state of rewards and punishments, has been as universal as the belief of a deity, and seems inseparable from it, and therefore must be considered as the sanction of the moral law. Shaftesbury inveighs severely against this as making man virtuous from a mercenary view; but there are two ways in which we may consider this matter, and in either light his objections have little force. (1) We may consider the primary obligations of virtue as founded upon a sense of its own excellence, joined with a sense of duty and dependance on the supreme being, and rewards and punishments as a secondary motive, which is found in fact, to be absolutely necessary to restrain or reclaim men from vice and impiety. Or (2) we may consider that by the light of nature as well as by revelation, the future reward of virtue is considered as a state of perfect virtue, and the happiness is represented as arising from this circumstance. Here there is nothing at all of a mercenary principle, but only an expectation that true goodness, which is here in a state of imperfection and liable to much opposition, shall then be improved to the highest degree, and put beyond any possibility of change.

We may add to these obligations the manifest tendency of a virtuous conduct to promote even our present happiness: this in ordinary cases it does, and when joined with the steady hope of futurity, does in all cases produce a happiness superior to what can be enjoyed in the practice of vice. Yet perhaps, the Stoics of old, who denied pain to be any evil, and made the wise man superior to all the vicissitudes of fortune, carried things to a romantic and extravagant height. And so do some persons in modern times, who setting aside the consideration of a future state, teach that virtue is its own reward. There are many situations in which, if you deprive a good man of the hope of future happiness, his state seems very undesirable. On the contrary, sometimes the worst of men enjoy prosperity and success to a great degree, nor do they seem to have any such remorse, as to be an adequate punishment of their crimes. If any should insist, that a good man has always some comfort from within and a bad man a self-disapprobation and inward disquiet, suited to their characters, I would say that this arises from the expectation of a future state, and a hope on the one side, and fear on the other, of their condition there.

Those who declaim so highly of virtue being its own reward in this life, take away one of the most considerable arguments, which from the dawn of philosophy, has always been made use of, as a proof of a future state, *viz.* the unequal distribution of good and evil in this life. Besides they do not seem to view the state of bad men properly. When they talk of remorse of conscience, as a sufficient punishment, they forget that this is seldom to a high degree, but in the case of some gross crimes. Cruelty and murder, frequent acts of gross injustice, are sometimes followed with deep horror of conscience; and a course of intemperance or lust is often attended with such dismal effects upon the body, fame and fortune, that those who survive it a few years, are a melancholy spectacle, and a burden to themselves and others. But it would be very loose morality, to suppose none to be bad men, but those who were under the habitual condemnation of conscience. On the contrary, the far greater part are blinded in their understandings, as well as corrupt in their practice—They deceive themselves, and are at peace. Ignorance and inattention keep the multitude at peace. And false principles often produce self-justification and ill-founded peace, even in atrocious crimes. Even common robbers are sometimes found to justify themselves, and say—I must live—I have a right to my share of provision, as well as that proud fellow that rolls in his chariot.

The result of the whole is that the obligation to virtue ought to take in all the following particulars: A sense of its own intrinsic excellence—of its happy consequences in the present life—a sense of duty and subjection to the Supreme Being—and a hope of future happiness, and fear of future misery from his decision.

Four

James Wilson (1742–1798)

James Wilson was born to a poor family in 1742 in the town of Carskerdo, Scotland. At the age of fifteen Wilson won a scholarship which enabled him to attend the nearby University of St. Andrews. Following his time at St. Andrews, Wilson enrolled at St. Mary's College divinity school in order to prepare for the ministry, but was forced to withdraw on account of financial difficulties caused by the death of his father.

In 1765, Wilson abandoned his plans for ministry and sailed for America in order to pursue a career as a merchant. Upon reaching the New World he began teaching as a tutor at the College of Philadelphia (now the University of Pennsylvania), where he was awarded an honorary MA in 1766, and then took up the study of law. After completing these studies, Wilson moved first to Reading, and then to Carlisle, Pennsylvania, in order to practice law.

The years between 1771 and 1777 were prosperous ones for Wilson. In 1771 Wilson married Rachel Bird, a wealthy heiress. Further, his acumen as a lawyer brought him both wealth and prestige. Wilson also began making a name for himself as a statesman during this period. In 1774, Wilson published a widely-read pamphlet asserting the independence of the colonies from Parliament, based on the political philosophy that all ruling power is derived from the consent of the governed. Following several terms as a representative in the local government of Pennsylvania, Wilson was elected as a delegate to the Continental Congress in 1775, where he became a signer of the Declaration of Independence.

Following the war, Wilson became convinced that the United States would be most prosperous under a strong federal government, in which the power of the legislative branch was balanced by empowered executive and judicial branches. Thus, he became an ardent proponent of the Federalist position at the Constitutional Congress and was instrumental in the US Constitution's ratification by Pennsylvania in 1787. In 1789, on account of both his political and legal talents, Wilson was appointed by George Washington as one of the first members of the Supreme Court.

Alongside his political and legal activities, Wilson was also a furious speculator and investor. From the early 1770s onward, he bought up enormous plots of land in the territories west of the colonies in the hopes of turning a profit as settlers pushed into the interior. From the 1780s on, he also invested in manufacturing ventures. Unfortunately for Wilson, the economic expansion of the United States fell well short of his optimism, and he was continually forced to finance his investments with large loans. By the late 1790s Wilson found himself unable repay his debts, and was therefore imprisoned. In 1798, during an imprisonment in North Carolina, penniless and largely forgotten, Wilson died following a stroke.

The selections extracted below come from a happier time in Wilson's life: during his brief tenure as the professor of law at the University of Philadelphia during the 1790–91 school year. Although these lectures were hastily written and unrevised by Wilson, and at times rely on Thomas Reid's works to the point of plagiarism, they capture the breadth and acuity of his thought. Furthermore, although forming only the first part of a planned three-part lecture series, they stand as one of the first attempts to develop a fully American philosophy of law.

Biographical Information: John K. Alexander, *American National Biography Online*.

READING VI

Sensation, Consciousness, and Memory[1]

'Know thou thyself' is an inscription peculiarly proper for the porch of the temple of science. The knowledge of human nature is of all human knowledge the most curious and the most important. To it all the other sciences have a relation; and though from it they may seem to diverge and ramify very widely, yet by one passage or another they still return.

In every art and in every disquisition, the powers of the mind are the instruments, which we employ; the more fully we understand their nature and their use, the more skillfully and the more successfully we shall apply them. In the sublimest arts, the mind is not only the instrument, but the subject also of our operations and inquiries. The poet, the orator, the philosopher work upon man in different ways and for different purposes. The statesman and the judge, in pursuit of the noblest ends, have the same dignified object before them. An accurate and distinct knowledge of his nature and powers, will undoubtedly diffuse much light and splendor over the science of law. In truth, law can never attain either the extent or the elevation of science, unless it be raised upon the science of man.

The knowledge of human nature is not more distinguished by its importance, than it is by its difficulty. Though the mind—the noblest work of God, which reason discovers—is of all objects the nearest to us, and seems the most within our view; yet it is no easy matter to attend to its operations and faculties, in such a manner as to obtain clear, full, and distinct conceptions concerning them. The consequence has been, that in no branch of knowledge have greater errors, and even absurdities, insinuated themselves, than in the philosophy of the human mind. Instead of proceeding slowly and cautiously by observation and experience, those who have written on this subject have adopted the more easy, but the less certain mode of process by hypothesis and analogy. The event has been such as might have been expected: those who have cultivated other sciences, have made progress,

---

[1] [Extracted from James Wilson (1804) 'Of Man, as an Individual', in *The Works of The Honourable James Wilson, L.L.D.*, Volume I, Philadelphia, PA: Lorenzo Press, pp. 229–49.]

because they have set out in the right road, and have consulted the proper guides: those who have speculated on human nature have, too many of them, been involved in a dark and inextricable labyrinth, because they commenced their journey in an improper direction, and have listened to the information of those, whose information was the result of conjecture and not of experience. But this darkness will not last forever. Some future sun of science will arise, and illuminate this benighted part of the intellectual globe. When the powers of the human mind shall be delineated truly and according to nature, those, whose vision is not distorted by prejudice, will recognize their own features in the picture. They will be surprised that things, in themselves so clear, could be so long involved in absurdity; and, when the truth is to be found in their own breasts, that they have been led so far from it by false systems and theories.

The only instrument, by which we can have any distinct notion of the faculties of our own and of others minds, is reflection. By this power, the mind makes its own operations the object of its attention, and views and examines them on every side. This power of reflection or self-examination, so absolutely indispensable in the investigation of what is so near and so important to us, is neither soon nor easily acquired or exerted. The mind, like the eye, contemplates, with facility, every object around it; but is with difficulty turned inward upon its own operations. Whoever has attempted to experiment on the philosophy of the mind—the only legitimate way in which a knowledge of it can be acquired—must have found how utterly impossible it is to make any clear and distinct observations on our faculties of thought, unless the passions, as well as the imagination, be silent and still. The materials on which we reflect are so minute, so mixed, and so volatile, that the strongest minds alone can, in any degree, arrange them, even in their quietest state. The least breath of passion moves and agitates them, so as to render everything distorted and deformed.

Reflection, like all our other powers, is greatly improved by exercise: it thus becomes habitual; the difficulty attending it daily diminishes; and the advantages resulting from it are many and great. One who is accustomed habitually to reflection, can think and speak with accuracy on every subject; and can judge and discriminate for himself in many cases, in which others must trust to notions borrowed, confused, and indistinct.

Assisting and subservient to accurate reflection, is the structure of language, which is of much use in developing the operations of the mind. The language of mankind is expressive of their thoughts. The various operations of the understanding, will, and passions have various forms of speech corresponding to them, in all languages; a due attention to the signs, throws light on the things signified by them. There are, in all languages, modes of speech, by which men signify their judgment, or give their testimony, or accept, or refuse, or command, or threaten, or supplicate, or ask information or advice, or plight their faith in promises or contracts. If such operations were not common to mankind, we should not find, in all languages, forms of speech by which they are expressed.

A system of human nature is not expected from this chair. The undertaking, indeed, is too vast for me; it is too vast for any one man, however great his genius or abilities may be. But it comes directly within our plan, to consider it so far as to have just conceptions of man in two most important characters, as an author, and as a subject of law; as accountable for his own conduct, as capable of directing the conduct both of himself and of others. The laws, which God has given to us, are strictly agreeable to our nature; they are adjusted with infallible correctness to our perfection and happiness. On those, which we make for ourselves, the same characters, as deeply and as permanently as possible, ought to be impressed. But how, unless we study and know our nature, shall we make laws fit for it, and calculated to improve it?

I mean not—for it would be uninstructive—to give you an account of the divisions and subdivisions, into which metaphysicians have attempted to class and arrange our mental powers and principles. No division has been more common, and, perhaps, less exceptionable, than that of the powers of the mind into those of the understanding and those of the will. And yet even this division, I am afraid, has led into a mistake. The mistake I believe to be this; it has been supposed, that in the operations ascribed to the will, there was no employment of the understanding; and that in those ascribed to the understanding, there was no exertion of the will. But this is not the case. It is probable, that there is no operation of the understanding, in which the mind is not in some degree active; in other words, in which the will has not some share. On the other hand, there can be no energy of the will, which is not accompanied with some act of the understanding. In the operations of the mind, both faculties generally, if not always, concur; and the distinction between them can be of no farther use, than to arrange each operation under that faculty, which has the largest share in it. Thus by the perceptive powers, we are supposed to acquire knowledge, and by the powers of volition, we are said to exert ourselves in action.

If even this division, long and generally received as it has been, has given occasion to a mistake; we have no great reason to indulge a partiality for others. The truth is, that they have been generally superficial and inaccurate; they have depended more on fancy than on nature; and have proceeded more from presumptuous attempts to accommodate the mind to a system, than from respectful endeavors to accommodate a system to the mind. Abhorrent from the first, restrained by propriety from aiming at the second; let my humble task be to select and make such observations concerning our powers, our dispositions, our principles, and our habits, as will illustrate the intimate connexion and reciprocal influence of religion, morality, and law.

Simplicity is the favorite object of system. In the material world, attachment to this simplicity misled the penetrating Descartes. Even the great Newton, patient, faithful, and attentive as he was in tracing nature's footsteps, was, on one occasion, almost seduced, by the same attachment, to follow hypothesis, the ape of nature. A body of morality, pretending to be complete, has sometimes been built on a single pillar of the inward frame: the entire conduct of life has been accounted for, at least the attempt has been made to account for it, from a single quality or power. Many systems of this kind have appeared, calculated merely to flatter the mind. According to some writers, man is entirely selfish; according to others, universal benevolence is the highest aim of his nature. One founds morality upon sympathy solely: another exclusively upon utility. But the variety of human nature is not so easily comprehended or reached. It is a complicated machine; and is unavoidably so, in order to answer the various and important purposes, for which it is formed and designed.

How wretched are oftentimes the representations and the imitations of nature's works! A puppet may make a few motions and gesticulations; but how unlike it is to that, which it represents! How contemptible, when compared to the body of a man, whose structure the more we know, the more we discover its wonders, and the more sensible we are of our ignorance! Is the mechanism of the mind so easily comprehended, when that of the body is so difficult? Yet, by some systems, which are offered to us, with pretensions the most lofty and magnificent, a few laws of association, joined to a few original feelings, explain the whole mechanism of sense, imagination, memory, belief, and of all the actions and passions of the mind. Is this the man that nature made? It is a puppet surely, contrived to mimic her work. The more we know of other parts of nature, the more we approve and admire them. But when we look within, and consider the mind itself, which makes us capable of all our prospects and enjoyments; if it is indeed what some late systems of high pretensions make it, we find we have only been in an enchanted castle, imposed upon by specters and apparitions. We blush to think how we have been deluded; we are ashamed of our frame; and can hardly forbear expostulating with our destiny. Is this thy pastime, O nature, to put such tricks upon a silly creature, and then take off the mask, and show him how he has been befooled? If this is the philosophy of human nature; my soul! enter thou not into her secrets. It is surely the forbidden tree of knowledge: I no sooner taste of it, than I perceive myself naked. —Such, in substance, has been the well founded expostulation against some of the late and famed theories concerning the human mind.[2] The theory, which we adopt, because we think it grounded in truth and reality, will open very different—the most enrapturing prospects.

The mind itself, indeed, is *one* internal principle: but its operations many, various, connected, and complicated: its

---

[2] [See Thomas Reid (1764) *Inquiry into the Human Mind on the Principles of Common Sense*, Chapter 1.]

perceptions are mixed, compounded, and decompounded, by habits, associations, and abstractions: its powers both of action and perception, on account either of a diversity in their objects, or in their manner of operating, are considered as separate and distinct faculties. This I take to be a just state of things with regard to the mind, and its perceptions, operations, and powers. But I think it is highly probable, that, in opposition to this account, the mind has been too often considered as distributed into different divisions and departments: and that the operations, in each department, have been considered as simple and unmixed. Each one of you, by recalling to remembrance your manner of thinking upon these subjects, will be able to say whether this has not been the case.

Again; the mind is an *active* principle. It has been the opinion of some modern philosophers, that, in thinking and sensation, the mind is merely passive. In all ages, and in all languages, the various modes of thinking have been expressed by words of active signification; such as seeing, hearing, reasoning, willing. It seems, therefore, to be the natural judgment of mankind, that the mind is active in its various ways of thinking; and for this reason, they are called its operations, and are expressed by active verbs. Sensation, imagination, memory, and judgment have, in all ages, been considered, by the vulgar, as *acts* of the mind. This is shown by the manner, in which they are expressed in all languages. When the mind is much employed in them, we say it is very active; whereas, if they were impressions only, as the *ideal* philosophy would lead us to conceive, we ought, in such a case, rather to say, that the mind is very passive. The paper which I hold in my hand was not active, when it received the characters written on it.

Man is composed of a body and a soul intimately connected; but at what time and in what manner connected, we do not know. In consequence of this connexion, the body lives and performs the functions necessary to life for a certain time; increases for a certain time in stature and in strength; is nourished with food, and is refreshed by sleep. In consequence of the same connexion, the body moves; the hands fulfill their various and active offices; the tongue expressive speaks; and the eyes sometimes still more expressive look.

The body, and the things of the body, are far from being beneath our regard. In its present state, it is a mansion well fitted for the temporary residence of its noble inhabitant: in its renewed state, it will be endowed with the power of retaining that fitness forever.

The fabric of the human mind, however, is more astonishing still. The faculties of this are, with no less wisdom, adapted to their several ends, than the organs of the other. Nay, as the mind is of an order higher than that of the body, even more of the wisdom and skill of the divine Architect is displayed in its structure. In all respects, fearfully and wonderfully are we made.[3]

From experience we find, that when external things are within the sphere of our perceptive powers, they affect our organs of sensation, and are perceived by the mind. That they are perceived we are conscious; but the manner in which they are perceived, we cannot explain; for we cannot trace the connexion between our minds and the impressions made on our organs of sense; because we cannot trace the connexion which subsists between the soul and the body. Frequent and laborious have been the attempts of philosophers to investigate the manner, in which things external are perceived by the mind. Let us imitate them, neither in their fruitless searches to discover what cannot be known; nor in framing hypotheses which will not bear the test of reason, or of intuition; nor in rejecting self-evident truths, which, though they cannot be proved by reasoning, are known by a species of evidence superior to any that reasoning can produce.

Many philosophers allege that our mind does not perceive external objects themselves; that it perceives only *ideas* of them; and that those ideas are actually in the mind. When it has been intimated to them, that, if this be the case; if we perceive not external objects themselves, but only ideas; the necessary consequence must be, that we cannot be certain that anything, except those ideas, exists; the consequence has been admitted in its fullest force. Nay, it has been made the foundation of another theory, in which it has been asserted, that men and other animals, the sun, moon, and stars, every-

---

[3] [Psalm 139:14.]

thing which we think we see, and hear, and feel around us, have no real existence; that what we dignify with such appellations, and what we suppose to be so permanent and substantial, are nothing more than 'the baseless fabric of a vision'[4]—are nothing more than ideas perceived in the mind. The theory has been carried to a degree still more extravagant than this; and the existence of mind has been denied, as well as the existence of body. We shall have occasion to examine these castles, which have not even air to support them. Suffice it, at present, to observe, that the existence of the objects of our external senses, in the way and manner in which we perceive that existence, is a branch of intuitive knowledge, and a matter of absolute certainty; that the constitution of our nature determines us to believe in our senses; and that a contrary determination would finally lead to the total subversion of all human knowledge. For this belief we cannot, we pretend not to assign an argument; it is a simple and original, and therefore an inexplicable act of the mind. It can neither be described nor defined. But one thing we shall engage to do, though, at present, we are not prepared for it. When those philosophers prove by argument, that we ought to receive the testimony of reason; we then will prove, by argument, that we ought to receive the testimony of sense. Till that time, let us receive the testimony of both, as of faculties, with which we have been endowed, for wise and benevolent purposes, by him who is all-true. The senses were intended by him to give us all that information of external objects, which he saw to be proper for us in our present state. This information they convey without reasoning, without art, without investigation on our part. They are five in number. Tastes are referred to the sense of tasting: odors, to that of smelling: sounds, to that of hearing: light and colors, to that of seeing: all other bodily sensations, to that of touch.

Our external senses are not indeed the most exalted of our powers; but they are powers of real use and importance; and, to powers of a more dignified nature, they are most serviceable and necessary instruments. It has been the endeavor of some philosophers to degrade them below that rank, in which they ought to be placed. They have been represented

---

[4] [Shakespeare, *The Tempest*, Act 4, Scene 1.]

as powers, by which we receive sensations only of external objects. Even this part of their service is far from being unimportant. The perception of external objects is a principal link of that mysterious chain, which connects the material with the intellectual world. But this, as I before mentioned, is not the whole of the functions discharged by the senses: they judge, as well as inform: they are not confined to the task of conveying impressions; they are exalted to the office of deciding concerning the nature and the evidence of the impressions, which they convey.

The senses are the vehicles of pleasures, less elevated indeed than those which are intellectual, still less elevated than those which are moral, but pleasures not beneath the regard of a rational and a moral mind. The pleasures of sense, it is true, ought, like everything else that is subordinate, to be prevented from transgressing their natural and proper bounds: but that is no reason why they should be either neglected or despised. To be without the senses even of tasting and smelling, would be a real misfortune, because it would be a real inconvenience, and would be attended with the loss of sensations innocent and agreeable. The organ of smelling is often the speediest and the surest instrument to prevent or to recover a person from a fainting fit. The senses are susceptible of improvement; and they ought to be improved; for they are the sources both of pleasures and of advantage. Some of the senses are the sources of pleasures of a very elegant kind. The ear is the welcome messenger of melody and harmony, as well as of sound: the eye, of beauty, as well as of light and colors: and the man who feels not agreeable emotions from the contemplation of beauty, and is not moved with concord of sweet sounds—I will not finish the fine poetical description—I will only say, that he has no reason to exult in the absence of those enjoyments. Both the eye and the ear are capable of being refined to a very great height. For this I need only appeal to judges of music, of painting, of statuary, of architecture. In many mechanic arts, a good eye, as it is called, is of excellent service. Gentlemen of the military profession—a profession which has something singular in it; a profession which should be learned, that it may never be used— know the importance of a military eye.

[...]

As the external senses convey to us information of what passes without us; we have an internal sense, which gives us information of what passes within us. To this we appropriate the name of consciousness. It is an immediate conception of the operations of our own minds, joined with the belief of the existence of those operations. In exerting consciousness, the mind, so far as we know, makes no use of any bodily organ. This operation seems to be purely intellectual. Consciousness takes knowledge of everything that passes within the mind. What we perceive, what we remember, what we imagine, what we reason, what we judge, what we believe, what we approve, what we hope, all our other operations, while they are present, are objects of this.

This, like many other operations of the mind, is simple, peculiar, inaccessible equally to definition and analysis. For its existence everyone must make his appeal to himself. Are you conscious that you remember, or that you think? We have already seen, that the existence of the objects of sense is one great branch of intuitive knowledge: of the same kind of knowledge, the existence of the objects of consciousness is another branch, more extensive and important still. When a man feels pain, he is certain of the existence of pain; when he is conscious that he thinks, he is certain of the existence of thought. If I am asked to prove that consciousness is a faithful and not a fallacious sense; all the answer which I can give is—I feel, but I cannot prove; I can find no previous truth more certain or more luminous, from which this can derive either evidence or illustration. But some such antecedent truth is necessarily the first link in a chain of proof. For proof is nothing else than the deduction of truths less known or less believed, from others that are more known or better believed. 'What can we reason, but from what we know?'[5] The immediate and irresistible conviction, which I have of the real existence of those things, of whose existence I am conscious, is a conviction produced by intuition, not by reason. He who doubted, or pretended to doubt, concerning every other information, deemed himself justified in taking

---

[5] [Alexander Pope (1733) 'An Essay on Man', Ep. 1, v. 18.]

for granted the veracity of that information, which was given to him by his consciousness. He was conscious that he thought; and therefore he was satisfied that he really thought. '*Cogito*'[6] was a first principle, which he who pronounced it dangerous and unphilosophical to assume anything else, judged it safe and wise to assume. And when he had once assumed that he thought, he gravely set to work to prove, that because he thought he existed. His existence was true, but he could not prove it; and all his attempts to prove it have been shown, by a succeeding philosopher, to be inconsistent with the rules of sound and accurate logic. But even this succeeding philosopher, who showed that Descartes had not proved his existence, and who, from the principles of his own philosophy could not assume this existence without proof — even this philosopher has assumed the truth of the information given by consciousness. 'Mr. Hume, after annihilating body and mind, time and space, action and causation, and even his own mind, acknowledges the reality of the thoughts, sensations, and passions, of which he is conscious.'[7] He has left them — how philosophically I will not pretend to say — to 'stand upon their own bottom, stripped of a subject, rather than call in question the reality of their existence'.[8] Let us felicitate ourselves, that there is, at least, one principle of common sense, which has never been called in question. It is a first principle, which we are required and determined, by the very constitution of our nature and faculties, to believe. Perhaps we shall find other first principles, which, by the same constitution of our nature and faculties, we are equally required and determined to believe. Such principles are parts of our constitution, no less than the power of thinking: reason can neither make nor destroy them: like a telescope, it may assist, it may extend, but it cannot supply natural vision.

Possessed of the senses and of consciousness; and believing, as we must believe, the truth of the information, which

---

[6] [From Descartes' famous maxim '*Cogito ergo sum*', 'I think therefore I am'. See Descartes (1637) *Discourse on Method*, IV and (1644) *Principles of Philosophy*, I.7.]

[7] [Thomas Reid (1785) *Essays on the Intellectual Powers of Man*, VI.v.]

[8] [Thomas Reid (1764) *Inquiry into the Human Mind on the Principles of Common Sense*, II.iii.]

they give, we cannot complain that our knowledge is a *baseless* fabric; but if we were possessed only of those powers, we might well complain, that our knowledge was a *fleeting* fabric. The moment that an external object is removed from the operation of our senses, that moment our perception of it is lost: the moment our attention is withdrawn from the consideration of any of the powers of the mind, that moment our immediate conception of it is gone. The external object may, indeed, return; but it will return as a stranger: the internal power may become again the object of our consciousness; but it will appear as an object hitherto unknown. As to the purpose of accumulating knowledge, every succeeding moment would be as the first moment of our existence. We should perceive what is present; but we should have no power of connecting what is present, with what is past. Without this connecting power, we should have no means of forming any conjecture concerning what is to come. But the divine hand that made us, leaves not its workmanship unfinished. We are endowed with a power, by which we have an immediate knowledge of things past. We are provided with a storehouse, fitted to preserve things new and old. And of this storehouse it is the extraordinary property, that the more it is filled with treasure, the more capacious and retentive it becomes. You know I speak of the memory. Much might be usefully said concerning this necessary and important power; but my plan, which comprehends such a variety of parts, forbids me to enlarge upon each of them.

Of the immediate cause of remembrance we know nothing: and all attempts to trace and discover that cause have, to say the least of them, proved vain and illusory: it is one of those things, of which we must be contented to remain ignorant. But while of some things we ought to acquiesce in our ignorance; of others, we should be satisfied with our knowledge: though we cannot assign a cause *why* we remember, we know the fact that we *do* remember; and we know likewise another fact, that our remembrance is true. What we distinctly remember, we believe as strongly as what we distinctly perceive. To give a reason why we believe the information of our perceptions, I have already declared myself incapable: the same declaration I now make, concerning the information of our memory. By the constitution of our nature, it is always accompanied with belief.

I had occasion to rescue the senses from the unjust disparagement, which they have sometimes suffered: let me now perform the same just office to the memory. You know it to be the fashion of some to exclaim, with a degree of affectation, how wretched their memories are. The design is not declared; but it is obvious. At the expense of their memory, they insinuate a compliment to their judgment: for it has somehow been received as an opinion, that a strong memory and a strong judgment have seldom been united in the same mind. Perhaps the beautiful lines of Mr. Pope may have contributed to give a currency to this sentiment: but the sentiment is ill-founded. I will, indeed, admit, on one hand, that a great memory is often found without a great genius: but I will not admit, on the other, that a great genius is often found without a great memory. The contrary I believe to be generally, I will not say always, the case. Men of the most extensive abilities have been men also of the most extensive memories: witness Themistocles, Cicero, Caesar, Bolingbroke. If these remarks be true, the compliment to judgment at the cost of memory is but a left-handed one. Instead of being rivals, judgment and memory are mutual assistants. Memory furnishes the materials which judgment selects, adjusts, and arranges. Those materials selected, adjusted, and arranged are more at the call of memory than before: for it is a well known fact, that those things, which are disposed most methodically and connected most naturally, are the most distinct, as well as the most lasting objects of remembrance: hence, in discourse, the utility as well as beauty of order. Strength, as well as clearness in our perceptions greatly aids the memory: hence, in discourse, the utility as well as beauty of vivacity. Agreeable emotions, attending our perceptions, contribute to render them both clear and strong: hence, in discourse, the utility as well as beauty of every chaste and elegant ornament. That which is conveyed through the channel of two senses makes a stronger and more lasting impression, than that which is conveyed through the channel of one: hence, in discourse, the utility as well as beauty of just and expressive action. To associate the pleasing with the useful, is Nature's example as well as precept.

I have already intimated that memory is greatly susceptible of improvement: it is so to a surprising degree. This improvement is acquired by vigorous but prudent exercise; and by habitual but lively attention. I assign limitations both to exercise and attention, because both are liable to run into excess. A memory overloaded will make but little useful progress either in literature or business. An attention overstrained is apt to degenerate into what is, with singular propriety, termed absence of thought. To counterfeit this absent kind of thoughtfulness, has been the affectation of those, who wish to be deemed deep thinkers, without the trouble of thinking. To feel it is frequently the lot of those, who think too much. But it is a failing, not an excellence: it is to be avoided, not to be courted. When it begins to steal upon a studious person, he should relieve his attention by changing its object.

In all the ways, in which the objects of our thoughts have hitherto presented themselves to us, they have been necessarily attended with the act or operation of belief. But they may be presented to us in another way, unaccompanied with that act or operation. Let me exemplify this by a set of very familiar instances: for things may be exemplified, that cannot be defined. You see this handkerchief. You are necessarily determined to believe that you see it. You remember that, but a moment ago, I showed you a handkerchief. You are now necessarily determined to believe that you saw it. In the first instance, the handkerchief was seen: that was necessarily accompanied with the belief of its then present existence. In the second instance, the handkerchief was remembered: that was necessarily accompanied with the belief of its past existence. You may hereafter think of a handkerchief, certainly without seeing, probably without recollecting, the handkerchief, which I just now showed you. In the first instance, the perception was accompanied with the belief of present existence: in the second instance, the remembrance was accompanied with the belief of past existence: in the third and last instance, the conception is not accompanied with any belief at all. Conception is an operation of the mind, by which we apprehend a thing, without any belief or judgment concerning it, without referring it to present or past existence. Every one is conscious that he can conceive a thousand things, of whose present or past existence he has not the least belief. You have seen a mountain: you have seen gold: you can conceive a golden mountain: but can you believe its existence?[9]

Conception enters into every operation of the mind. Our senses and our consciousness cannot convey to us information concerning any object, without, at the same time, giving some conception of that object. If we remember anything, we must have some conception of that, which we remember. In conception there is neither truth nor falsehood; for conception neither affirms nor denies. But though all the other operations of the mind include conception; conception itself may exist, detached from all the others, excepting consciousness. By logicians, conception is frequently called *simple apprehension*.[10]

The powers of sensation, of consciousness, and of memory are exerted upon objects which exist, or have existed. Conception is often exerted upon objects, which have neither past, nor present, nor even future existence. The creative powers of conception and description possessed by Shakespeare were, by no means, confined to actual existence, past, present, or to come.

READING VII

Judgment, Reason, and Common Sense[11]

Judgment is an important operation of the mind; and is employed upon the materials of perception and knowledge. It is generally described to be, that act of the mind, by which one thing is affirmed or denied of another. But this description is, in one respect, too limited; in another, it is too extensive. It is too limited in this respect, that though our judgments, when expressed, are indeed expressed by affirmation or denial, yet it is not necessary to a judgment that it be expressed at all.

---

9 [See David Hume (1739) *A Treatise on Human Nature*, I.i.1.]
10 [See Thomas Reid (1785) *Essays on the Intellectual Powers of Man*, IV.i.]
11 [Extracted from James Wilson (1804) 'Of Man, as an Individual', in *The Works of The Honourable James Wilson, L.L.D.*, Volume I, Philadelphia, PA: Lorenzo Press, pp. 249–81.]

Men may judge without affirming or denying anything; nay, they may judge contrary to what they affirm or deny. The description is too extensive in this respect, that it includes testimony as well as judgment. When a judge pronounces his decree, he delivers it in the affirmative or negative: when a witness delivers his testimony, he uses the affirmative or negative likewise. Judgment and testimony are, however, operations very different from one another: wrong judgment is only an error: false testimony is something more.

In persons arrived at the years of discretion, their perceptions, their consciousness, their memory are objects of their judgment. Evidence is the ground of judgment; and where evidence is, it is impossible not to judge.

To every determination of the mind concerning what is true or what is false, the name of judgment may be assigned. Some consider knowledge as a separate faculty, conversant about truth and falsehood: perhaps it is more accurate to consider it as a species of judgment; for without judgment, how can there be any knowledge?[12] Judgments are intuitive, as well as discursive, founded on truths that are self-evident, as well as on those that are deduced from demonstration, or from reasoning of a less certain kind. The former, or intuitive judgments, may, in the strictest sense, be called the judgments of nature.

Sense and judgment are sometimes used, especially by some modern philosophers, in contradistinction to each other—very improperly. In common language, and in the writings of the best authors, sense always implies judgment: a man of sense is a man of judgment: common sense is that degree of judgment, which is to be expected in men of common education and common understanding.

With the power of judging, the power of reasoning is very nearly connected. Both powers are frequently included under the general appellation of reason. But reasoning is strictly the process, by which we pass from one judgment to another, which is the consequence of it. In all reasoning, there must be one proposition, which is inferred, and another, at least, from which the inference is made.

---

[12] [See John Locke (1690) *An Essay Concerning Human Understanding*, IV.xvi.]

Reason as well as judgment, has truth and falsehood for its objects: both proceed from evidence; both are accompanied with belief.

The power of reasoning is frequently selected as the characteristic quality, which distinguishes the human race from the inferior part of the creation. From nature the capacity of reasoning is unquestionably derived; but it may be wonderfully strengthened, improved, and extended by art. Imitation and exercise are the two great instruments of improvement.

In a chain of reasoning, the evidence must proceed regularly and without interruption from link to link: the evidence of the last conclusion can be no greater than that of the weakest link in the chain; because if even the weakest link fails, the whole chain is broken.

In reasoning, the most useful and the most splendid talent is the invention of intermediate proofs. In all productions of the understanding, invention is entitled to the highest praise. It implies a luminous view of the object proposed, and sagacity and quickness in discerning, selecting, and employing, to the utmost advantage, the means that are best fitted for accomplishing that object. In the assemblage of those qualities consists that superiority of understanding, which is denominated genius.

Reasoning is distinguished into two kinds; that, which is demonstrative; and that, which is only probable.[13] In demonstrative reasoning there are no degrees; the inference, in every step of the series, is necessary; and it is impossible but that, from the premises, the conclusion must flow. Hence demonstrative reasoning can be applied only to such truths as are necessary; not to such as are contingent.

With regard to reasoning, which is only probable, the connexion between the premises and the conclusion is not a necessary connexion. Probability is susceptible of numerous and widely differing degrees of strength and weakness. The degrees of evidence are measured by their effect upon a clear, a sound, and an unprejudiced understanding. Every degree of evidence produces a proportioned degree of knowledge and belief.

---

[13] [See Thomas Reid (1785) *Essays on the Intellectual Powers of Man*, VII.i–iii.]

Probable evidence may be distributed into a number of different kinds. One, and a very important one, is that of human testimony. On this a great part of human knowledge depends. History and law resort to it for the materials of decision and faith. To examine, to compare, and to appreciate this kind of evidence is the business of the judge, the juryman, the counsel, and the party. Without some competent discernment concerning it, no man can act with common prudence or safety in the ordinary occurrences of life.

Another kind of probable evidence is, the opinion of those, who are professional judges of the point in question. In England, a reference is sometimes made to the judges for their opinions in a matter of law. On a trial, recourse is frequently had to the professional sentiments of a physician. A shoemaker could point out to Apelles[14] himself a defect in the picture of a shoe. A tyrant, nurtured and practiced in the tyrant's art, could, at the first glance, discover a mistake in the representation of a decollated head.

A third kind of probable evidence is that, by which we recognize the identity of the same thing, and the diversity of different things. This kind of evidence is of the greatest consequence in the affairs of life. By it, the identity of persons and things is determined in courts of justice. In acquiring, retaining, and applying this kind of evidence, there is a wonderful diversity of talents in different men. Some will recollect and distinguish almost all the faces they have ever seen: others are much more slow, and much less retentive in this species of recollection and discrimination.

There are many other kinds of probable evidence, that well deserve the study of the lawyer, the philosopher, and the man. But this is not the proper occasion to attempt an enumeration of them.

Every free action has two causes, which cooperate in its production. One is moral; the other is physical: the former is the will, which determines the action; the latter is the power, which carries it into execution. A paralytic may will to run: a person able to run, may be unwilling: from the want of will in one, and the want of power in the other, each remains in his place.

---

[14] [Apelles of Kos: a famous painter from 4th century BC Greece.]

Our actions and the determinations of our will are generally accompanied with liberty. The name of liberty we give to that power of the mind, by which it modifies, regulates, suspends, continues, or alters its deliberations and actions. By this faculty, we have some degree of command over ourselves: by this faculty we become capable of conforming to a rule: possessed of this faculty, we are accountable for our conduct.

But the existence of this faculty has been boldly called in question. It has been asserted, that we have no sense of moral liberty; and that, if we have such a sense, it is fallacious.

With regard to the first question, let every one ask it of himself. Have I a sense of moral liberty? Have I a conviction that I am free? If you have; this sense—this conviction is a matter of fact, or an object of intuition; and vain it is to reason against its truth or existence.

If it exists; why is it to be deemed fallacious? Are there peculiar marks of deception discoverable in it? Can any reason be assigned why we should suspect it, and not every other sense or power of our nature? He that made one, made all. If we are to suspect all; we ought to believe nothing.

But by what one especial power are we told that we ought to suspect all others? On which is this exclusive character of veracity impressed? If Nature is fallacious; how do we learn to detect the cheat? If she is a juggler by trade; is it for us to attempt to penetrate the mysteries of her art, and take upon us to decide when it is that she presents a true, and when it is that she presents a false appearance? If she is false in every other instance, how can we believe her, when she says she is a liar?

But she does not say so. She is, and she claims to be honest; and the law of our constitution determines us to believe her. When we feel, or when we perceive by intuition, that we are free; we may assume the doctrine of moral liberty, as a first and self-evident, though an undemonstrable principle.

I have frequently mentioned *first principles*. The evidence, on which they ought to be received, well deserves discussion and attention. This is a subject which has been greatly misunderstood, and, perhaps, misrepresented. It is a subject, in which inferences, destructive of all knowledge and virtue, have been drawn, with all the pomp and parade of metaphysical sagacity. It is a subject, concerning which proper conceptions are essentially necessary to the progress of all science, that is truly valuable. They are peculiarly necessary in the study of law, in which evidence bears such an active and distinguished part. To believe our senses—to give credit to human testimony, has been considered as unphilosophical, and, consequently, irrational, if not absurd. The connexion, on this subject, between the principles of law, of philosophy, and of human nature has never, so far as I know, been sufficiently traced or explained.

Of some philosophers of no small fame, and of no small influence in propagating a certain fashionable—creed, I was going to say; but that would be peculiarly improper—system I will call it, by a particular indulgence—of such philosophers it has been the favorite doctrine, that reason is the supreme arbitress of human knowledge; that by her solely we ought to be governed; that in her solely we ought to place confidence; that she can establish first principles; that she can ascertain and correct the mistakes of common sense.

Reason is a noble faculty, and when kept within its proper sphere, and applied to its proper uses, exalts human creatures almost to the rank of superior beings. But she has been much perverted, sometimes to vile, sometimes to insignificant purposes. By some, she has been chained like a slave or a malefactor; by others, she has been launched into depths unknown or forbidden.

Are the dictates of our reason more plain, than the dictates of our common sense? Is there allotted to the former a portion of infallibility, which has been denied to the latter? If reason may mistake; how shall the mistake be rectified? Shall it be done by a second process of reasoning, as likely to be mistaken as the first? Are we thus involved, by the constitution of our nature, in a labyrinth, intricate and endless, in which there is no clue to guide, no ray to enlighten us? Is this true philosophy? Is this the daughter of light? Is this the parent of wisdom and knowledge? No. This is not she. This is a fallen kind, whose rays are merely sufficient to shed a 'darkness visible'[15] upon the human powers; and to disturb the security and ease enjoyed by those, who have not become

---

[15] [See John Milton (1674) *Paradise Lost*, I.lxiii.]

apostates to the pride of science. Such degenerate philosophy let us abandon: let us renounce its instruction: let us embrace the philosophy which dwells with common sense.

This philosophy will teach us, that first principles are in themselves apparent; that to make nothing self-evident is to take away all possibility of knowing anything; that without first principles, there can be neither reason nor reasoning; that discursive knowledge requires intuitive maxims as its basis; that if every truth would admit of proof, proof would extend to infinity; that, consequently, all sound reasoning must rest ultimately on the principles of common sense — principles supported by original and intuitive evidence.

In the investigation of this subject, we shall have the pleasure to find, that those philosophers, who have attempted to fan the flames of war between common sense and reason, have acted the part of incendiaries in the commonwealth of science; that the interests of both are the same; that, between them, there never can be ground for real opposition: that, as they are commonly joined together in speech and in writing, they are inseparable also, in their nature.

We assign to reason two offices, or two degrees. The first is, to judge of things self-evident. The second is, from self-evident principles, to draw conclusions, which are not self-evident. The first of these is the province, and the sole province, of common sense, and, therefore, in its whole extent, it coincides with reason; and is only another name for one branch or one degree of reason. Why then, it may be said, should it have a particular name assigned to it, since it is acknowledged to be only a degree of reason? To this it may be answered, why would you abolish a name, which has found a place in all civilized languages, and has acquired a right by prescription? But this degree of reason ought to be distinguished by a particular name, on two accounts. 1. In the greatest part of mankind, no other degree of reason is to be found. It is this degree of reason, and this only, which makes a man capable of managing his own affairs, and answerable for his conduct towards others. 2. This degree of reason is purely the gift of heaven; and where heaven has not given it, no education can supply it; though, where it is given, it may, in a certain degree, be improved. But the second degree of reason is learned by practice and rules, where the first is wanting.

From the age of Plato down to the present century, it has been the opinion of philosophers, that nothing is perceived but what is in the mind which perceives it: that the mind takes no direct cognizance of external things; but that it perceives them through the medium of certain shadows or images of them: those images were called by the ancients *species, forms, phantasms;* by the moderns they are called *ideas.*

On this foundation the systems of Descartes and Locke have been built. The doctrines of Mr. Locke have been received, not only in England, but in many other parts of Europe, with unbounded applause; and to his theory of the human understanding the same kind of respect and deference has been paid, as to the discoveries of Sir Isaac Newton in the natural world.

The school of Mr. Locke has given rise to two sects: at the head of one are Berkeley and Hume: at the head of the other are Hartley and Priestley.

In the extension of Mr. Locke's principles, the Bishop of Cloyne conceived that he saw reason to deny the reality of matter; and to resolve all existence into mind. In his own sublime language, he thought he discovered, 'that all the choir of heaven and furniture of the earth; all those bodies that compose the frame of the universe, are merely ideas, and exist only in the mind'.[16]

Mr. Hume, proceeding on the same principles of reasoning, advances boldly a step farther: he thinks he sees reason for denying the existence of mind as well as of matter; he annihilates spirit as well as body; and reduces mankind—I use his own words—to 'a bundle or collection of different perceptions, which succeed each other with an inconceivable rapidity, and are in a perpetual flux and movement'. 'There is properly no simplicity in the mind at one time; nor identity in it at different times; whatever natural propensity'—tis indeed natural—'we may have to imagine that simplicity

---

[16] [George Berkeley (1710) *A Treatise Concerning the Principles of Human Knowledge*, vi.]

and identity: they are successive perceptions only, that constitute the mind.'[17]

On the other hand, Dr. Hartley, assuming the existence of an immaterial principle, and of an external world, has endeavored to trace the connexion between them. By a chain of hypotheses, he has attempted to illustrate the nature of the impressions, which the senses receive from external objects; the laws, by which those impressions influence our ideas; and the rules of association, by which these ideas are connected in our mind. He has thus formed a system, which, in the opinion of some enlightened men, explains, in a satisfactory manner, most of the operations of the thinking faculty.

Dr. Priestley has embraced these doctrines with his usual warmth; and has propagated them with his well known zeal. He is of [the] opinion, however, that they ought to be further simplified. A principle, separate from body, he contends is an incumbrance on Dr. Hartley's system. On the principles of deduction, satisfactory to him, he asserts, that to matter, we should ascribe the capacity of intelligence, as well as the property of gravitation. Thought he believes to arise necessarily from a certain organization of the brain; and, resting on this, he denies the existence of an immaterial principle.

Different—exceedingly different indeed—nay, totally irreconcilable are these illustrious men in the conclusions, which they draw. But however widely they differ, however impracticable it may be to reconcile them with regard to their conclusions; they all agree concerning their fundamental principles. They all agree in *assuming* the *existence* of *ideas*. This is the fundamental principle of Mr. Locke's philosophy.

Strange has been the fate of this principle! Strange have been the vicissitudes, with which it has been attended! Strange have been the revolutions, which it has been thought capable of producing! What a powerful engine it has been! In skillful and experienced hands, how tremendous have been its operations! Wielded by one philosopher, it attaches itself solely to matter, and destroys mind. Wielded by another, it attaches itself solely to mind, and destroys matter. Wielded

---

[17] [David Hume (1739) *A Treatise on Human Nature*, I.iv.6. Note: the second quote appears immediately after the first in the 1739 edition of the *Treatise*, but does not appear in modern editions.]

by a third, it becomes equally fatal to matter and mind: by a single fiat of uncreating omnipotence, it strikes body and spirit, time and space into annihilation; and leaves nothing remaining but impressions and ideas!

We have hitherto been apt, perhaps, with unphilosophic credulity, to imagine, that thought supposed a thinker; and that treason implied a traitor. But correct philosophy, it seems, discovers, that all this is a mistake; for that there may be treason without a traitor, laws without a legislator, punishment without a sufferer. If, in these cases, the *ideas* are the traitor, the legislator, the sufferer; the author of this discovery ought to inform us, whether ideas can converse together; whether they can possess rights, or be under obligations; whether they can make promises, enter into covenants, fulfill, or break them; whether, if they break them, damages can be recovered for the breach. If one set of ideas make a covenant; if another successive set—for be it remembered they are all in succession—break the covenant; and if a third successive set are punished for breaking it; how can we discover justice to form any part of this system? These professional questions naturally suggest themselves.

[...]

Shall I be permitted to ask [...a] question [...]? These images, and species, and phantasms of the ancients; these ideas of the moderns— did they ever exist? You will unquestionably be surprised when I tell you, that though, from the time of Plato and Aristotle to the time of Berkeley and Hume, ideas and species have been supposed to lie at the foundation of the philosophy of the human mind, and, consequently, of all philosophy and knowledge; yet that foundation has never, till lately, been examined; but that the existence of ideas and species has always been assumed as a doctrine taken for granted. You will, perhaps, be further surprised, on being told, that, when lately the rubbish, which, during the long course of two thousand years, had covered and concealed the foundations of philosophy, was removed; and when those foundations were examined by an architect of uncommon discernment and skill; no such things as the ideas of the moderns, or the species of the ancients were to be discovered there.

'I acknowledge', says the enlightened and candid Dr. Reid,[18] 'that I never thought of calling in question the principles commonly received with regard to the human understanding, until the *Treatise of Human Nature* was published.' This is the performance of Mr. Hume, from which I cited a passage a little while ago. It appeared in the year 1739. 'The ingenious author', continues Dr. Reid, 'of that treatise, upon the principles of Locke, who was no sceptic, hath built a system of skepticism, which leaves no ground to believe any one thing rather than its contrary. His reasoning appeared to me to be just: there was, therefore, a necessity to call in question the principles, upon which it was founded; or admit the conclusion.'

[...]

The fruits of [Reid's] inquiries have been published; and richly deserve your perusal and attention. Others have sown and cultivated the same seeds of knowledge, with the most encouraging success; and there is reason to hope, that the philosophy of human nature will not much longer continue the reproach of the human understanding.

Monopoly and exclusive privilege are the bane of everything—of science as well as of commerce. The skeptical philosophers claim and exercise the privilege of assuming, without proof, the very first principles of their philosophy; and yet they require, from others, a proof of everything by reasoning. They are unreasonable in both points. Some things, which ought to be believed, ought to be believed without proof. The first principle of their philosophy—the existence of ideas— is none of those things. If it be true; it is a discursive, not an intuitive truth; and, therefore, it can be proved. For this reason, unless it be proved, it should not be believed.

After having mentioned the skeptical philosophers, it is with a degree of reluctance that I so soon introduce the respected name of Mr. Locke. I introduce him not as one of those philosophers, but as one, who has unfortunately given

---

[18] [Thomas Reid (1785) *Inquiry into the Human Mind on the Principles of Common Sense*, 'Dedication'.]

a sanction to principles, the consequences of which he certainly did not foresee. But from his principles, those consequences have been ably and unanswerably drawn by others. His principles, therefore, ought to be minutely examined, that we may see whether, on a strict examination, they will stand the test.

I shall examine his leading principle by the very test, which he himself proposes for its trial. Cautious and candid as he was, it is very remarkable, that, while he recommends it to others to be careful in the admission of principles, he admits his own leading principle without sufficient examination and care. 'I take leave to say' — I use his own words — 'I take leave to say, that everyone ought very carefully to beware what he admits for a principle, to examine it strictly, and see whether he certainly knows it to be true of itself by its own evidence; or whether he does only, with assurance, believe it to be so upon the authority of others.'[19] And yet he begins his observations on ideas and their original, by assuming their existence, as his leading principle. 'Every man being conscious to himself that he thinks; and that which his mind is applied about, whilst thinking, being the *ideas* that are *there*, tis past doubt, that men have in their minds several ideas [...]: it is, in the *first* place, then, to be inquired *how* he comes by them.'[20]

With all deference for the character and talents of Mr. Locke — and I have, indeed, a high respect for them — I think that a previous inquiry ought to have been made — *Does* he come by them? To assume, without proving, that the things, which the mind is applied about, whilst thinking, are the ideas that are *there*; is certainly to assume too much.

In another place, he expresses a hope, that it will be received as an intuitive truth — as one of that species of intuitive truths, which arise from consciousness. 'I presume', says he, 'it will be easily granted me, that there are such ideas in men's minds.'[21] Why so easily granted? Why should the leading principle of a philosophy, which, if true, necessarily

---

[19] [John Locke (1690) *An Essay Concerning Human Understanding*, IV.xx.8.]
[20] [John Locke (1690) *An Essay Concerning Human Understanding*, II.i.1.]
[21] [John Locke (1690) *An Essay Concerning Human Understanding*, 'Introduction'.]

draws us to such consequences as have been represented — why should such a leading principle be taken on trust? 'Because', continues Mr. Locke, 'every one is conscious of them in himself.'[22]

Here is a fair and candid appeal: for if every one is conscious of ideas in his own mind, he must believe that such ideas are *there:* for consciousness is unquestionably a first principle of evidence. In this appeal I have the pleasure of joining with Mr. Locke. In one thing we certainly agree — the object of both is to discover the truth. Of this truth, you shall be the judges, or rather the triers[23] between us; for consciousness is a matter of fact.

But before we enter upon the trial of this appeal, let us be sure that the point to be tried is clearly ascertained and understood: let us not be misled by verbal ambiguity, nor drawn into the field of verbal disputation. Many errors, and some of no inconsiderable importance, have arisen from the vague, the doubtful, or the inaccurate application of the term *idea.*

By ideas are sometimes meant the acts or operations of our minds in perceiving, remembering, or imagining objects. In this sense, the existence of ideas is far from being called in question. We are conscious of them every day and every hour of our lives.

Sometimes *idea* is used to denote *opinion* — Thus, when we speak of the ideas of Cicero; we mean his opinions or doctrines.

But there is a third sense, in which the term *idea* has been used. It has been used to denote those images and pictures of things, which, and not the things themselves, are the immediate objects perceived by the mind. Those, who speak the most intelligibly, explain their doctrine in this manner. Suppose me to look at a mirror; and, while I am looking at it, suppose a person to come behind me; I see, in the mirror, not the person himself, but his image. In the same manner, when, without a mirror, I am supposed to see a house or a tree; I see only an image of those objects in my mind. This image is the immediate object of my perception.

---

[22] [John Locke (1690) *An Essay Concerning Human Understanding*, I.i.8.]
[23] [A 'trier' is a judge or jury responsible for deciding matters of fact.]

It is in this last sense, now explained, that an appeal is made to your consciousness for the truth of the existence of ideas.

You look at me: now I call for your conscious verdict. Are you conscious, that you really see me: or are you conscious, that you see, not me, but only a certain image or picture of me, imprinted upon your own minds? If the latter; your consciousness decides in favor of Mr. Locke: if the former; it decides in favor of me. In whose favor does your verdict decide? Before you finally declare it, it may, perhaps, be urged, that you perceive me by means of intervening resemblances of me, distinctly painted on the retinae of your eyes.

This shows, that I am willing to give the cause an impartial trial, nay, an advantageous one, on the side of my admired antagonist. From those parts only of our knowledge, which are disclosed by the sense of seeing, could this objection be urged.

I admit, that the resemblances mentioned are distinctly painted on the retinae of your eyes. But suffer me to ask you —do you *perceive* those resemblances, so painted? I presume you do not: for the existence of those resemblances was never, so far as I know or have heard, perceived by any of the innumerable race of men: it was not so much as suspected, till in the last century. Then the discovery was made by Kepler: but even to Kepler the discovery was not disclosed by consciousness: it was the result of deep and accurate researches into the philosophy of vision.

But I have not yet done with my answer to this objection. That you do not perceive me by the intervention of any perception of the resemblances painted on the retinae of the eyes, is evident from two circumstances. In the first place, the resemblances of me are painted on the retina of both eyes: therefore, if you saw me through the intervention of those resemblances, you would see me double. In the second place, the resemblances of me on the retinae are inverted: therefore, if you saw me through the intervention of those resemblances, you would see me turned upside down.

Are you now ready finally to declare your verdict? Do you perceive me? Or do you only perceive, in your own minds, an image or picture of me?

I presume I may say, that the existence of ideas is not the dictate of consciousness. Is the existence of ideas entitled, in any other manner, or from any other source, to be considered as an intuitive truth? I have not heard it suggested. If it is a truth, and not an intuitive one; it is a truth capable of being proved: if it is capable of being proved; it ought to be proved, as we have already said, before it be believed.

A proof has been attempted: let us examine it. 'No being, it is said, can act or be acted upon, but where it is; and, consequently, our mind cannot act upon, or be acted upon by any subject at a distance.'[24]

This argument possesses one eminent advantage: its obscurity, like that of an oracle, is apt to impose on the hearer, who is willing to consider it as demonstration, because he does not, at first, discover its fallacy. Let it undergo a fair examination; let it be drawn out of its obscurity: let it be stated and analyzed in a clear point of view. Then it will appear as follows.

'No subject can be perceived, unless it acts, upon the mind, or is acted upon by the mind: but no distant object can act upon the mind, or be acted upon by the mind; for no being can act but where it is: therefore the immediate object of perception must be something in the mind, so as to be able to act upon, or to be acted upon by the mind.'[25]

Now you see, fairly stated in all its parts, the argument, which is supposed to prove the necessity of phantasms or ideas in the mind, as the only objects of perception. It is singularly unfortunate for this argument, that it concludes directly against the very hypothesis, of which it is the only foundation: for how can phantasms or ideas be raised in the mind by things at a distance, if things at a distance cannot act upon, or be acted upon by the mind.

Again; the argument assumes a proposition as true, without evidence—that no distant subject can act upon, or be acted upon by the mind. This proposition requires evidence; for it is not intuitively certain. Till this proposition, therefore,

---

[24] [Thomas Porterfield (1752) 'An Essay Concerning the Motions of our Eyes'. Wilson takes the quote from Reid's *Essays on the Intellectual Powers of Man*, II.xiv.]

[25] [Henry Home (Lord Kames) (1762) *Elements of Criticism*, II.Appendix.14.n.]

be proved, every man may rationally rely upon the conviction of his senses, that he sees and hears objects at a distance.

But further; to render the foregoing argument conclusive, it ought to be proved, that when we perceive objects, either they act upon us, or we act upon them. This is not self-evident; nor is it proved. Indeed reasons may be well offered against its admission.

When we say, that one being acts upon another, we mean that some power is exerted by the agent, which produces, or tends to produce a change in the thing acted upon. Now, there appears no reason for asserting, that, in perception, either the object acts upon the mind, or the mind upon the object. An object, in being perceived, does not act at all. I perceive the desk before me; but it is perfectly inactive; and, therefore, cannot act upon my mind. Neither does the mind, in perception, act upon the object. To perceive an object is one thing: to act upon it is another thing. To say, that I act upon the paper before me, when I look at it, is an abuse of language. We have, therefore, no evidence, that, in perception, the mind acts upon the object, or the object upon the mind; but strong evidence to the contrary. The consequence is, that the very foundation of the only argument brought to prove the existence of ideas is sandy and unsound.

Thus the first principle of the ideal philosophy is supported neither by intuition nor by proof. On what pretension, then, can it lay any just claim to our regard?

And yet this principle, unsupported, absurd, and unphilosophical as it is, will, I believe, be found to be the sole foundation laid, so far as any is laid, in our law books, for the philosophy of the law of evidence. My Lord Chief Baron Gilbert, the most approved, and deservedly the most approved writer on this part of the law, grounds his general observations on the doctrine of Mr. Locke, that knowledge is nothing but the perception of the agreement or disagreement of our *ideas*.[26]

In one of my early lectures, I made the following observations. 'Despotism, by an artful use of "superiority" in politics; and skepticism, by an artful use of "ideas" in metaphysics, have endeavored—and their endeavors have freq-

---

[26] [Lord Chief Jeffrey Gilbert (1754) *The Law of Evidence*, three volumes.]

uently been attended with too much success—to destroy all true liberty and sound philosophy. By their baneful effects, the science of man and the science of government have been poisoned to their very fountains. But those destroyers of others have met, or must meet with their own destruction.'[27] I have put you in possession of materials to judge for yourselves whether these observations are or are not well founded.

At first sight, it would seem strange that the principles of law, as they are laid down in a book, which is very generally received for authority, should be destructive of liberty; and that the principles of the philosophy of the human mind, as they likewise are generally received and taught, should be subversive of all truth and knowledge. But after what we have seen; is it not as true as strange?

This investigation has cost me some trouble: to you I hope it will be attended with some advantage. I thought it my duty to make and to communicate it; because, without it, any superstructure of system, which I could build, would not satisfy me as resting on a solid foundation. Could I have been justified in palming upon you a system leaning on such principles as do not satisfy myself?

I know very well, that, in the business of life, the dictates of common sense will always, and that in the business of government, the spirit of liberty will sometimes prevail over false theories of politics and philosophy. But is this a reason why those false theories should be received, or encouraged, or propagated? Ought not our conduct as men and as citizens to receive benefit instead of detriment from the systems of our education? One, whose practice is in diametrical opposition to his principles, stands always in an awkward, often in a painful, sometimes in a dangerous situation.

I have said, that the spirit of liberty will sometimes prevail over false theories of politics. Unhappily I could not say more: I could not say, generally: far less could I say, always. Let us look around us and behold the sons of men, who inhabit this globe. What an immense proportion of them are the wretched slaves of perverted opinion, of perverted system, of perverted education, and of perverted example in

---

[27] [James Wilson (1804) 'Of the General Principles of Law and Obligation', in *The Works of The Honourable James Wilson, L.L.D.*]

matters relating to the principles of society, and the rights of the human kind!

I hope I have now shown, that the philosophers before mentioned unreasonably claimed the exclusive privilege of assuming the first principle of their philosophy, without proof: I now proceed to show, that they are equally unreasonable in requiring, from others, a proof of everything by reasoning.

The defects and blemishes of the received philosophy, which have most exposed it to ridicule and contempt, have been chiefly owing to a prejudice of the votaries of this philosophy in favor of reason. They have endeavored to extend her jurisdiction beyond its just limits; and to call before her bar the dictates of common sense. But these will not submit to this jurisdiction: they plead to its authority; and disdain its trial; they claim not its aid; they dread not its attacks.

In this unequal contest between reason and common sense, the former will always be obliged to retreat both with loss and with dishonor; nor can she ever flourish, till this rival-ship is dropped, till these encroachments are given up, and till a cordial friendship is restored. For, in truth, reason has no other root than the principles of common sense: it grows out of them: and from them it draws its nourishment.

There are some common principles, which are the foundation of all science, and of all reasoning. Before men can argue together, they must agree in such principles; for it is impossible for two to reason, but from principles held by them in common. Such common principles seldom admit of direct proof; they need none; they are such as men of common understanding will acknowledge as soon as they are proposed and understood.

Such principles, when we have occasion to use them in science, are called *axioms*. Upon such, the finest, the most elaborate, and the most sublime reasonings in mathematics are founded.

In every other science, as well as in mathematics, there are some common principles, upon which all the reasonings in that science are grounded, and into which they may be resolved. If these were pointed out and considered, we should be better able to judge concerning the strength and certainty of the conclusions in that science.

It is not impossible, that what is only a vulgar prejudice may be mistaken for a first principle. Nor is it impossible, that what is really a first principle, may, by the enchantment of words, have such a mist thrown about it, as to hide its evidence, and make a man of candor doubt concerning it.

The peripatetic philosophy, instead of being deficient, was redundant in first principles; instead of rejecting those, which are truly such, it adopted, as such, many vulgar prejudices and rash judgments.[28] This seems, in general, to have been the spirit of ancient philosophy.

How naturally one extreme produces its opposite! Descartes, at the head of modern reformers in philosophy, anxious to avoid the snare, in which Aristotle and the peripatetic had been caught—that of admitting things too rashly as first principles—resolved to doubt of everything, till it was clearly proved. He would not assume, as a first principle, even his own existence. In what manner he supposed nonexistence could institute, or desire to institute a series of proof to prove existence or anything else, we are not informed.

He thought he could prove his existence by his famous enthymeme—*Cogito, ergo sum*.[29] I think, therefore, I exist. Though he would not assume the existence of *himself* as a first principle, he was obliged to assume the existence of his *thoughts* as a first principle. But is this entitled to any degree of preference? Can one, who doubts whether he exists, be certain that he thinks? And may not one, who, without proof, takes it for granted that he thinks—may not such an one, without the imputation of unphilosophic credulity, take it for granted, likewise without proof, that he exists?

In every just proof, a proposition less evident is inferred from one, which is more evident. How is it more evident that we think, than that we exist? Both are equally evident: one, therefore, ought not to be first assumed, and then used as a proof of the other.

But further; if we attend to the strict rules of proof; the existence of Descartes was not legitimately inferred from the existence of his thoughts. If the inference is legitimate; it

---

[28] [See Thomas Reid (1785) *Essays on the Intellectual Powers of Man*, VI.vii.]

[29] [See Note 6 above.]

must become legitimate by establishing this proposition—that thought cannot exist without a thinking being. But did Descartes, or has any of his followers proved this proposition? They have not proved it: they cannot prove it. Mr. Hume has denied it; and has triumphantly challenged the world to establish it by proof. The basis of his philosophy is, as we have already seen—'that a train of successive perceptions constitute the mind'.

Let me not here be misunderstood. When I say, that the existence of a thinking principle, called the mind, has not been and cannot be proved; I am far from saying, that it is not true, that such a thinking principle exists. I know—I feel—it to be true; but I know it not from proof: I know it from what is greatly superior to proof: I *see* it by the shining light of intuition.

Why will philosophers, by a preposterous pride, wish and endeavor to be indebted, for the discovery of everything, to the feeble and glimmering rays of their own tapers, when they have only to throw the window open, and they will behold everything illuminated by the splendor of the meridian sun?

Let me, upon this subject, further observe, that strongly as Descartes was seized with this phobia of first principles, he was obliged, in one instance at least, to suffer the detested liquid to touch his lips. *Cogito*, says he: I think. You think! How do you prove that! You, who will not believe your own existence without proof—can you consistently dispense with the proof of the existence of your thoughts? He is obliged to submit to the inconsistency. He assumes the existence of his thoughts, as a first principle. Why did he not pursue the same course with regard to other intuitive truths?

As the last observation on this subject, I beg leave to take notice, that, in this remarkable enthymeme, Descartes assumed the very thing to be proved. *Cogito. I* think. Who *are you*? Existence is implied in the very proposition, that *one* thinks.

To the distinction between first principles and those principles, which may be ascribed to the power of reasoning, it is not a just objection, that there may be some judgments, concerning which we may be doubtful, to which class they should be referred. In painting and in nature, two colors, very different, may so run into one another, as to render it difficult to perceive where one ends and the other begins.

Let us then conclude—for we may safely conclude—that all knowledge, obtained by reasoning, must be built on first principles. When we examine, by analysis, the evidence of any proposition; we find, either that it is self-evident; or that it rests upon one or more propositions, which support it. The same thing may be said of the propositions, which support it; and of those again, which support them. But we cannot go back, in this tract, to infinity. Where, then, must the analysis stop? When we come to propositions, which support all that are built upon them, but are themselves supported by none: in other words, when we come to self-evident propositions.

All first principles must be the immediate dictates of our natural faculties; nor is it possible that we should have any other evidence of their truth. In different sciences, the faculties, which dictate these first principles, are very different: the eye, in astronomy and optics: the ear, in music: the moral sense, in morals.

Some first principles yield conclusions, which are certain; others yield such only as are probable. In just reasoning, the strength or weakness of the conclusion will always correspond to the strength or weakness of the principles, on which it is grounded. But the lowest degree of probability, as well as absolute certainty, must be grounded ultimately on first principles.

After hearing so much concerning first principles, the question will naturally suggest itself—are they ascertained and pointed out? That they were so, is most ardently to be desired. In mathematics, they have been so, as far back as the annals of literature can carry us. And the consequence has been, that, in mathematics, we find no sects, or contrary systems. This science, founded upon first principles, as upon a rock, has been increased from age to age, till it has become the loftiest and most solid fabric, which human reason can boast.

Till within these two hundred years, natural philosophy was in the same fluctuating state with the other sciences. Every new system pulled up the old one by the roots. The great Lord Bacon first marked out the only foundation, on which natural philosophy could be built. His celebrated successor, Sir Isaac Newton, gave the first and noblest examples of that chaste induction, of which his guide in the principles of science could only delineate the theory. He reduced the principles of Lord Bacon into a few axioms, which he calls *'regulæ philosophandi'*,—rules of philosophizing. From these, together with the phenomena observed by the senses, which he likewise assumes as first principles, he deduces, by strict reasoning, the propositions of his philosophy; and, in this manner, has erected an edifice, which stands immovable upon the basis of first and self-evident principles. This edifice has been enlarged by the accession of new discoveries, made since his time; but it has not been subjected to alterations in the plan.

The other sciences have not, as yet, been so fortunate as those of mathematics and natural philosophy. Indeed the other sciences, compared with these, have this disadvantage, that it is more difficult to form distinct and determinate conceptions of the objects, about which they are employed. But this difficulty, though great, is not insurmountable: it may afford a reason why the other sciences have had a longer infancy; but it can afford none, why they may not, at last, arrive at maturity by the same steps as those of a quicker growth.

If the same unanimity concerning first principles could be introduced into the other sciences, as in those of mathematics and natural philosophy; this might be considered as a new era in the progress of human reason.[30]

Some first principles I have already had occasion to notice: in the course of my system, others will come forward into view; and will receive particular attention; especially in the important law of evidence, upon which the practical use of the whole municipal law entirely rests. For the facts must be ascertained by evidence, before they are susceptible of an application of the law. '*Ex facto oritur jus.*'[31] How can facts be satisfactorily established, unless the genuine philosophy of evidence be known?

Investigation will, perhaps, disclose to us, that this part of philosophy has been best known, where the knowledge of it has been least expected.

---

[30] <Reid's Inq. 483.>
[31] ['Law arises out of facts.']

Five

Samuel Stanhope Smith (1751-1819)

Samuel Stanhope Smith, son of a Presbyterian minister, was born in Peaqua, Pennsylvania in 1751. From the ages of six to sixteen, Stanhope Smith studied Latin and Greek at an academy run by his father. In 1767, on account of his academic proficiency, he was admitted directly to the junior class at the College of New Jersey (now Princeton University).

Stanhope Smith graduated with an A.B. in 1769 and, following a short stint as a teacher at his father's academy, became a tutor at the College of New Jersey in 1771. While working at the college, he also began studying theology under its president, John Witherspoon. Although Stanhope Smith intended to pursue a career in academics, a bout of tuberculosis inspired him to pursue missionary work. Accordingly, after receiving ordination in the Presbyterian church, he moved to rural Virginia to work as a minister.

Soon, however, Stanhope Smith was enticed to return to academia. In 1775, the Presbytery persuaded Stanhope Smith to oversee the foundation and operation of Prince Edward Academy (now Hampden-Sydney College). That same year, Stanhope Smith married John Witherspoon's daughter, Ann.

In 1779, following a successful run at the helm of Prince Edward Academy, Stanhope Smith was convinced by his father-in-law to return to Princeton and succeed him as professor of moral philosophy at the College of New Jersey. Despite his personal connections to the school, Stanhope Smith must have been wary, for the college had suffered much on account of the revolutionary battles that had taken place in and around Princeton. Among the difficulties confronted by the college in 1779 were a lack of funds, the total destruction of its library, and the partial destruction of its main building, Nassau Hall. Managing these difficulties increasingly fell on Stanhope Smith as Witherspoon remained occupied with his political duties. In order to overcome the school's financial impediments, Stanhope Smith frequently bought materials and books for the college and students with his own funds.

Between 1781 and 1795, Stanhope Smith took on several roles at the college, serving not only as a professor, but also as clerk of the board of trustees, treasurer, and vice president. Following Witherspoon's death in 1794, Stanhope Smith was elected to the presidency of the college. His tenure was not a happy one. In 1795, Smith appointed an undergraduate instructor in natural science; in the United States a heretofore unprecedented move which proved popular with the students but upset the religiously conservative trustees. Then, in March of 1802, a fire nearly destroyed the newly rebuilt Nassau Hall. Although the allegations were never proven, several students were implicated for arson and suspended. These events and other matters continued to divide the students and trustees until, in March 1807, a large student-led riot broke out on the campus. Although the riot was quickly put down, the damage done to the College of New Jersey's reputation was substantial, and led to a decline in both enrolment and funding. In 1812, Stanhope Smith retired in order to work on revising his lectures, from which the selections below have been taken.

Biographical Information: Edward L. Lach, Jr., *American National Biography Online.*

READING VIII

The Active Powers of Human Nature[1]

Having thus far considered those principles in human nature by which we become furnished with ideas, the elements of

---

[1] [Extracted from Samuel Stanhope Smith (1812) 'Lecture XI', in *The Lectures, Corrected and Improved, which have been Delivered for a Series of Years in the College of New Jersey on the Subjects of Moral and Political Philosophy*, 2 Volumes, Volume I, New York: Whiting & Watson, Trenton, NJ: James J. Wilson, pp. 223–48.]

all our knowledge, — I proceed, in the next place, to point out those physical and moral powers, or properties, which are the immediate springs and incentives of action in man. Our perceptions, which are derived through the channels of sensation, external, or internal, might be a source of enjoyment to ourselves, but would contribute little to the use and happiness of the world, unless the various faculties of our nature were put into vigorous movement by the active principles with which it is endued. These principles may all, perhaps, be embraced under the following analysis; — propensity — instinct — habit — sentiment — imagination — affection or desire — reason — and volition.[2] On each of these I shall content myself with making only a few observations, except the last, which, as it is a subject that has greatly agitated the metaphysical world, I shall treat with somewhat greater extent.

Propensity may be defined to be a natural tendency to perform certain actions, or to seek for certain enjoyments, prior to reflection, or to any experience we have had of the good or ill effects of those actions, or of those enjoyments. Seldom are men prompted to that course of conduct which may be most beneficial to themselves, or to society, from abstract considerations of utility: they must be strongly incited, antecedently, at least, to the commanding influence of a virtuous education, by some powerful impulse of nature, which acts more directly and immediately than the deliberate and slow conclusions of reason; that is, by some passion, or by some present propensity. Even the necessity of preserving life and health would not always find us sufficiently attentive to its duties without the stimulus of hunger and thirst. — Propensities are divided into the bodily, mental, and mixed. — The propensities which have their seat chiefly in the body, are more usually termed *appetites,* from the strength of desire which they commonly imply. The mental propensities are natural and strong tendencies of the mind to particular exertions of its powers, which have this property in common with the former, that they promote to their respective actions and pursuits, antecedently to reflection and experience. Among these may be ranked curiosity to know, ambition to excel, the love of imitation, and, in many cases, a strong and

---

[2] [The first five of these are treated in this reading. Volition is the topic of the next reading.]

peculiar direction of the mental faculties, which usually indicates a genius, or capacity for excelling in particular arts. The mixed propensities, in the gratifications which they solicit, partake almost equally of the pleasures of sense and intellect. Such are those which appear in the protection, caresses and love of children in the inclinations to society, and especially, the society of the sexes, on which the union and civilization of mankind chiefly depend.

There is an essential difference between the propensities which have their seat in the mind, and those which spring from the body, in the constancy of their action. The former are as equable as all the other operations of the mind; the latter arise only at intervals according to the wants of the body; and when their immediate purposes are obtained, they are, for a season, wholly suspended. To attempt to continue, or to force indulgence after the proper ends of nature are fulfilled, is generally followed by satiety and disgust. The propensities to particular kinds of food or drink, depend at first, chiefly on natural taste, but are afterwards formed more frequently by custom. Custom strengthens natural and often creates artificial tastes, and sometimes, to objects originally unpleasant, more powerful than the natural. No principles in human nature require to be observed, in their commencement and their progress, with stricter vigilance, or to be put under severer restraint, than our corporeal appetites. Virtue has acquired an important conquest when prudence and habit have limited their wants to the point of temperate indulgence.

Among our mental propensities, all those which tend immediately to the happiness of mankind, and originate from the benevolent feelings of the heart, react with pleasure on ourselves by promoting our own happiness. On the other hand, those which have an injurious tendency, however they may yield a certain gratification in the moment of passion, or under the irritations of provocation, will ever be followed, especially in a generous mind, by painful reflection. A proof how much we are formed for social duties, and for social happiness.

Propensity is sometimes confounded with another principle of action, denominated *instinct*. They are, on several accounts, nearly allied, particularly as they prompt to action, antecedently to reflection, and proceed to their end without the aid of reason. Instinct is a kind of mechanical operation, producing actions relative to our preservation, or enjoyment, simply under the impulse of a strong natural feeling, in which the higher powers of the mind have not any concern. It is from this principle that the child applies its mouth to the breast of its mother. It knows not the consequence of this action; but the Author of nature has prompted the infant to it for its nourishment, while it has not wisdom to obtain it by any other way. The operations of suction and deglutition, are performed by a very complicated machinery. The infant is unacquainted with the structure of the organ, or the effect of action; but, by a single act of desire, or volition, stimulated by hunger, the whole is put into regular and perfect movement. Many are the actions of men, in situations in which they cannot be supposed to exercise their reason at the moment, which are the result of this principle. But because the inferior animals cannot, in any case, possess the guidance and defense of reason, the Creator has endowed them, for their safety, with a proportionally greater number of instincts than man; or at least than man, who is early put under the direction of a superior principle, is ever called upon, in the ordinary avocations of life, to exercise. Instinct is generally more uniform and certain in its operation than reason: for reason depending for its improvement, and its proper exercise, on the sagacity, diligence, and faithfulness of man, is often liable to defect or error; but instinct, being the provision of nature herself, always goes directly to its end. We see with what uniformity and truth each animal pursues that course of life for which it was destined; — how unerringly it selects that food which is proper for its subsistence; — and constructs those habitations which are adapted to its state, and its necessities. The works of man vary with his means of culture and science, with his state of society, and with a thousand circumstances which impress their influence upon the operations of reason; but these animals conduct their works with the same perfection in every age. The bee constructs her cells, and the spider his web, without change and without error.[3]

---

[3] I am aware that in different climates, and in different situations, we frequently perceive some variation in the instinctive operations of

Although propensity and instinct, in several particulars, resemble one another, there appears to be this difference between them, that the former expresses that internal impulse which prompts us to seek an object for some want that it relieves, or some gratification that it yields; the latter relates chiefly to the manner of accomplishing its end, which is uniform in all animals of the same species. Children have a propensity to seek for nourishment, but it is by instinct, as I have said, that they apply their mouths to the breast. By instinct the bee collects her honey, and deposits it in her wonderful cells, which also by instinct she has framed; whence in the season that forbids her further labors she satisfies the propensities of hunger. And, in like manner, the spider instinctively frames his web for the purpose of taking the insects which he has a propensity to devour.

Our sensations, and propensities, lay a foundation for dividing all objects into two general classes, which we denominate good and evil. All those which afford agreeable sensations, or which are adapted to gratify our natural propensities, we place in the former class; those, on the other hand, which affect us with painful, or disagreeable sensations, or which contradict or violate our propensities, we arrange in the latter. Whatever, therefore, contributes to our own preservation or comfort, or to that of our fellow men,—whatever tends to promote the interest of society,—whatever is supposed to advance the perfection of the individual, or to confer eminence and distinction in the estimation of the world, is to be placed in the catalogue of goods; and all that is contrary to these belongs to the class of evils. When we follow only the guidance of nature in making this distribution, we shall seldom greatly err. But when, in the progress of life, in consequence of any irregular indulgences, certain appetites acquire an undue ascendancy, our judgments of things become, in the same degree, perverted.

Another principle which prompts, as well as facilitates the actions of men, is habit. In its primary signification, habit respects chiefly that facility and perfection in performing an action which is the result of frequent repetition. But the ease

---

the same animal to adapt them to the necessity of his new state. But in similar situations these variations are as uniform as the original impulse, and indicate only the guidance of nature.

of execution commonly produces pleasure in the performance. And we find it to be a law of our nature that we are most happy when occupied in that course of life which custom has rendered habitual. This principle has a powerful influence over human nature, not only in creating exquisite nicety of execution in the operations of the arts, but in giving direction to all the talents of the mind, and in forming both the moral and intellectual character of man. As youth is the period of life most susceptible of habit, and that on which the whole mold and fashion of its after periods principally depends, it is of the utmost importance that the earliest habits of youth, and even of childhood, be well regulated. *Choose in the beginning,* said a virtuous ancient, *the best course of life, and custom will render it the most pleasing.*[4]

The power of habit, the extent of its influence, and the immense complexity of its operations, are seldom minutely adverted to, or duly estimated. Examples of its efficacy which we rarely behold, and the process of which we do not understand, forcibly attract our notice, and excite our wonder. We regard with astonishment, for instance, the feats of rope-dancing, and the tricks of legerdemain; but we hardly reflect on the complicated variety of attentions, perhaps not less surprising, only that they are common, which are blended in one act by habit, in the most simple expression of our thoughts in conversation:—the connection of the arbitrary sounds which form our words with our thoughts,—the just and graceful articulation of them,—their mutual relations in grammatical construction,—their combination and arrangement in perfect logical propositions,—the means which must have been employed in forming just conceptions of the subjects of discourse in the mind, and discriminating them from such as are erroneous,—with a multitude of other effects, which, when accurately considered, render it wonderful that they should be so quickly, and even instantly combined in the imagination, and so promptly expressed by the tongue of the speaker. How much more wonderful the habitual powers of the orator managing in debate the affairs of a great nation, bringing into act in one moment the rich stores of his memory, the immense extent of his foresight, the vast com-

---

[4] [Pythagoras, *From Stobæus*, § 125.]

pass of his reflection and reading, and the infinite attentions demanded by his subject, by the rules of his art, and the audience he is addressing! A great writer has declared that, if it were not so frequently witnessed, it might well be esteemed a prodigy.[5] What application and wisdom then, what circumspection and prudence, what unwearied assiduity, ought to be employed in forming the intellectual and moral habits of youth, on whom the future welfare of their country depends! —What encouragement to hope from the well-directed influence of habit, for the most useful and elegant attainments in literature, or the most commanding abilities in the management of public affairs?

The next of our active principles which I have mentioned is *sentiment:* a principle embracing those movements of the mind which have more commonly been considered by philosophers among our passions. And although they have in some respects an affinity with them; yet have they so much of a distinctive peculiarity as well entitles them to be ranked as a separate class of our active principles.

Sentiment may be defined to be an emotion of the mind relative to good or evil, present or future, in ourselves or others.[6] It produces a state of feeling rather predisposing to action in a certain direction, than exciting to any immediate effort.

A few examples will probably render the nature of this principle better understood. The import of good and evil having been before explained, we may employ them now as known and general terms in our definitions.—The possession, or the near and certain expectation of what is esteemed to be good, creates that agreeable and sprightly state and emotion of the mind which we call *joy*. The deprivation of good, or the actual suffering of evil, produces those distressing emotions which make up the sentiment of *grief*. The prospect of good to be enjoyed, or evil to be escaped,—the probable apprehension of losing the possession of some favorite good, or suffering the pressure of some dreaded evil, creates those emotions or states of the mind which we distinguish by the names of *hope* and *fear*.—Many writers have formerly

---

[5] Dr. Reid. Third essay on the active powers of man.
[6] See Ferguson's *Institutes* under the head of sentiment, from whom also are taken most of the following examples.

proposed dividing all our sentiments, and even the whole system of our passions and affections into the classes of *joy* and *sorrow*. — The names of these divisions have certainly been very inaccurately applied. For small undoubtedly is the resemblance between the sentiments of joy and sorrow, and many of those emotions which are respectively classed under them; between the former, for example, and the emotions of insolence and pride, — and between the latter, and those of displeasure, or of scorn.

Without attempting any scientific distribution and arrangement of our various sentiments, all that I propose is to give only a few examples in order to beget precision in the use of terms appropriate to this branch of our constitution. — When we contemplate our own safety, and the circumstances which contribute to render it stable, we feel the sentiment of *security*. In great success we perceive the sentiment of *exultation*. In adverse or disastrous circumstances, according to the degree of danger which accompanies them, we perceive those of *apprehension, terror, despair*. When we behold others receiving an accession to their happiness, between whom and ourselves there is no rival-ship, or cause of disaffection, we indulge the sentiment of *congratulation*. In their distresses, on the other hand, we feel that of *sympathy* or *compassion*.

When men contemplate any excellent qualities in themselves, they perceive the sentiments of *self-approbation*, — of *elation of mind*, — of *conscious worth*. — Defects and vices, on the contrary, when they are perceived, produce the sentiments of *shame, compunction, self-reproach, remorse*. Superiority to others, in qualities especially which attract the esteem or admiration of the world, produce, according to the moral disposition of the mind in which they reside, the sentiment of *dignity*, of *pride*, of *vanity*, or *insolence*. — The sentiments arising from the view of the superiority of other men are different, according to the state of our affections towards them, and according as the comparison is made between them and ourselves, or between them and others. If we love them, we feel for them the sentiments of *deference, respect, esteem, veneration;* — if we dislike them, the sentiment of *envy* is too apt to affect the mind that is not under the guard of virtuous principles, or governed by a dignified self-respect. — When the comparison is made with others, the superiority of those whom we esteem produces *exultation*, — of those who have provoked our enmity, *animosity* or *regret*.

After proposing these few examples, simply in illustration of this principle in the constitution of human nature, I shall conclude the imperfect summary by remarking, that, among all our sentiments, which, in their full extent, are almost infinitely various, none have a greater influence on the character and conduct of mankind, except, perhaps, those of conscience, or are more closely allied to virtue, than those of *honor* and *shame*. These emotions are indeed awakened, not so much by the consideration of the rectitude or criminality of actions, as by the general estimate entertained of them in the public opinion: yet are they useful auxiliaries to virtue, inasmuch as the public opinion is, in most instances, nearly coincident with the laws on which the public morals, which are, in fact, those of the public interest, are founded. This, however, is not a genuine and universal rule, since the splendor, or éclat of an action is too often found to outweigh its morality.

In comparing the sentiments of honor and of virtue, of guilt and of shame, we will perceive that those of virtue produce more tranquility of mind, — those of honor more elevation; the sentiments of guilt create greater compunction, those of shame deeper humiliation.

The imagination, which is that active principle that forms the next object of our consideration, is defined by Dr. Ferguson to be the faculty of creating in the mind the images of objects, or scenes which have no real existence in nature; or of representing real objects, and scenes invested with all their circumstances and qualities; those circumstances and qualities, especially which escape the notice of ordinary observers, and strike only the finer or secondary powers of sensation, such as beauty, sublimity, proportion, grace, or harmony.

This definition is not intended to imply that the ideas, or materials which compose the pictures created by the imagination, have not entered the mind through the ordinary organs of sense, and been derived like our other ideas from actual scenes, and objects in nature; but the manner in which they are put together in the fancy, for example, of the poet or the painter, forms a picture which has no real archetype without, to which it can be referred. In the Paradise of

Milton, or the island of Calypso, as described by Fenelon, there is not an idea which has not been derived from trees, flowers, streams, or groves which exist in different parts of nature; but never were they arranged in the same order, or with the same enchanting effect as in the imagination of the poet.—This is what is intended by Dr. Ferguson when he says that the imagination is the faculty of creating scenes or objects which *have no real existence in nature*. But it will perhaps convey a better conception of this part of our constitution, to consider the imagination, with professor Dugald Stewart,[7] as a complex power, consisting of fancy, taste, and judgment. A man of fancy has a quick and lively perception of those secondary sensations or qualities, which we denominate beauty, sublimity, grace, proportion, with others of the same class, derived from all the various objects in nature, and; the power of calling them up with and variety adapted to the illustration and embellishment of every subject. But this luxuriant power is apt to shoot wild, and to fill the mind with a confusion of beauties, unless it be combined with judgment and taste to select those which are most proper for the occasion, and arrange them in such order as to form the most agreeable pictures in the mind. From this description, the imagination may be called the *picture-making* faculty of the soul. In the delineation of real scenes, as well as in creating such as are new, or have no existence in nature, it frames its descriptions chiefly by touching those vivid secondary sensations which its subject is calculated to excite, rather than by retracing the mere impressions of external sense. We may explain this difference by supposing on one hand the recital of a plain, judicious traveller, who aims simply at giving a geographical description of the surface of a beautiful country which shall be accurate in all its parts; on the other hand, the picture of a poet of genius presenting to us the same scene. He draws the landscape with equal accuracy, but with a coloring of fancy entirely new. He employs words that glow, and images that make us feel their beauties, touching every finer chord of internal sensation.

The materials out of which the pictures of the imagination are framed, are limited entirely by Mr. Addison to such as

---

[7] *Elements of the Philosophy of the Human Mind*, VII.

enter the mind through the eye. 'We cannot', says he, 'have a single image in the fancy that did not make its first entrance through the sight.'⁸ Perfectly according with this opinion is that of Dr. Reid of Glasgow. — 'Imagination properly signifies a lively conception of objects of sight.'⁹ This is certainly a slight inadvertence in that elegant critic, and that profound philosopher. For, although much the most numerous and various classes of the ideas, which enter into the combinations of the imagination, have been introduced by this sense, and although the term itself seems to have been originally borrowed from the images of sight; yet undoubtedly it embraces all the perceptions introduced by any other of our faculties which may contribute to form agreeable pictures in the fancy. — In the following beautiful passage from the first eclogue of Virgil, the poet draws upon the ear in the sweet languor of nature just inclining to repose, and the pensive emotions of the heart, for the finest images in this simple and delightful scene!

> *Hinc tibi, quæ semper vicino ab limite sepes,*
> *Hyblæis apibus florem depasta salicti,*
> *Sæpe levi somnum suadebit inire susurro.*
> *Hinc alta ab rupe canet frondator ad auras;*
> *Nec tamen interea raueæ, tua cura, palumbes,*
> *Nec gemere aeria cessabit turtur ab ulmo.*[10]

In the beautiful episode of Orpheus and Euridice in the fourth book of his *Georgics*, the pensive powers of music furnish out almost entirely the exquisite picture. And in Thomson's *Summer*, we are indebted for our pleasures in the grove, or orchard of Pomona, in the torrid climes, not less to the fragrance, and rich tastes, than to the blended beauties of the leaves, the flowers, and fruits.

---

[8] [Joseph Addison (1712) 'On the Pleasures of the Imagination, First Essay'.]
[9] [Thomas Reid (1785) *Essays on the Intellectual Powers of Man*, V.vi.]
[10] [On this side, as of old, on your neighbor's border, the hedge
whose willow blossoms are sipped by Hybla's bees
shall often with its gentle hum soothe you to slumber;
on that, under the towering rock the woodman's song shall fill the air;
while still the cooing wood pigeons, your pets,
and the turtle dove shall cease not their moaning from the elm tops.
— Virgil, *Eclogue* I.53-8.]

The imagination is the principal power employed in invention; and by it the character of the genius is chiefly formed, whether it delight to dwell among the light and gay beauties of nature, to retire to her sober and pensive scenes, or to soar amidst the most magnificent and sublime of her works. To it the philosopher, the orator, the artist, as well as the poet, are indebted for many of the principal excellencies of their arts. The logician depends on it for the discovery of those intermediate ideas which help to conduct him to his conclusions!—The philosopher for those analogies which extend the sphere, and promote the accuracy of his reasonings; the orator for his allusions, his figures, his arguments, and those persuasive topics which assist him most directly in his access to the heart; and the artist for those delicate touches, those enchanting graces, and those appropriate groups which so much delight the fancy and the sense.

As a vivid imagination is the faculty chiefly employed in invention, and associated with virtue, it is a powerful engine of doing good; although it has unhappily been often abused, by ingenious vice, with too fatal success, in undermining the principles, and depraving the affections of incautious youth. To poets, orators, painters, and other liberal artists, however, it ought to be no small encouragement to give their talents a useful direction, to reflect that the most beautiful efforts of the imagination have always appeared in works which contribute to innocent entertainment, or are calculated to awaken social, benevolent, and virtuous affections; and human nature is so constituted that the productions of genius fitted to promote these ends, will always meet with the most general and lasting approbation of mankind.

Imagination I have called the picture-making faculty of the mind. And every work of genius may be considered as one picture, the parts of which are connected by certain natural relations. They are not loosely and arbitrarily brought together without any sympathy or congeniality between the ideas, which, in every production of taste, ought more or less directly, to tend to one definite end, and ultimately to be combined into one consistent whole. The mind is generally inclined to pursue its thoughts in some train; and it rarely happens, that in passing from one subject to another, we cannot discern some connection between the different parts, or that in the groups which it assembles together there are not some principles of union which have led to the association.

It has been a subject of enquiry among philosophers what are the principles of association among our ideas that most naturally guide the train of the mind's thoughts, especially in the excursions of a poetic imagination, or the investigations of science. Mr. Hume among the moderns, is the first, perhaps, who has attempted to give a regular analysis of these principles, which he endeavored to reduce to the three following; resemblance, contiguity in time or in place, and cause and effect; by which last he means, according to his philosophy, only antecedents and consequents. Writers, since Mr. Hume's time, have considerably increased the number of these associating principles. It has not, however, been pretended that a complete enumeration of them has yet been made. And as every possible relation among the objects of our thoughts, and even among the words in which our thoughts are expressed, may be a ground of association, such an entire enumeration cannot easily be accomplished. Our ideas may often be associated by resemblance or by opposition in the sounds of the words, and sometimes in the letters of the words which convey them to the ear. Not infrequently, as has been remarked by Dr. Stewart, the grammatical figure of alliteration may bring words and thoughts together which have hardly any other link of connection; a remarkable example of which we have in the following line of Mr. Pope's, in his *Rape of the Lock*;

> Puffs, powders, patches, — bibles, billet doux.[11]

An extensive collection of these associating principles may be found in Dr. Campbell's *Philosophy of Rhetoric*. A few only of the principal I shall barely suggest, referring for the illustration and application of them to the operations of taste and genius to that judicious author. — The first of these, and as far as works of fancy are concerned, perhaps the most important is, *resemblance*. Resembling qualities easily suggest themselves to writers who have made the wide extent of nature their study, and are familiar with the copies of her

---

[11] [billet-doux: a love letter.]

works so beautifully traced by the fine writers of the ancient or modern areas of literature.

Under *resemblance* may be comprehended *analogy*, which implies, not the perfect similitude of parts, but a similitude of relations among different objects. These are a fruitful source of emblematic representations, of allegories, comparisons, metaphors, and many of the finest figures of speech. Under this principle also is embraced *similarity of emotion*, comprehending all those objects which tend to excite resembling thoughts, emotions and feelings in the mind. For example, the resembling state of mental feeling and emotion created by gentle breezes, murmuring rivulets, and the melody of birds, would very naturally conspire to associate them together with other objects of a like tendency, in the description of rural scenes. — One of the finest examples, perhaps, in any language, of this similarity of emotion associating in the mind objects which have not any other point of resemblance, is that in the poems of Ossian in which the poet compares the *music of Carol* to the *memory of past joys*. The music of Carol, says he, *is like the memory of past joy, pleasing and mournful to the soul*.[12]

The author of *the Seasons*, in an address to a lady, presents to us an image of the same kind, beautiful in the thought, but perhaps too obscure in the expression; for all the associations of a poetic fancy should be the most easy and natural: —

> Oh thou, whose tender serious eye
> Expressive speaks the soul I love,
> The gentle azure of the sky,
> The pensive shadows of the grove.[13]

The emotion created by her eye, the index of her soul resembles that awakened by the serene blue of the heavens, while retired beneath some pensive shade.

Another principle of association is *contrast*, or *opposition*. Opposites are found naturally to recall one another. Contrast is the source of many beauties in the arts; and the figure of *antithesis*, by the sparkling collision of thoughts, often yields peculiar pleasure to the imagination. In philosophy, distinctions, exceptions, discriminations, so necessary to the precise

---

[12] [Ossian (James Macpherson) (1765) '*The Death of Cuthullin*'.]
[13] [James Thomson (1726?) 'Song'.]

and accurate discussion of the greater part of subjects in this science, depend on this principle. The orator often resorts to it in the elucidation of the topics which he handles; and often in his most pathetic addresses to the passions. Other principles, directed to the same end, we find in the contiguity of objects in place, and in time; in fitness and congruity of parts, either in single images, or in more extended views: in the simple ode, or the complex epic, or drama.—*Custom* and *habit* are not less natural and important conductors to the train of thought. The connections in the relations of our ideas which we have been accustomed to pursue, almost spontaneously offer themselves to the mind. The thoughts easily retrace their former channels. Hence the importance of a certain course of studies, of certain habits of reflection, of an extensive intercourse with society, and the world, and of customarily exercising the imagination, and the understanding on those subjects on which men expect to be called either to write, or to speak. Such habitual employments of the mind will facilitate its command over all its necessary exertions when required, whether they consist in the closer application of its reasoning powers, or in the freer and more picturesque excursions of fancy.

Strong feelings, passions, or emotions, although they cannot properly be called principles of association among our ideas, yet are undoubtedly calculated to call up in the mind, with peculiar vivacity and strength, all those ideas which are in any way connected with the emotion, and tend to increase its force. They are calculated likewise to assist the powers of expression, and to give to those ideas an easy and impressive utterance in words. Hence the poet or the orator, before he begins to write or to speak, should study to kindle his mind with his subject, and to awaken all those perceptions, and emotions which it ought, or is naturally fitted to excite. Where there is natural genius, the true inspiration of the poet and the orator is *feeling*. The same observation is, perhaps, not less applicable to the sculptor, and the painter.

Another class of associating principles there is, almost exclusively connected with philosophic investigation; such as, the relations of *cause* and *effect*, of the *means* and the *end*, of the *premises* and the *conclusion*. In pursuing these connections the philosopher is expected to lay down a regular plan, and to follow it with rigorous exactness, rarely permitting any digressions for the purpose of embellishment, or of relieving the fatigue of attention, by the pleasant pictures of fancy. The principles of resemblance, analogy and contrast, and others that have been mentioned before, leave the mind in a more free and easy state, and therefore more especially belong to the province of poetic imagination. It deserves to be remarked of these trains of associated ideas, and the remark serves, in some degree, to characterize the different genius of poetry and philosophy, that the mind in passing along them has power to select any single idea at pleasure, although connected with its principal, by the slightest association, and making it the origin of a new train, to conduct the fancy in this manner, by different steps, through a wide and diversified field, till, by artfully seizing, at length, some related image, it is led back by an easy and natural transition, to the subject from which it had digressed. A beautiful example of this regular play of the imagination, if I may so call it, is given by Virgil in the end of the first book of his *Georgics*, a work that is full of the finest specimens of a cultivated and digressive fancy. He was pointing out to the husbandman the usual prognostic of the weather, so important to be foreseen by the cultivator of the earth; he passes thence to those meteors, and atmospheric phenomena which the superstition of Rome regarded as indications of civil revolution, and public disasters; this introduces the direful presages which were said to have preceded the death of Caesar; whence the transition was easy to the civil wars that followed, and the battles of Pharsalia and Philippi. And here we cannot but admire the art with which the poet returns to his subject—'the *time*', says he, 'will come when the rustic laborer in these fields, will raise from the earth the rusty weapons with his crooked plough, and with his heavy harrows strike the empty helms of fallen heroes, while he admires the huge bones turned forth from their graves'; which affords a natural introduction to the continuance of his agricultural labors.[14] There is something apparently casual in the order, and transitions of our thoughts, though strictly connected with the train of our associations, when the mind is in that easy and natural state

---

[14] [Virgil, *Gregorics*, I.493–7.]

in which poetry is enjoyed with the greatest pleasure, which is never allowed in philosophic reasoning.

READING IX

Volition[15]

The will is that power of the soul, and volition the exercise of that power which is the immediate cause of action in man. Propensities, affections, and other active principles in our nature, may stimulate the mind to action, and thus prove motives to the exercise of its voluntary powers. These internal emotions, therefore, and the various external objects which tend to incite them, may be regarded as primary and remote causes of our actions; but the immediate and proximate cause, is volition.

The nature of the will is understood, as far as we understand any of the acts or powers of our own minds, only by consciousness. The plainest and most unlettered man perfectly conceives the meaning of these phrases, *I will*, and *I will not*. And the nature of this faculty, as of every other power of the soul, is understood only in its acts.

The principal inquiry on this subject which merits your attention, relates to *the freedom of the will*, as it is generally expressed; or, as it ought, perhaps, to be more definitely stated, *the freedom of the mind in her volitions.* — It is an inquiry on which volumes have been written by the most acute and distinguished metaphysicians, and moralists. And, as they have embraced directly contradictory opinions upon the question, or have come in their conclusions to opposite results, it is probable that there is some peculiar subtlety in the subject, or that they have set out in the discussion on erroneous principles, or embarrassed it by the introduction of the peculiar tenets of their respective sects of philosophy or religion. — One party maintain not only that the will is free in acting, but that it determines its own acts. Another party contend that the will is, in all cases, determined by motives; that

---

[15] [Extracted from Samuel Stanhope Smith (1812) 'Lecture XIII', in *The Lectures, Corrected and Improved, which have been Delivered for a Series of Years in the College of New Jersey on the Subjects of Moral and Political Philosophy*, 2 Volumes, Volume I, New York: Whiting & Watson, Trenton, NJ: James J. Wilson, pp. 275-99.]

it cannot act in any other way; and that, therefore, it must necessarily be determined by the strongest motive, or the last motive in the view of the mind at the time of acting. — That is, laying aside all consideration of the interior energy or power of the soul over its own acts, the will is, by a separate mechanism, subjected to the impulse and control of motives, as the water wheel, to use Dr. Priestley's own analogy, is to the force and gravity of the fluid that turns it round.

One would think, indeed, that it is a question of the utmost simplicity, and the most obvious solution. It is a question strictly of experience; and to experience alone we ought to appeal for its decision. Every man is conscious to himself that he acts freely; and that, in all ordinary cases, when he is not under the impulse of some violent passion, or under the commanding influence of some inveterate habit, he has it in his power to pursue a directly contrary course of action, from that to which he is invited by the present predominant motive. But philosophers have opposed speculation to fact; and commencing with an erroneous principle, that the acts of the will must be determined solely, and irresistibly by the motives before it, as they are presented in the order of nature, they have been led to conclusions contrary to nature and experience. We seem to be free, they say, yet, we are only borne along by a powerful stream to which we make no resistance because it concurs with our inclinations; but which, otherwise, it would be vain to attempt to resist. In the beginning, permit me to observe, that the decision of this question involves considerations of no small importance to morals. The doctrine of necessity, when pursued to its ultimate consequences, appears to destroy all moral distinctions, and to take away merit from virtue, and demerit from vice. I am aware that notwithstanding the errors of speculation, nature will often find means to enforce the practical dictates of truth and reason. Many of those philosophers who have most strenuously contended to bind the moral world under the chain of a speculative necessity, not only obey the laws of virtue themselves, but, would reprehend any departure from them in others, no less severely than the advocates of a rational liberty. It is, however, too much to be apprehended that the greater part of the modern disciples of this school, have intended to annihilate the true distinction between vice and virtue, except so far as it may be made a convenient political engine of public order. On the regulation of individual manners it has certainly an unfavorable aspect. Those writers who have embraced the system of necessity, connecting it at the same time with the principles of religion, have endeavored, except Dr. Priestley, and a few others, to state a distinction between physical and moral necessity. After all the explanations, however, which have been given of these phrases, they appear to amount only to this, that the one is the necessity of matter, the other, the necessity of mind. The consequences of the doctrine on the merit and demerit of virtue and vice, seem not to have been, clearly at least, guarded against by the friends of the latter phraseology. If by moral necessity were intended to be expressed the extreme difficulty of changing, or correcting old and inveterate habits, we could admit it as a justifiable figure of speech. But if it be meant to indicate a real necessity, in vicious men of acting immorally, resulting from a depraved disposition of the heart, which is natural, constitutional, incurable, I see not how the term, so circumstanced, at all relieves the consequences, as to the accountability or guilt of the agent, imputable to the principle of physical necessity. To say that the course of immoral action being voluntary, is therefore criminal, is merely an abuse of words, when the will itself, in the language of these writers, is infused by the author of our being; at best, is the necessary result of the moral constitution of man.[16]

The controversies concerning liberty and necessity have been extended to so great a length, that it would be impossible, in a course of lectures like the present, to give even a

---

[16] It will be easily perceived that, in these reflections, there is an oblique reference to the extravagant, not to say atheistical tenets of some metaphysical divines. I mean not, however, to enter into any religious discussion. The depravity of human nature, which the scriptures teach, and which experience proves, I am very far from denying, but would strenuously assert. But can any moral necessity be attached to man's condition of depravity, which was not attached to his original state of innocence and perfection? Or do these writers forget their own principle that man has been placed in a new state of trial, under a dispensation of grace? But can any trial be imposed on a subject bound under the chains of an *invincible* necessity, though softened under the deceptive name of *moral*?

concise abridgment which would be intelligible, and satisfactory, of the various reasonings which have been held on one side and on the other. They have, besides, been so mingled with the doctrines of religion, converting the simplicity of the gospel into a system of abstruse metaphysics, that it is become almost dangerous to touch a subject on which each party claims a merit for detecting a latent heterodoxy under the most guarded and philosophic expression of truth. We often see, moreover, speculations so bold, and hear a language so presumptuous, with regard to the power, liberty and prescience of the Deity, as are sufficient to deter us from a subject, simple and obvious in itself, but puzzled by a vain philosophy, and no less vain theology, in which men, in proportion to their ignorance, affect to be acquainted with the inscrutable mysteries of the divine nature, and the way in which infinite wisdom is present with the human will.

All that I propose upon the subject is to state in a few plain propositions, and in as clear and comprehensive a manner as I am able, as far as human duty is concerned, what I conceive to be the truth upon this question, which has been rendered obscure only in consequence of too much subtlety.

And, in the first place, it is of importance to correct an error in language, which has probably contributed, in some measure, to involve the question of *liberty and necessity* in that obscurity with which it has been so remarkably surrounded.—The *freedom of the will*, is a phrase which has been familiarly employed by all parties, and the propriety of which seems not to have been questioned by any. But volition being only an act of the mind, liberty cannot be so properly predicated of it, as of the mind which exercises that act. —When we speak of liberty, or necessity, as predicable of the *will*, there are only two forms of discourse which the advocates of the respective sides of this question employ;—the one, that the *will* determines itself;—the other, that it is solely determined by motives,—both equally unphilosophical and false.

If we ask how the will forms any determination? If the question is not an absurdity, because the will is itself the determination of the mind, we would be obliged to answer by an identical proposition, that it is by an act of volition. If then we admit that the will determines itself, it can only be, if the phrase have any meaning, by a previous act of volition. And if we inquire by what is this act determined? we must in the same manner answer, by one still prior—which would lead us through an infinite series of volitions to determine one free act.

If, with the other sect of philosophers, we admit that the will is solely determined by motives, there is no avoiding the consequence that we are not free; but that all our actions are necessarily subject to the direction and control of that power, whatever it is, which orders the train of events, that is, the succession of motives, in the midst of which we are placed. The will not having any power of deliberating, or suspending its own actions, if there is no controlling power in the mind, it must, like the magnetic needle, be subject to the minutest force impressed, or the minutest excess of force between two opposite motives. On this supposition, the will, in all the ordinary train of life, pressed on every side, by motives of different degrees of strength, ought to be found in a continual vibratory state, till some one, more powerful than the rest, fixes its choice, or till it is disposed to settle on the last, which happens, at any moment, to be within its view. If the will, which has no power of deliberating, but solely of acting, is determined entirely by motives, it must be merely the victim of events, or the slave of inclination, appetite, or passion, as it arises.

We shall, perhaps, arrive at clearer ideas upon this subject, and approach nearer the truth, by rejecting the phraseology of both parties, and, instead of admitting the hypothesis, either that the will determines itself, or that it is determined by the last or strongest motive in the mind, to lay it down as a principle upon this question, that the mind alone determines the acts of the will, as it does all its other operations.

If it be asked what advantage is gained by this change in the language usually employed upon this subject? For if it be admitted as a principle that the mind determines the will, must it not be by a previous act of volition, involving a similar absurdity to that which we have just rejected? I answer, by no means.—Although the mind determines all our other voluntary operations by the agency of the will; yet it does not thus determine the acts of the will. An act of the will is the determination of the mind with regard to some other object; not with regard to itself. The volitions of the mind are the effect of its own internal energy, not by a previous volition, but by an original, innate power over its own actions, of which every man who reflects upon himself is conscious, but which, like all the other primary perceptions, and operations of our nature, it is not easy, perhaps not possible, to express in words, except by identical propositions.

But if the mind is determined in its volitions by the influence of motives, will not the same consequences follow as have been shown to result from the determination of the will by the same means? The will being merely an act, without the power of deliberation or resistance, must implicitly obey, according to its nature, the power which governs it. But the soul being endowed with the faculty of deliberating, judging, comparing, and estimating motives before it acts, demonstrates in the exercise of this power the freedom of its actions. If motive necessarily govern the mind, then the present motive at each instant, when there is none stronger to counterbalance it, or that among several motives which has any surplus of strength above its antagonists, must immediately, and antecedently to all deliberation, determine its action. But the exercise of its deliberative powers affords sufficient proof, that it still possesses the faculty of commanding its own actions. True it is, the mind seldom or never acts without some present motive, that is, without some end in view at the time, although Dr. Reid has rendered it probable that, on many occasions, it forms determinations without motive, by the immediate energy of its own self-control; yet no one motive, nor any assemblage of motives, has power to compel it to act in this or that particular direction. We can still deliberate, compare, judge, reason, concerning their respective value, and the degree of influence which they ought to possess. And when, at length, we yield to the influence of any one, we feel that we yield it a free homage; we can resist it; we are sensible of a power to follow the leading or impulse of any other motive within the contemplation of the mind; or even of any which, though not present, we can call up at pleasure. Thus, though always situated in the midst of various motives, addressed to the principles of appetite, affection, passion, duty, prudence, interest, pleasure, yet are we always able to judge among them with freedom, and to admit or reject them at pleasure. The mind is placed as a judge listening to the pleas of different advocates, and when he has heard them, deciding with magisterial authority between them.

If it be asked, what influence, then, do motives possess over the determinations of the mind?—Only a moral and persuasive influence. Inclination, or duty present, on one side, or on the other, their respective claims, which are, in no case irresistible, unless we may, in some instance, except the effects of violent passion, or of inveterate habit, when the mind contemplates, weighs them, and on the result forms its resolution; a resolution which on all the common occasions of life, it forms with promptness; on others, with more deliberation; but on all with perfect freedom.—Some writers, among whom we may name with distinction Priestley, and Helvétius, represent human nature, even in the exercise of its moral and rational powers, as so entirely mechanical, that in the whole process of reasoning, no less than in the decisions of the will, it is subject to the certain, though unconscious control of necessity. The language of others seems to admit of freedom in the exercise of our powers, of deliberation and judgment, but, when the decision of the mind is made up, that is, when the motive is completely formed, then the correspondent act of the will must necessarily ensue. They compare the will to a balance in which the least preponderance of weight must turn the scale. And, if it were possible that motives perfectly equal in all respects, could be thrown into it, then it must be suspended in total inaction, like the schoolmen's ass between two bundles of hay. All this subtlety of reasoning and deduction, I am persuaded, is contrary to experience, and to our natural feelings of liberty. This, indeed, is not denied by many of the most strenuous advocates of the necessitarian philosophy; though, like lord Kames, they say, the sense of liberty is only a delusive feeling, implanted by the Author of nature, more effectually to accomplish the purposes of our own moral machinery.

In the discussion of every subject, we should endeavor to fix, in the beginning, some clear and determinate principles, that may lay a firm foundation on which our reasonings, and conclusions may rest. Our present subject, although it has been much embarrassed by erroneous hypothesis, and by subtle and abstruse speculations, affords some elementary propositions as precise and clear as those of any metaphysical question whatever. A few of these you will permit me here to state, giving them a very brief illustration, as it is not my intention to go into an extensive investigation of this much-agitated question, but only to open such an introduction to it as may assist your future enquiries.[17]

In the first place, it is acknowledged that, in the various operations of the mind in which the influence of the will is concerned, we are usually sensible of the solicitation of some motive more gentle, or more powerful; that is, in every thing that we do, we have commonly some end in view, — the gratification of some propensity, or affection, — the indulgence of some inclination, — or obedience to some dictate of reason or of conscience.

In the next place, although these motives prompt to action, and, in many cases, direct the tenor of our actions, yet do we never perceive that they impose upon the mind any necessary constraint in acting. This is a subject on which experience must be the sole test of truth. No speculative or abstracted deductions of reasoning, should ever be permitted to establish a conclusion in opposition to the simple and obvious perceptions of our own consciousness. For whatever be the action to which we are solicited, and by whatever strength of motive we are drawn, we find, unless it be in some paroxysms of violent passion, that we are able to suspend acting; we can act in a manner directly contrary to the attraction of the primary motive. — It has been objected to the argument which we would derive in favor of liberty from the power of suspending or altering any of our actions, that it does not in the least impair the principle of necessity; for the new act is the effect of some new motive, if it were only to make an experiment of our own power, which now in its turn possesses the necessitating influence. — I answer, that if the motive to this suspending act, were to make trial of our own power, the experiment surely has been completely succ-

---

[17] Those who have leisure to enter profoundly into the question, may consult Leibniz, Clarke, Locke, Hartley, Helvétius, Priestley, Kames, President Edwards, and Dr. Reid of Glasgow.

essful. But if the advocate of necessity rests the decision of the question on the necessary force of this last motive, here also his argument fails; for again we can suspend the action, and again, and again, as often as the trial is made. And although liberty does not consist in suspending or changing the course of an action merely for the sake of exercising our self-command: yet the power of suspension or of change which we always feel that we possess, whenever we please to exert it, is a decisive proof that the mind, in acting, is not subject to the constraints of necessity; but, on the contrary, is perfectly free in yielding to the persuasive influence of any motive.

In the third place, the mind has the power of beginning action, or exerting the acts of its will by its own intrinsic energy. Surrounded by an infinite variety of motives in the structure of the world, in the state of society, and in the propensities, dispositions, and inclinations of our own nature, it has power to choose among them at pleasure; it can even change, at the slightest command of its will, the train of motives which it will at any time suffer to be present to its view. All this it does by its own inherent self-command. Motives may incite and awake the mind into action; but they are subject to the control of the mind. And this control it exercises, not, as I have before said, by any previous act of volition, but by that internal energy and power which the mind possesses over the will of which every man who reflects upon himself must be conscious, but which he cannot in any other way explain but by referring to that common feeling of human nature. After taking a survey of the motives before it, and contemplating them as far as it deems necessary to forming a decision, it resolves: that resolution is its will; in which it acts like a master who has power to resolve in different ways, concerning the objects of its choice, not like a slave who is constrained to resolve only in one way.

The power of beginning action without being itself impelled by any extraneous impulse, is one of the principal distinctions between spirit and matter. Matter, that is impelled by other matter, receives an impetus according to the quantity and direction of the force with which it is impressed. And without the impression of some external force it is inert. But mind is essentially active; it is capable of beginning motion, and of communicating motion to other things, antecedently to the action of any anterior force upon it. Otherwise how shall we account for all the motions of the universe? How account for creation itself? For we cannot surely be under the necessity here of combating the atheistical absurdity of *fate*, and making all existence depend upon an abstract and unintelligible idea. The Infinite and Eternal Mind, the author of all power and wisdom, has given existence and motion to all things by that intrinsic power which mind possesses over matter, and over its own movements. He could not originally have been moved by any consideration, extraneous to himself. If motive can be ascribed to the Deity, the motive, the power, and the wisdom in him must have been simultaneous and co-eternal with his existence; or if we can conceive of any order in the divine mind, power, and wisdom in him must have been prior to any system of motives that could arise out of the arrangement of the universe; for that arrangement, and every motive of action resulting from it, must have first been conceived, and received effect from him. He was self-determined by his own sovereign power and wisdom, conceiving most freely the system, to which he freely gave existence. To say, with Leibniz, that there was a best in the plan and idea of the universe antecedent to the act of the Creator, which of necessity his infinite power converted into fact, seems certainly a very unfounded principle. Much more consistent it is with our apprehensions of the wisdom, power, and perfection of the Deity, to believe that he could have conceived an infinite variety of systems, any of which should have been equal in its structure to that which he has formed; but, in his sovereign pleasure, he gave effect only to that which exists. No antecedent motive in the state of the universe influenced his action. He created all motives; and in its conformation, and arrangement, only gave existence to his own idea. As an inherent self-determining power is essential to the infinite mind by which he controls all the movements of the universe; so has he given to man to possess an image of that power, in the control that he enjoys over his own will and over all the actions of his mind, as well as of his body.

In all disquisitions concerning the will, it ought perhaps to be laid down as a primary principle, than which there can be no axiom in science more evident, that the mind is perfectly free in her volitions. It stands on the same footing with the clearest testimonies of sense and consciousness. This, indeed, is confessed by some of the most strenuous advocates of necessity; although in order to preserve their theory they are obliged to maintain that it is a delusive feeling. They lay it down as a maxim that the human mind acts and can act only in consequence of motives; whence, as they conceive, results this necessary consequence, that it must be determined by the strongest motive, or at least by the last motive immediately present to its view before acting. Whence arises this ulterior consequence, that, the train and order of motives being arranged by another power than man's, his mind, in all its acts, is subjected to the law of an imperious necessity, over which it can have no control.

This naked and bald idea of necessity, in its evident tendency, goes to destroy all moral distinctions; but we have the pleasure of perceiving that nature, in her care for human happiness, often contradicts, by her practical dictates, the errors of a too subtle speculation. And some distinguished philosophers have had the candor to acknowledge that, however certain their principles appear in theory, they are not able to carry their conclusions into practical life. The invincible feelings of liberty, every moment stand in the way of their uncomfortable speculations. Not a few of these hardy philosophers, however, like the French Helvétius, and the British Kames, boldly avow the moral results of their system, and declare virtue and vice to be only names invented for the use and convenience of society. If the existence, or the happiness of society depends so much upon these names, there can hardly be conceived, one would think, a stronger argument for the reality of the things. But if we degrade a consciousness so clear and determinate into a deceitful feeling, by what criterion shall we admit any principle of science to the rank of an axiomatic or first truth? Is there any proposition, or even any perception of sense, more clear, or more irresistibly convincing than this, that we are free in acting? The clear and ultimate perceptions of nature are the foundations of all truth and certainty in reasoning.

Before I conclude my reflections on this question, I must observe that liberty, as a principle of moral action, has a much more extensive power than merely controlling our general conduct within a certain sphere, according to our present inclinations and dispositions. It extends to the power of resisting our inclinations, of correcting any habits of thinking and acting which may be in opposition to our duty, interest, or pleasure; and in a word, of changing our moral dispositions. Of this we need no other proof than the obvious effects of moral culture. The most ignorant mind may become enlightened, the most rude and uncultivated taste refined, and the most vicious disposition reformed. And this effect we see produced simply by presenting clear ideas, and distinct examples of virtue, and of taste before it; and by illuminating and directing it in the free and proper exercise of its natural faculties and powers. It is true, when any violent passion has seized, or any inveterate prejudice, or habit, has in a manner incorporated itself with the soul, it becomes extremely difficult, and, in some cases, almost impossible to effect a favorable change. But the ideas of difficulty, and of necessity, are totally distinct. And surely the increasing strength of all moral habits arising from time, and by indulgence, conformably to universal experience, is an argument against the fatalists; unless they will imagine a useless distinction of grades in necessity, where every grade is uncontrollable perdition.

An argument is sometimes employed on this subject which would operate against all power of moral reform in vicious men, unless there be presupposed in them a miraculous change, that is, a change wholly independent on all natural means of instruction and cultivation in the moral dispositions of the heart. Without such a change, it is asserted, in which, however, the will of the agent cannot have any concern but that of a passive subject, no moral motive can have effect in producing the habits and principles of virtue. A man of depraved affections, it is said, is blind to the proper beauty of virtue; and has, moreover, an aversion to the purity of its sentiments, and to the restraints which it imposes on his inclinations. On both these grounds, therefore, in the first place, want of discernment of the excellence of virtue, which will hinder the effect of any motive drawn from that source; and, in the next place, aversion from its restraints, and from the purity of its sentiments, he will be hostile to every virtuous reform, and therefore incapable of true virtue, as long as he is left merely to the action of his own natural powers. — This is a mistaken view of human nature. There are principles in the moral constitution of man, which lead even the vicious to understand, and approve a degree of virtue beyond their own present attainments, and enable then to perceive, at least, some faint and dawning rays of its beauty and excellency through the mists of their passions, before they are enamored of its perfection. Here, then, we behold a vantage ground, in advance of their actual state of morals, on which moral culture, reason and reflection can take hold to carry forward to an ulterior point, their improvements in knowledge and virtue. And as these improvements proceed, the same means of assisting their progress continually advance before them.

In this process of the mind there is a striking analogy between the cultivation of morals and of taste. The uncultivated mind is blind to the finer and more delicate beauties of taste, as the immoral heart is to the excellencies of virtue. It prefers a ruder and coarser execution in all the works of art; because it is not yet prepared to understand and relish those of a higher and more perfect order. Still, however, there are principles in the rudest mind which give a perception of beauty and elegance, in examples properly placed before it, always in advance of its own present state of improvement, and its present powers of execution in the liberal arts. And in these principles we discern the means of still further improvements. These reflections exhibit a proof of the moral freedom of man, and of power over his own actions, to fulfil his duties, and, notwithstanding his present imperfections, to advance in the career of moral and mental cultivation, that ought to be very consoling to human nature. If well founded, they overturn the foundation of all the gloomy speculations of necessity and fatalism.

Appendix

Although I rely with confidence on the practical reasonings which establish the freedom of human action, and would by all means avoid placing speculation on any footing of equality with fact, and the practical feelings of nature, there is one speculative argument for the doctrine of necessity drawn from divine prescience which it may be proper not wholly to omit. — The knowledge of future events, it is said, can be founded only on the certain connection of causes with their effects; and this certainty, it is further added, can have no other foundation than the necessary operation and influence of the cause. Any contingency in the event, which they suppose to be an unavoidable consequence of the liberty of moral action, removes the sole ground on which prescience can rest.

How presumptuously will weak man speak of the incomprehensible nature and operations of the Deity, as if there could be any resemblance between the knowledge and action of the divine mind, and that of any of his creatures! Can we suppose that he reasons, like man; that he depends for his knowledge of future events on the concatenation of causes with effects, of premises with their conclusion; and is obliged to proceed with the progressive step of mortals, along his chain of inferences? — While we reject this unworthy conception of the Infinite, and Eternal, Mind, it becomes us, on the other hand, reverently to believe that he is always present to every moment of duration, to every point of infinite space: and that his knowledge, instead of consisting of a train of induction, is immediate, intuitive, and from eternity, ever present with the future as with the past, with the freest action as with the most necessary event.

These philosophers repeat the assertion, that choice, or volition, without the necessary determination of motive, is mere caprice, or the uncertainty of pure accident. It cannot, therefore, be the cause of a virtuous act, which must always arise from good motives; nor can it be an object of knowledge to any being. I answer that the persuasive influence which we attribute to motives relieves the principle from both these consequences. The persuasion of right motives is the only ground of virtue; which would be destroyed by necessity. The same influence would be an ample ground of certainty to a mind which like that of the Deity should be able accurately to estimate the minutest relations of motives to the tempers, characters, and circumstances of men. A familiar example though derived from our imperfect foresight, may serve to illustrate this conclusion. When we thoroughly know the dispositions of our children, or our intimate friends, although they sometimes disappoint the anticipations which we frame of their actions, yet, in general we can, without much hazard of mistake, predict, in given situations, what conduct they will hold;—not surely from any knowledge which we possess of the necessary connection of motives with their ends, for they frequently disappoint us, but from our acquaintance, generally, with the persuasive influence of such motives, on such dispositions. And there are many occasions on which we can rely with confidence on that moral certainty which is the result of the free operation of moral causes.

Were, then, the prescience of the Divine Mind, who knows the minutest movements of the human heart, the slightest and most complicated influences of the infinitely various motives that address it, governed like that of man, by reasonings, inferences, or experience, how infallible might be his assurance, although not built upon the laws of necessity, but guided only by his perfect knowledge of their moral and persuasive powers?—But, as I have already said,—away with such unworthy conceptions and reasonings concerning the Infinite, Eternal, Omnipresent Mind!—All knowledge with him is intuition. It is connate with his existence. All eternity,—the future, as well as the past, is ever present to his immediate view.

Six

Archibald Alexander (1772–1851)

Archibald Alexander was born in 1772 in Lexington, Virginia. In 1781 he matriculated at Liberty Academy (now Washington and Lee College), and after graduation moved to Spottsylvania County, Virginia in order to work as a tutor for a wealthy Presbyterian family. While there, Alexander witnessed Baptist revivals: an event which led him to question his religious beliefs and practice. Intrigued by the enthusiasm of the Baptist evangelicals but concerned over what he felt was a lack of sophistication in their preaching, Alexander decided to return to Liberty Academy in order to pursue an education in theology.

Upon returning to Liberty, Alexander prepared for a career in ministry by studying under William Graham, a noted Presbyterian minister and educator, who had also been a student of John Witherspoon. Under Graham, Alexander was exposed both to Calvinist theology and the philosophy of the Scottish Enlightenment. Following graduation, Alexander worked as a minister for six years—first as an itinerant and then as the pastor of a linked charge in Charlotte County, Virginia. In 1797 he became the president of Hampden-Sydney College; a position he held until 1806.

Over the next few years, Alexander served the Presbyterian church in various capacities. In 1801 Alexander was selected by the Presbyterian church to oversee the partial unification of the denomination with the Congregationalist church of Connecticut. Then, in 1807 Alexander returned to ministry by becoming the pastor of the prestigious Third Street

Presbyterian Church in Philadelphia. In 1808, however, Alexander set the course for the rest of his life when he preached a sermon in favor of the creation of a new Presbyterian seminary. Finding no one better qualified than Alexander himself to run the institution, the Presbyterian church established Princeton Theological Seminary in 1812. In its first year, Alexander was the sole faculty member of the seminary; but under his leadership the size of the student body and faculty rapidly increased during the school's first years.

As an educator, Alexander stood firmly in the tradition of Witherspoon and Graham, extolling both a thoroughgoing Calvinist theology and Common Sense philosophy. During the conflict between the conservative Old Light and liberal New Light Presbyterians over the importance of the Calvinist Westminster Confession in the Presbyterian church, Alexander initially held back, but eventually sided with the former. Conservative by nature, Alexander was both a proponent of colonization and of the institution of slavery.

During his life, Alexander wrote many widely-read sermons and several well-received books. The following selection is extracted from his first book, *A Brief Outline of the Evidences of the Christian Religion*, published in 1825. Although Alexander is not much read today, his work and teaching inspired several generations of theologians, including his former student Charles Hodge, who went on to establish the school of Princeton Theology.

Biographical Information: James H. Moorhead, *American National Biography Online*.

READING X

Miracles[1]

I do not know that any one has denied that a miracle would be credible, if exhibited to our senses. A man might, indeed, be deceived by an illusion arising from some disorder in his senses; but if he was conscious of being in a sound state of body and mind, and should witness not only one, but a var-

---

[1] [Extracted from Archibald Alexander (1825) 'Section IV: Miracles are Capable of Proof from Testimony', in *A Brief Outline of the Evidences of the Christian Religion*, 2nd Edition, Princeton, NJ: Princeton Press, pp. 56–75.]

iety of miracles; not only a few times, but for years in succession; and if he should find, that all around him had the same perceptions of these facts as himself, I need not say, that it would be reasonable to credit his senses, for the constitution of his nature would leave him no choice: — he would be under the necessity of believing what he saw with his eyes, heard with his ears, and handled with his hands. But are there facts which a man would credit on the evidence of his senses, which can, by no means, be rendered credible by the testimony of any number of witnesses? Then there might be facts, the knowledge of which could never be so communicated as to be worthy of credit. According to this hypothesis, the constitution of our nature would require us to withhold our assent from what was true, and what others knew to be true. If a thousand persons of the strictest veracity should testify, that they had repeatedly witnessed a miracle, and if all circumstances should concur to corroborate their testimony, yet upon this principle it would be unreasonable to credit them, even if they should consent to die in confirmation of what they declared to be the fact. This is the ground taken by Mr. Hume, in his boasted argument against miracles. But it appears to me, that every man, previously to examination, must be convinced that it is false; for it is contrary to common sense, and universal experience of the effect of testimony. The true principle on this subject, is, *that any fact which would be believed on the evidence of the senses, may be reasonably believed on testimony.* For there may be testimony of such a nature, as to produce conviction as strong as any other conceivable evidence; and such testimony in favor of a miracle, would establish it as firmly as if we had witnessed it ourselves. But, notwithstanding that this is the conclusion of common sense and experience, the metaphysical argument of Mr. Hume has had the effect of perplexing, and unsettling the minds of many; and as he boasts, that 'it will be useful to overthrow miracles as long as the world endures',[2] it seems necessary to enter into an examination of his argument, that we may be able to expose its fallacy. This has already been done, in a convincing manner, by several men,[3] eminent for

---

[2] [All quotations from Hume are drawn from (1748) 'Section X: Of Miracles', in *An Enquiry Concerning Humans Understanding*.]

[3] Dr. Campbell, Prof. Vince, Mr. Adams, Dr. Douglas.

their learning and discrimination; and if their works were read by all who peruse Hume, I should think it unnecessary to add a single word on the subject. But it may not be without its use, to present the substance of their refutation, in a condensed form, for the sake of those who will not take the trouble to go through a minute and extended demonstration.

The argument of Mr. Hume will be best exhibited in his own words. 'A miracle', says he, 'supported by any human testimony, is more properly a subject of derision, than of argument. No testimony for any kind of miracle can ever possibly amount to a probability.' — 'We establish it as a maxim, that no human testimony can have such force, as to prove a miracle, and make a just foundation for any system of religion.' —

> Our belief or assurance of any fact from the report of eye witnesses, is derived from no other principle, than experience; that is, our observation of the veracity of human testimony, and of the usual conformity of facts to the reports of witnesses. Now, if the fact attested partakes of the marvelous, if it is such as has seldom fallen under our own observation; here is a contest of two opposite experiences, of which the one destroys the other, as far as its force goes. Further, if the fact affirmed by the witnesses, instead of being only marvelous is really miraculous; if, besides, the testimony considered apart, and in itself, amounts to an entire proof; in that case there is proof against proof, of which the strongest must prevail. — A miracle is a violation of the laws of nature; and as a firm and unalterable experience has established these laws, the proof against a miracle from the very nature of the fact is as entire as any argument from experience can possibly be imagined. And if so, it is an undeniable consequence, that it cannot be surmounted by any proof whatever from testimony. A miracle, therefore, however attested, can never be rendered credible, even in the lowest degree.

Here we have the substance of Mr. Hume's argument, on which I propose to make some remarks, intended to show that its whole plausibility depends on the assumption of false principles, and the artful use of equivocal terms.

1. Some prejudice is created in the minds of the unsuspecting reader, by the definition of a miracle here given. It is called 'a violation of the laws of nature', which carries with it an unfavorable idea, as though some obligation was violated,

and some injury was done. But the simple truth is, that the laws of nature are nothing else than the common operations of divine power in the government of the world, which depend entirely, for their existence and continuance, on the divine will; and a miracle is nothing else, than the exertion of the same power in a way different from that which is common; or it may be a mere suspension of that power, which is commonly observed to operate in the world.

2. Mr. Hume's argument will apply to the evidence of the senses as well as to that derived from testimony, and will prove (if it prove anything) that it would be impossible to believe in a miracle if we should witness it ever so often. 'The very same principle of experience', says he, 'which gives us a certain degree of assurance in the testimony of witnesses, gives us also, in this case, another degree of assurance against the fact which they endeavor to establish, from which contradiction there arises necessarily a counterpoise, and mutual destruction of belief and authority.' The very same counterpoise and mutual destruction of belief must also occur between the assurance derived from the senses, and that derived from experience. The reason why testimony cannot be believed in favor of a miracle, is not, according to Mr. Hume, because it has no force; for taken by itself, it may be sufficient to produce assurance; but let this assurance be as strong as it may, it cannot be stronger than that derived from universal experience. 'In that case', says he, 'there is proof against proof.' Now it is evident that upon these principles, the same *equilibrium* from contradictory evidence must take place, between experience and the senses. If one evidence be stronger than another, 'the strongest must prevail, but with a diminution of force in proportion to that of its antagonist'. But in the case of the senses, and a firm and unalterable experience, the evidence is perfect on both sides, so that the 'counterpoise and mutual destruction of belief' must occur. According to this metaphysical balance of Mr. Hume, a miracle could not be believed if we witnessed it ever so often; for although there is a great weight of evidence on each side, yet as there is an equilibrium, neither can have any influence on our assent. Whether Mr. Hume would have objected to this conclusion, does not appear; but it is manifest that it logically follows from his argument, as much as in the case to which

he has applied it. And here we see to what pitch of skepticism his reasoning leads.

3. Mr. Hume makes an unnecessary distinction between that which is *marvelous,* and that which is *miraculous;* for although there is a real difference, yet as to his argument, there is none. The force of his reasoning does not relate to events as being *miraculous,* but as being opposite to universal experience. If the conclusion, therefore, be correct, it will equally prove, that no testimony is sufficient to establish a natural event, which has not before been experienced. If ever so many witnesses should aver, that they had seen meteoric stones fall from the clouds, or the galvanic fluid melt metals, yet if we have never experienced these things ourselves, we must not believe them.

4. The *opposite* or *contrary* experience of Mr. Hume, in regard to miracles, can mean nothing more, than that such things have not been experienced. There is no other opposite experience conceivable, in this case, unless a number of persons present, at the same time, should experience opposite impressions. The distinction, which he artfully makes, in relation to 'the king of Siam, who refused to believe the first reports concerning the effects of frost', between *that which is contrary* to experience, and *not conformable* to experience, is without foundation. For a fact cannot be contrary to experience in any other way, than by being *not conformable* to it. There neither is, nor can be, any experience against miracles, except this, that they have not occurred in our own experience or that of others. When the proposition of our author is expressed in language free from ambiguity, it will amount to this, that what has never been experienced, can never be believed on any testimony; than which nothing can easily be conceived more false. In what a situation must man have been, at the beginning of the world, if he had adopted the principles of this skeptic.

5. Mr. Hume uses the word *experience* in a twofold sense, changing from one to the other, as best suits his purpose. Sometimes it means, *personal* experience, and at other times, and more commonly, the experience of the whole world. Now, if it be taken to mean our own individual experience, the argument will be, that no fact which we ourselves have not witnessed, can be established by testimony; which if

correct, would cut off, at a stroke, the greater part of human knowledge. Much the most numerous class of facts are those which we receive upon the testimony of others, and many of these are entirely different from anything that we have personally experienced. Many learned men never take the trouble to witness the most curious experiments in philosophy, and chemistry; yet they are as well satisfied of the truth, as if they had personal experience of it.

But although an argument founded on an opposition between testimony and experience, in order to be of any validity, must relate to *personal experience*; yet Mr. Hume commonly uses the term to signify the experience of all men in all ages. This extensive meaning of the term must be the one which he affixes to it in most places of his essay; because, it is an experience by which we know that the laws of nature are uniform and unalterable; and he has given an example which clearly determines the sense of the word, 'that a dead man should come to life,' says he, 'has never been witnessed in any age or country'.

Now, according to this use of the word, what he calls an argument, is a mere assumption of the point in dispute; what logicians call, a *petitio principii;* a begging of the question. For what is the question in debate? Is it not whether miracles have ever been experienced? And how does Mr. Hume undertake to prove that they never did exist? By an argument intended to demonstrate that no testimony can establish them; the main principle of which argument is, that all experience is against them. If miracles have ever occurred, they are not contrary to universal experience; for whatever has been witnessed at any time, by any person, makes part of universal experience. What sort of reasoning is it, then, to form an argument against the truth of miracles, founded on the assumption, that they never existed? If it be true, as he says, 'that it has never been witnessed in any age or country that a dead man should come to life', then, indeed, it is useless to adduce testimony to prove, that the dead have on some occasions, been brought to life. If he had a right to take this for granted, where was the use of such a parade of reasoning on the subject of testimony? The very conclusion to which he wished to come, is here assumed, as the main principle in the argument. It is, however, as easy to deny as to affirm; and we do utterly deny the truth of his position; so that after all, we are at issue, precisely on the point, where we commenced. Nothing is proved by the argument which promised so much, except the skill of the writer in sophistical reasoning.

6. Our author falls into another mistake, in his reasoning. The object is to prove, that testimony in favor of miracles, can never produce conviction, because it is opposed by uniform and unalterable experience. But how do we know what this universal experience is? Is it not by testimony, except within the narrow circle of our own personal experience? Then it turns out, that the testimony in favor of miracles is neutralized or overbalanced, by other testimony. That is, to destroy the force of testimony, he assumes a principle founded on testimony. It is admitted, that when testimony is adduced to establish any facts, if other and stronger testimony can be brought against them, their credibility is destroyed. But if I bring testimony for a fact, and someone alleges that he can show that this testimony is unworthy of credit, because he can bring witnesses to prove that many persons in different countries and ages never saw any such thing: to such a person I would reply, that even if these witnesses declared the truth, it could not overthrow the positive testimony which I had adduced, as they did not contradict the facts asserted; and, besides, it must he determined, which witnesses are most credible, yours or mine. Just so it is, in the case of Mr. Hume's argument. He sets up uniform experience against testimony, and gives a preponderance to the former, on the ground, that witnesses are known sometimes to lie; but all that he knows of what has happened in other ages and countries, is by testimony; and they who give this testimony are as fallible as others; therefore, there existed no ground for preferring the evidence of experience, to testimony. Besides, he is not in possession of testimony to establish a thousandth part of what has been experienced; and as far as it goes, it amounts to no more than *non-experience;* a mere negative thing, which can never have any weight to overthrow the testimony of positive witnesses. In a court of justice, such a method of rebutting testimony, would be rejected as totally inadmissible. If we had sufficient evidence of a fact of any kind, *that* testimony would not be invalid-

ated, if it could be proved, that no person in the world had ever witnessed the like before. This want of previous experience naturally creates a presumption against the fact, which requires some force of evidence to overcome: — but in all cases, a sufficient number of witnesses, of undoubted intelligence and veracity, will be able to remove the presumption and produce conviction.

7. Mr. Hume lays it down as a principle, that our belief in testimony arises from 'experience; that is, observation of the veracity of human testimony'. But this is not correct. Our belief in testimony is as natural and constitutional as our belief in our senses. Children, at first, believe implicitly all that is told them; and it is from experience that they learn to distrust testimony. If our faith in testimony arose from experience, it would be impossible to acquire any knowledge from instruction. If children were to believe nothing that was told them, until they had made observations on the veracity of human testimony, nothing would ever be believed; for they would never arrive at the maturity and judgment necessary to make observations on a subject so complicated.

But although, I perceive, Mr. Hume's object in wishing to establish this false principle, was, to exalt the evidence of what he calls *experience,* above testimony; yet I think, if we should concede it to him, it could answer him no purpose, since we have shown, that this experience itself, depends on testimony. Whatever use he can make of this principle, therefore, against testimony, can be turned against himself since his knowledge of what the experience of the world is, can only be obtained by the report of witnesses, who, in different ages have observed the course of nature.

8. Mr. Hume, on reflection, seems to have been convinced, that his argument was unsound, for in a note appended to his essay 'On Miracles', he makes a concession, which entirely overthrows the whole. But mark the disingenuity, or shall I not rather call it, the malignity of the man against religion, which is manifested in this only evidence of his candor. He concedes that there may be miracles of such a kind, as to admit of proof from human testimony, in direct contradiction to his reiterated maxims, and in complete repugnance to all his reasoning; but he makes the concession with the express reservation, that it shall not be applied to the support

of religion. He, however, not only makes this concession, but gives an example of such a miracle, and of the testimony which he admits to be sufficient to establish it. 'Suppose', says he, 'all authors in all languages agree, that from the first of January, 1600, there was a total darkness all over the earth for eight days; suppose that the tradition of this event is still strong and lively among the people; that all travelers bring us accounts of the same tradition, &c. — it is evident that our Philosophers ought to receive it for certain.' And this is a part of the same Essay, in which it is said, *'that a miracle, supported by any human testimony is more properly a subject of derision than argument'*. *'No kind of testimony for any kind of miracle can possibly amount to a probability, much less to a proof.'* It might appear, that after so complete a renunciation of the principle which at first he so strenuously asserted, we might have spared ourselves the pains of a formal refutation. But not so. The author is resolved, that his concession shall be of no service whatever to religion. Hear his own words; 'But should this miracle be ascribed to any new system of religion; men in all ages have been so imposed upon by ridiculous stories of that kind, that this very circumstance would be full proof of a cheat, and sufficient with all men of sense, not only to make them reject the fact, but even reject it, without further examination.' I have heard of a maxim, which, I believe, the Jesuits introduced, that that might be true in philosophy, which was false in theology; but I never could have expected that a philosopher, a logician, and a metaphysician too, would utter anything so unreasonable, and so marked with prejudice, as the declaration just quoted. The fact was admitted to have such evidence that even philosophers ought to receive it as certain; but not if it is ascribed to a new religion. On this subject no evidence is sufficient. It is perfectly unexceptionable in philosophy; but in religion a sensible man will reject it, whatever it may be; even without further examination. The circumstance of its being a miracle connected with religion, is sufficient, in his opinion, to prove it a cheat, however complete the testimony. The world, it seems, has been so imposed on by ridiculous stories of this kind, that we must not even listen to any testimony in favor of religious miracles. This author would indeed reduce the advocates of religion to an awkward dilemma. They are called upon to produce evidence for their religion, but if they adduce it, sensible men will not notice it; even if it is good everywhere else, it must go for nothing in religion. Upon these principles, we might indeed give up the contest; but we are not willing to admit that this is sound logic, or good sense. The reason assigned for proscribing, in this summary way, all the testimony in favor of religion, will apply to other subjects. Men have been imposed on by ridiculous stories in philosophy, as well as religion; but when evidence is proposed, shall we not even examine it, because there have been impositions? This is the very reason why we should examine with care, that we may distinguish between the true and the false.

If it were true, that miracles had often been ascribed to new religions, it would not prove that there never were any true miracles, but rather the contrary; just as the abounding of counterfeit money, is evidence that there is some genuine; for that which has no existence is not counterfeited. But the clamor, that has been raised by infidels about new religions being commonly founded on miracles, or the pretense of miracles, has very little foundation in fact. Besides the Jewish and Christian religions, (which are indeed parts of the same) it would, I believe, be difficult to point out any other, which claims such an origin.

After all that has been said of the false maxims of the Jesuits, I doubt whether any one could be selected so perfectly at war with reason, as this of the Scotch philosopher: nay, I think I may challenge all the enemies of revelation, to cull from any Christian writer, a sentence, so surcharged with prejudice.

But, to do justice to Mr. Hume; although he seems to have closed the door against all discussion, on our part; yet, in one of his general maxims, he leaves us one alternative. The maxim is this, 'that no testimony is sufficient to establish a miracle, unless it be of such a kind, that its falsehood would be more miraculous than the fact'. An ingenious writer[4] has undertaken to meet Mr. Hume on his own ground, and has endeavored to prove, that the testimony of the apostles and early Christians, if the facts reported by them were not true,

---

[4] Dr. Gleig.

is a greater miracle than any which they have recorded. But the maxim, as stated by Mr. Hume, is not correct. With the change of a single word, perhaps, it may be adopted, and will place the question on its proper ground. The change which I propose, is, to substitute the word *improbable,* for *miraculous.* And it will then read, *no testimony is sufficient to establish a miracle unless the testimony be of such a kind, that its falsehood would be more improbable, than the fact which it endeavors to establish.* The ground of objection to the word *miraculous,* is, that it involves a false principle, which is, that facts are incredible in proportion as they are miraculous; which principle, he, in several places avows, and which is, indeed, a cardinal point in his system of evidence. But it is not true. There are many cases which might be proposed, in which, of two events one of which must be true, that which is miraculous is more probable than the one which is merely natural. I will mention only one at present. Man was either immediately created by God, or he proceeded from some natural cause. Need I ask which of these is most probable? And yet the first is miraculous, the second not. The plain truth is, that in all cases, the fact which has most evidence is most probable, whether it be miraculous or natural. And when all evidence, relating to a proposition, is before the mind, that is true which is easiest to be believed; because it is easier to believe with evidence, than against it.

We are willing, therefore, that this maxim, as now stated, should be the ground of our decision, and we pledge ourselves to prove, that the falsehood of the miracles of the Gospel, would be more improbable, and consequently more incredible, than the truth of the facts recorded in them. But this discussion will be reserved for another place. To conclude this section; since then it has been shown, that there is no antecedent presumption against miracles from the nature of God, or from the laws by which he governs the universe;—since a miraculous fact is not more difficult to be accomplished by omnipotence, than any other; since miracles are no further improbable than as they are unusual;—since they are the most suitable and decisive evidences which can be given of a revelation;—since, even by the concession of Mr. Hume himself, there may be sufficient testimony fully to establish them; and since the many false pretenses to miracles, and the general disposition to credit them, are rather proofs that they have existed, than the contrary, we may safely conclude, that Mr. Hume's argument, on this subject, is sophistical and delusive; and that it is so far from being true, as he alleges, that they are incredible, whatever may be their evidence, when brought to support religion, that this is, of all others, that department, in which they are most reasonable and credible.

Seven

William Ellery Channing (1780–1842)

William Ellery Channing was born in Newport, Rhode Island in 1780 to a well-connected Federalist family. His father, William Channing, was a personal friend to both George Washington and Chief Justice John Jay. His grandfather, William Ellery, had signed the Declaration of Independence. In 1798, after graduating from Harvard University, Channing moved to Richmond, Virginia, in order to work as a tutor. Although his hometown of Newport had been an important port in the trans-Atlantic slave trade, it was in Virginia that Channing developed his lifelong anti-slavery views.

In 1803 Channing moved to Boston in order to become the minister of the Federal Street Church, where he soon became a leader in the burgeoning Unitarian movement. Three events in particular show his deep and abiding influence. First, 1816, Channing helped found Harvard Divinity School, in order to train liberal ministers. Second, in 1819, Channing provided the movement with a foundational text when he published his sermon for the ordination service of Jared Sparks, entitled 'Unitarian Christianity'. Here, Channing emphasized that Unitarianism not only entailed a rejection of Calvinist ideas of predestination and the traditional Christian doctrine of the Trinity, but also the affirmation of the essential goodness of human beings and the virtuous guidance of reason. Finally, in 1820, Channing organized the Berry

Street Conference, which led to the foundation of the American Unitarian Association in 1825.

Rejecting the Calvinism of his upbringing, Channing advocated a theology that emphasized free will and excluded both the doctrine of original sin and the special divinity of Jesus Christ. Despite these positions, however, Channing insisted that his theology was not a break from Christianity as such, and accordingly affirmed the divine inspiration of the Bible. Channing's theology also contained a political dimension. Believing strongly in the equality of all persons, Channing became a fierce advocate for the education of all children regardless of class, a friend to the feminist movement, and a well-known critic of slavery.

In 1835, Channing laid out his considered criticism of the last in his book *Slavery*, from which the following selections have been extracted. In this work, Channing argues that slavery is morally indefensible on account of the equal freedom and worth of rational beings. In its appeal to the common sentiments of humankind, and the reliability of intuitive principles, it shows the influence of the philosophy of the Scottish Enlightenment, and particularly that of Francis Hutcheson, which Channing studied while at Harvard.

Although Channing never formally joined the abolitionist movement, and at times publicly opposed its political strategies, Channing's anti-slavery views were seen by his congregation in Boston as dangerously radical, and led to his resignation from ministry in 1840. Not only known for his theological and political work, Channing was also widely influential as a proponent of enlightened humanism and liberalism. As such, he provided inspiration both to contemporaries such as the poet Henry Wadsworth Longfellow, and a new generation of New England intellectuals, including the Transcendentalist Ralph Waldo Emerson.

Biographical Information: Daniel Walker Howe, *American National Biography Online*.

READING XI

Slavery[1]

The slave-holder claims the slave as his property. The very idea of a slave is, that he belongs to another, that he is bound to live and labor for another, to be another's instrument, and to make another's will his habitual law, however adverse to his own. Another owns him, and of course has a right to his time and strength, a right to the fruits of his labor, a right to task him without his consent, and to determine the kind and duration of his toil, a right to confine him to any bounds, a right to extort the required work by stripes, a right, in a word, to use him as a tool, without contract, against his will, and in denial of his right to dispose of himself or to use his power for his own good.

'A slave', says the Louisiana Code, 'is in the power of the master to whom he belongs. The master may sell him, dispose of his person, his industry, his labor; he can do nothing, possess nothing, nor acquire anything, but which must belong to his master.' 'Slaves shall be deemed, taken, reputed, and adjudged', say the South Carolina laws, 'to be chattels personal in the hands of their masters, and possessions to all intents and purposes whatsoever.' Such is slavery, a claim to man as property.

Now this claim of property in a human being is altogether false, groundless. No such right of man in man can exist. A human being cannot be justly owned. To hold and treat him as property is to inflict a great wrong, to incur the guilt of oppression.

This position there is a difficulty in maintaining on account of its exceeding obviousness. It is too plain for proof. To defend it is like trying to confirm a self evident truth. To find arguments is not easy, because an argument is something clearer than the proposition to be sustained. The man, who, on hearing the claim to property in man, does not see and feel distinctly that it is a cruel usurpation, is hardly to be reached by reasoning, for it is hard to find any plainer principles than what he begins with denying. I will endeavor, however, to illustrate the truth which I have stated.

---

[1] [Extracted from William E. Channing (1835) 'Chapter I: Property', in *Slavery*, Boston, MA: James Munroe & Company, pp. 13–29.]

1. It is plain, that, if one man may be held as property, then every other man may be so held. If there be nothing in human nature, in our common nature, which excludes and forbids the conversion of him who possesses it into an article of property; if the right of the free to liberty is founded, not on their essential attributes as rational and moral beings, but on certain adventitious, accidental circumstances, into which they have been thrown; then every human being, by a change of circumstances, may justly be held and treated by another as property. If one man may be rightfully reduced to slavery, then there is not a human being on whom the same chain may not be imposed. Now let every reader ask himself this plain question: Could I, can I, be rightfully seized, and made an article of property; be made a passive instrument of another's will and pleasure; be subjected to another's irresponsible power; be subjected to stripes at another's will; be denied the control and use of my own limbs and faculties for my own good? Does any man, so questioned, doubt, waver, look about him for an answer? Is not the reply given immediately, intuitively, by his whole inward being? Does not an unhesitating, unerring conviction spring up in my breast, that no other man can acquire such a right in myself? Do we not repel indignantly and with horror the thought of being reduced to the condition of tools and chattels to a fellow-creature? Is there any moral truth more deeply rooted in us, than that such a degradation would be an infinite wrong? And if this impression be a delusion, on what single moral conviction can we rely? This deep assurance, that we cannot be rightfully made another's property, does not rest on the hue of our skins, or the place of our birth, or our strength, or wealth. These things do not enter our thoughts. The consciousness of indestructible rights is a part of our moral being. The consciousness of our humanity involves the persuasion, that we cannot be owned as a tree or a brute. As men we cannot justly be made slaves. Then no man can be rightfully enslaved. In casting the yoke from ourselves as an unspeakable wrong, we condemn ourselves as wrong doers and oppressors in laying it on any who share our nature. It is not necessary to inquire whether a man, by extreme guilt, may not forfeit the right of his nature, and be justly punished with slavery. On this point crude notions prevail. But the discuss-

ion would be foreign to the present subject. We are now not speaking of criminals. We speak of innocent men, who have given us no hold on them by guilt; and our own consciousness is a proof, that such cannot rightfully be seized as property by a fellow-creature.

2. A man cannot be seized and held as property, because he has rights. What these rights are, whether few or many, or whether all men have the same, are questions for future discussion. All that is assumed now is, that every human being has *some* rights. This truth cannot be denied, but by denying to a portion of the race that moral nature which is the sure and only foundation of rights. This truth has never, I believe, been disputed. It is even recognized in the very codes of slave-legislation, which, while they strip a man of liberty, affirm his right to life, and threaten his murderer with punishment. Now, I say a being having rights cannot justly be made property; for this claim over him virtually annuls all his rights. It strips him of all power to assert them. It makes it a crime to assert them. The very essence of slavery is, to put a man defenseless into the hands of another. The right claimed by the master, to task, to force, to imprison, to whip, and to punish the slave, at discretion, and especially to prevent the least resistance to his will, is a virtual denial and subversion of all the rights of the victim of his power. The two cannot stand together. Can we doubt which of them ought to fall?

3. Another argument against property is to be found in the essential equality of men. I know that this doctrine, so venerable in the eyes of our fathers, has lately been denied. Verbal logicians have told us that men are 'born equal', only in the sense of being equally born. They have asked whether all are equally tall, strong, or beautiful; or whether nature, Procrustes-like,[2] reduces all her children to one standard of intellect and virtue. By such arguments it is attempted to set aside the principle of equality, on which the soundest moralists have reared the structure of social duty; and in these ways the old foundations of despotic power, which our fathers in their simplicity thought they had subverted, are laid again by their sons.

---

[2] [In Greek mythology Procrustes was an outlaw blacksmith who made his victims fit exactly on an iron bed by either violently stretching them or shortening them by amputating their legs.]

It is freely granted, that there are innumerable diversities among men; but be it remembered, they are ordained to bind men together, and not to subdue one to the other; ordained to give means and occasions of mutual aid, and to carry forward each and all, so that the good of all is equally intended in this distribution of various gifts. Be it also remembered, that these diversities among men are as nothing in comparison with the attributes in which they agree, and it is this which constitutes their essential equality. All men have the same rational nature, and the same power of conscience, and all are equally made for indefinite improvement of these divine faculties, and for the happiness to be found in their virtuous use. Who, that comprehends these gifts, does not see that the diversities of the race vanish before them? Let it be added, that the natural advantages, which distinguish one man from another, are so bestowed as to counterbalance one another, and bestowed without regard to rank or condition in life. Whoever surpasses in one endowment is inferior in others. Even genius, the greatest gift, is found in union with strange infirmities, and often places its possessors below ordinary men in the conduct of life. Great learning is often put to shame by the mother-wit and keen good sense of uneducated men. Nature, indeed, pays no heed to birth or condition in bestowing her favors. The noblest spirits sometimes grow up in the obscurest spheres. Thus equal are men; and among these equals, who can substantiate his claim to make others his property, his tools, the mere instruments of his private interest and gratification? Let this claim begin, and where will it stop? If one may assert it, why not all? Among these partakers of the same rational and moral nature, who can make good a right over others, which others may not establish over himself? Does he insist on superior strength of body or mind? Who of us has no superior in one or the other of these endowments: Is it sure that the slave or the slave's child may not surpass his master in intellectual energy or in moral worth? Has nature conferred distinctions which tell us plainly, who shall be owners and who be owned? Who of us can unblushingly lift his head and say that God has written 'Master' there? Or who can show the word 'Slave' engraven on his brother's brow? The equality of nature makes slavery a wrong. Nature's seal is affixed to no instrument, by which property in a single human being is conveyed.

4. That a human being cannot be justly held and used as property is apparent from the very nature of property. Property is an exclusive, single right. It shuts out all claim but that of the possessor. What one man owns cannot belong to another. What, then, is the consequence of holding a human being as property? Plainly this. He can have no right to himself. His limbs are, in truth, not morally his own. He has not a right to his own strength. It belongs to another. His will, intellect, and muscles, all the powers of body and mind which are exercised in labor, he is bound to regard as another's. Now, if there be property in anything, it is that of a man in his own person, mind, and strength. All other rights are weak, unmeaning, compared with this, and in denying this all right is denied. It is true that an individual may forfeit by crime his right to the use of his limbs, perhaps to his limbs, and even to life. But the very idea of forfeiture implies that the right was originally possessed. It is true that a man may by contract give to another a limited right to his strength. But he gives only because he possesses it, and gives it for considerations which he deems beneficial to himself; and the right conferred ceases at once on violation of the conditions on which it was bestowed. To deny the right of a human being to himself, to his own limbs and faculties, to his energy of body and mind, is an absurdity too gross to be confuted by anything but a simple statement. Yet this absurdity is involved in the idea of his belonging to another.

5. We have a plain recognition of the principle now laid down, in the universal indignation excited towards a man who makes another his slave. Our laws know no higher crime than that of reducing a man to slavery. To steal or to buy an African on his own shores is piracy.[3] In this act the greatest wrong is inflicted, the most sacred right violated. But if a human being cannot without infinite injustice be seized as property, then he cannot without equal wrong be held and used as such. The wrong in the first seizure lies in

---

[3] [Participation in the international slave trade was outlawed in the United States in 1808. The buying and selling of slaves already in America was not outlawed until 1865, with the ratification of the Thirteenth Amendment.]

the destination of a human being to future bondage, to the criminal use of him as a chattel or brute. Can that very use, which makes the original seizure an enormous wrong, become gradually innocent? If the slave receive injury without measure at the first moment of the outrage, is he less injured by being held fast the second or the third? Does the duration of wrong, the increase of it by continuance, convert it into right? It is true, in many cases, that length of possession is considered as giving a right, where the goods were acquired by unlawful means. But in these cases the goods were such as might justly be appropriated to individual use. They were intended by the Creator to be owned. They fulfill their purpose by passing into the hands of an exclusive possessor. It is essential to rightful property in a thing, that the thing from its nature may be rightfully appropriated. If it cannot originally be made one's own without crime, it certainly cannot be continued as such without guilt. Now, the ground, on which the seizure of the African on his own shore is condemned, is, that he is a Man, who has by his nature a right to be free. Ought not, then, the same condemnation to light on the continuance of his yoke? Still more. Whence is it that length of possession is considered by the laws as conferring a right? I answer, from the difficulty of determining the original proprietor, and from the apprehension of unsettling all property by carrying back inquiry beyond a certain time. Suppose, however, an article of property to be of such a nature that it could bear the name of the true original owner, stamped on it in bright and indelible characters. In this case, the whole ground, on which length of possession bars other claims, would fail. The proprietor would not be concealed or rendered doubtful by the lapse of time. Would not he, who should receive such an article from a robber or a succession of robbers, be involved in their guilt? Now, the true owner of a human being is made manifest to all. It is himself. No brand on the slave was ever so conspicuous as the mark of property which God has set on him. God, in making him a rational and moral being, has put a glorious stamp on him, which all the slave-legislation and slave-markets of worlds cannot efface. Hence no right accrues to the master from the length of the wrong which has been done to the slave.

6. Another argument against the right of property in man may be drawn from a very obvious principle of moral science. It is a plain truth, universally received, that every right supposes or involves a corresponding obligation. If, then, a man has a right to another's person or powers, the latter is under obligation to give himself up as a chattel to the former. This is his duty. He is bound to be a slave; and bound not merely by the Christian law which enjoins submission to injury, not merely by prudential considerations, or by the claims of public order and peace; but bound because another has a right of ownership, has a moral claim to him, so that he would be guilty of dishonesty, of robbery, in withdrawing himself from this other's service. It is his duty to work for his master, though all compulsion were withdrawn; and in deserting him he would commit the crime of taking away another man's property, as truly as if he were to carry off his owner's purse. Now, do we not instantly feel, can we help feeling, that this is false? Is the slave thus morally bound? When the African was first brought to these shores, would he have violated a solemn obligation, by slipping his chain, and flying back to his native home? Would he not have been bound to seize the precious opportunity of escape? Is the slave under a moral obligation to confine himself, his wife, and children, to a spot where their union in a moment may be forcibly dissolved? Ought he not, if he can, to place himself and his family under the guardianship of equal laws? Should we blame him for leaving his yoke? Do we not feel, that, in the same condition, a sense of duty would quicken our flying steps? Where, then, is the obligation which would necessarily be imposed, if the right existed which the master claims? The absence of obligation proves the want of the right. The claim is groundless. It is a cruel wrong.

7. I come now to what is to my own mind the great argument against seizing and using a man as property. He cannot be property in the sight of God and justice, because he is a rational, moral, immortal being; because created in God's image, and therefore in the highest sense his child; because created to unfold Godlike faculties, and to govern himself by a divine law written on his heart, and republished in God's Word. His whole nature forbids that he should be seized as property. From his very nature it follows, that so to seize him

is to offer an insult to his Maker, and to inflict aggravated social wrong. Into every human being God has breathed an immortal spirit more precious than the whole outward creation. No earthly or celestial language can exaggerate the worth of a human being. No matter how obscure his condition. Thought, reason, conscience, the capacity of virtue, the capacity of Christian love, an immortal destiny, an intimate moral connection with God, here are attributes of our common humanity which reduce to insignificance all outward distinctions, and make every human being unspeakably dear to his Maker. No matter how ignorant he may be. The capacity of improvement allies him to the more instructed of his race, and places within his reach the knowledge and happiness of higher worlds. Every human being has in him the germ of the greatest idea in the universe, the idea of God; and to unfold this is the end of his existence. Every human being has in his breast the elements of that divine, everlasting law, which the highest orders of the creation obey. He has the idea of duty; and to unfold, revere, obey this is the very purpose for which life was given. Every human being has the idea of what is meant by that word, truth; that is, he sees, however dimly, the great object of divine and created intelligence, and is capable of ever-enlarging perceptions of truth. Every human being has affections, which may be purified and expanded into a sublime love. He has, too, the idea of happiness, and a thirst for it which cannot be appeased. Such is our nature. Wherever we see a man, we see the possessor of these great capacities. Did God make such a being to be owned as a tree or a brute? How plainly was he made to exercise, unfold, improve his highest powers, made for a moral, spiritual good! And how is he wronged, and his Creator opposed, when he is forced and broken into a tool to another's physical enjoyment!

Such a being was plainly made for an end in himself. He is a person, not a thing. He is an end, not a mere instrument or means. He was made for his own virtue and happiness. Is this end reconcilable with his being held and used as a chattel? The sacrifice of such a being to another's will, to another's present, outward, ill-comprehended good, is the greatest violence which can be offered to any creature of God. It is to degrade him from his rank in the universe, to make him a means, not an end, to cast him out from God's spiritual family into the brutal herd.

Such a being was plainly made to obey a law within Himself. This is the essence of a moral being. He possesses, as a part of his nature, and the most essential part, a sense of duty, which he is to reverence and follow, in opposition to all pleasure or pain, to all interfering human wills. The great purpose of all good education and discipline is, to make a man master of himself, to excite him to act from a principle in his own mind, to lead him to propose his own perfection as his supreme law and end. And is this highest purpose of man's nature to be reconciled with entire subjection to a foreign will, to an outward, overwhelming force, which is satisfied with nothing but complete submission?

The end of such a being as we have described is manifestly improvement. Now, it is the fundamental law of our nature, that all our powers are to improve by free exertion. Action is the indispensable condition of progress to the intellect, conscience, and heart. Is it not plain, then, that a human being cannot, without wrong, be owned by another, who claims, as proprietor, the right to repress the powers of his slaves, to withhold from them the means of development, to keep them within the limits which are necessary to contentment in chains, to shut out every ray of light and every generous sentiment, which may interfere with entire subjection to his will?

No man, who seriously considers what human nature is, and what it was made for, can think of setting up a claim to a fellow-creature. What! Own a spiritual being, a being made to know and adore God, and who is to outlive the sun and stars! What! Chain to our lowest uses a being made for truth and virtue! Convert into a brute instrument that intelligent nature on which the idea of duty has dawned, and which is a nobler type of God than all outward creation! Should we not deem it a wrong which no punishment could expiate, were one of our children seized as property, and driven by the whip to toil? And shall God's child, dearer to him than an only son to a human parent, be thus degraded? Everything else may be owned in the universe; but a moral, rational being cannot be property. Suns and stars may be owned, but not the lowest spirit. Touch anything but this. Lay not your hand on God's rational offspring. The whole spiritual world cries out, Forbear! The highest intelligences recognize their own nature, their own rights, in the humblest human being. By that priceless, immortal spirit which dwells in him, by that likeness of God which he wears, tread him not in the dust, confound him not with the brute.

We have thus seen that a human being cannot rightfully be held and used as property. No legislation, not that of all countries or worlds, could make him so. Let this be laid down, as a first, fundamental truth. Let us hold it fast, as a most sacred, precious truth. Let us hold it fast against all customs, all laws, all rank, wealth, and power. Let it be armed with the whole authority of the civilized and Christian world.

I have taken it for granted that no reader would be so wanting in moral discrimination and moral feeling, as to urge that men may rightfully be seized and held as property, because various governments have so ordained. What! Is human legislation the measure of right? Are God's laws to be repealed by man's? Can government do no wrong? What is the history of human governments but a record of wrongs? How much does the progress of civilization consist in the substitution of just and humane, for barbarous and oppressive laws? Government, indeed, has ordained slavery, and to government the individual is in no case to offer resistance. But criminal legislation ought to be freely and earnestly exposed. Injustice is never so terrible, and never so corrupting, as when armed with the sanctions of law. The authority of government, instead of being a reason for silence under wrongs, is a reason for protesting against wrong with the undivided energy of argument, entreaty, and solemn admonition.

READING XII

Conscience and Prejudice[4]

I have endeavored to show in the preceding sections that slavery is a violation of sacred rights, the infliction of a great wrong. And here a question arises. It may be asked, whether,

---

[4] [Extracted from William E. Channing (1835) 'Chapter III: Explanations', in *Slavery*, Boston, MA: James Munroe & Co., pp. 54–62.]

by this language, I intend to fasten on the slave-holder the charge of peculiar guilt. On this point great explicitness is a duty. Sympathy with the slave has often degenerated into injustice towards the master. I wish it, then, to be understood, that, in ranking slavery among the greatest wrongs, I speak of the injury endured by the slave, and not of the character of the master. These are distinct points. The former does not determine the latter. The wrong is the same to the slave, from whatever motive or spirit it may be inflicted. But this motive or spirit determines wholly the character of him who inflicts it. Because a great injury is done to another, it does not follow that he who does it is a depraved man; for he may do it unconsciously, and, still more, may do it in the belief that he confers a good. We have learned little of moral science and of human nature, if we do not know that guilt is to be measured, not by the outward act, but by unfaithfulness to conscience; and that the consciences of men are often darkened by education, and other inauspicious influences. All men have partial consciences, or want comprehension of some duties. All partake, in a measure, of the errors of the community in which they live. Some are betrayed into moral mistakes by the very force with which conscience acts in regard to some particular duty. As the intellect, in grasping one truth, often loses its hold of others, and by giving itself up to one idea, falls into exaggeration; so the moral sense, in seizing on a particular exercise of philanthropy, forgets other duties, and will even violate many important precepts in its passionate eagerness to carry one to perfection. Innumerable illustrations may be given of the liableness of men to moral error. The practice, which strikes one man with horror, may seem to another, who was born and brought up in the midst of it, not only innocent, but meritorious. We must judge others, not by our light, but by their own. We must take their place, and consider what allowance we in their position might justly expect. Our ancestors at the North were concerned in the slave-trade. Some of us can recollect individuals of the colored race, who were torn from Africa, and grew old under our parental roofs. Our ancestors committed a deed now branded as piracy. Were they, therefore, the offscouring of the earth? Were not some of them among the best of their times? The administration of religion in almost all past ages has been a violation of the sacred rights of conscience. How many sects have persecuted and shed blood! Were their members, therefore, monsters of depravity? The history of our race is made up of wrongs, many of which were committed without a suspicion of their true character, and many from an urgent sense of duty. A man born among slaves, accustomed to this relation from his birth, taught its necessity by venerated parents, associating it with all whom he reveres, and too familiar with its evils to see and feel their magnitude, can hardly be expected to look on slavery as it appears to more impartial and distant observers? Let it not be said that when new light is offered him he is criminal in rejecting it. Are we all willing to receive new light? Can we wonder that such a man should be slow to be convinced of the criminality of an abuse sanctioned by prescription, and which has so interwoven itself with all the habits, employments, and economy of life, that he can hardly conceive of the existence of society without this all-pervading element? May he not be true to his convictions of duty in other relations, though he grievously err in this? If, indeed, through cupidity and selfishness, he stifle the monitions of conscience, warp his judgment, and repel the light, he incurs great guilt. If he want virtue to resolve on doing right, though at the loss of every slave, he incurs great guilt. But who of us can look into his heart? To whom are the secret workings there revealed?

Still more. There are masters who have thrown off the natural prejudices of their position, who see slavery as it is, and who hold the slave chiefly, if not wholly, from disinterested considerations; and these deserve great praise. They deplore and abhor the institution; but believing that partial emancipation, in the present condition of society, would bring unmixed evil on bond and free, they think themselves bound to continue the relation, until it shall be dissolved by comprehensive and systematic measures of the state. There are many of them who would shudder as much as we at reducing a freeman to bondage, but who are appalled by what seem to them the perils and difficulties of liberating multitudes, born and brought up to that condition. There are many, who, nominally holding the slave as property, still hold him for his own good and for the public order, and would blush to retain him on other grounds. Are such men to be set down among the unprincipled? Am I told that by these remarks I extenuate slavery? I reply, slavery is still a heavy yoke, and strips man of his dearest rights, be the master's character what it may. Slavery is not less a curse, because long use may have blinded most, who support it, to its evils. Its influence is still blighting, though conscientiously upheld. Absolute monarchy is still a scourge, though among despots there have been good men. It is possible to abhor and oppose bad institutions, and yet to abstain from indiscriminate condemnation of those who cling to them, and even to see in their ranks greater virtue than in ourselves. It is true, and ought to be cheerfully acknowledged, that in the slave-holding States may be found some of the greatest names of our history, and, what is still more important, bright examples of private virtue and Christian love.

There is, however, there must be, in slave-holding communities a large class which cannot be too severely condemned. There are many, we fear, very many, who hold their fellow-creatures in bondage, from selfish, base motives. They hold the slave for gain, whether justly or unjustly they neither ask nor care. They cling to him as property, and have no faith in the principles which will diminish a man's wealth. They hold him, not for his own good or the safety of the state, but with precisely the same views with which they hold a laboring horse, that is, for the profit which they can wring from him. They will not hear a word of his wrongs; for, wronged or not, they will not let him go. He is their property, and they mean not to be poor for righteousness sake. Such a class there undoubtedly is among slave holders; how large their own consciences must determine. We are sure of it; for under such circumstances human nature will and must come to this mournful result. Now, to men of this spirit, the explanations we have made do in no degree apply. Such men ought to tremble before the rebukes of outraged humanity and indignant virtue. Slavery, upheld for gain, is a great crime. He, who has nothing to urge against emancipation, but that it will make him poorer, is bound to immediate emancipation. He has no excuse for wresting from his brethren their rights. The plea of benefit to the slave and the state avails him nothing. He extorts, by the lash, that labor to which he has no claim, through a base selfishness. Every morsel of food, thus forced from the injured, ought to be bitterer than gall. His gold is cankered. The sweat of the slave taints the luxuries for which it streams. Better were it for the selfish wrongdoer of whom I speak, to live as the slave, to clothe himself in the slave's raiment, to eat the slave's coarse food, to till his fields with his own hands, than to pamper himself by day, and pillow his head on down at night, at the cost of a wantonly injured fellow-creature. No fellow-creature can be so injured without taking terrible vengeance. He is terribly avenged even now. The blight which falls on the soul of the wrongdoer, the desolation of his moral nature, is a more terrible calamity than he inflicts. In deadening his moral feelings, he dies to the proper happiness of a man. In hardening his heart against his fellow-creatures, he sears it to all true joy. In shutting his ear against the voice of justice, he shuts out all the harmonies of the universe, and turns the voice of God within him into rebuke. He may prosper, indeed, and hold faster the slave by whom he prospers; but he rivets heavier and more ignominious chains on his own soul than he lays on others. No punishment is so terrible as prosperous guilt. No fiend, exhausting on us all his power of torture, is so terrible as an oppressed fellow-creature. The cry of the oppressed, unheard on earth, is heard in heaven. God is just, and if justice reign, then the unjust must terribly suffer. Then no being can profit by evildoing. Then all the laws of the universe are ordinances against guilt. Then every enjoyment, gained by wrongdoing, will be turned into a curse. No laws of nature are so irrepealable as that law which binds guilt and misery. God is just. Then all the defenses, which the oppressor rears against the consequences of wrongdoing, are vain, as vain as would be his strivings to arrest by his single arm the ocean or whirlwind. He may disarm the slave. Can he disarm that slave's Creator? He can crush the spirit of insurrection in a fellow-being. Can he crush the awful spirit of justice and retribution in the Almighty? He can still the murmur of discontent in his victim. Can he silence that voice which speaks in thunder, and is to break the sleep of the grave? Can he always still the reproving, avenging voice in his own breast?

I know it will be said, 'You would make us poor'. Be poor, then, and thank God for your honest poverty. Better be poor than unjust. Better beg than steal. Better live in an almshouse, better die, than trample on a fellow-creature and reduce him to a brute, for selfish gratification. What! Have we yet to learn that 'it profits us nothing to gain the whole world, and lose our souls'?[5]

Let it not be replied, in scorn, that we of the North, notorious for love of money, and given to selfish calculations, are not the people to call others to resign their wealth. I have no desire to shield the North. We have, without doubt, a great multitude, who, were they slave-holders, would sooner die than relax their iron grasp, than yield their property in men to justice and the commands of God. We have those who would fight against abolition, if by this measure the profit of their intercourse with the South should be materially impaired. The present excitement among us is, in part, the working of mercenary principles. But because the North joins hands with the South, shall iniquity go unpunished or unrebuked? Can the league of the wicked, the revolt of worlds, repeal the everlasting law of heaven and earth? Has God's throne fallen before Mammon's? Must duty find no voice, no organ, because corruption is universally diffused? Is not this a fresh motive to solemn warning, that, everywhere, Northward and Southward, the rights of human beings are held so cheap, in comparison with worldly gain?

---

[5] [See Matthew 16:26, Mark 8:36, and Luke 9:25.]

Eight

Alexander Campbell (1788–1866)

Alexander Campbell was born in County Antrim, Ireland, in 1788. The son of a Presbyterian minister, Campbell was educated in literature, classics, and philosophy at his father Thomas Campbell's preparatory school. During these years, Campbell was also formed by the turbulent political struggles between Irish Protestants and Roman Catholics, including the violent suppression of the 1798 Irish Rebellion. In 1807, Campbell's father immigrated to the United States with the intention of moving his family over the next year. When the rest of the Campbell family attempted to cross the Atlantic in 1808, however, their ship wrecked off the Isle of Islay, and they were forced to wait out the winter in Glasgow. While there, Campbell attended classes at Glasgow University, where he was exposed to the philosophy of the Scottish Enlightenment.

Upon reaching the United States, Campbell joined his father in the newly formed Christian Association of Washington, Pennsylvania. Among the central tenets of this association, as expounded by Thomas Campbell, were the preaching of the gospel, Christian unity, and a return to the practices of the church described in the New Testament book of Acts. All of these views were motivated by the belief that the progress of technology, science, and political freedom were evidences of Christ's imminent return.

In 1811, the Christian Association church was reorganized, and became the founding congregation of the Disciples of Christ. Three years later, Campbell succeeded his father as the leader of the church. After a series of failed attempts at unification with the Baptists throughout the 1820s Campbell united his Disciples movement with the Christian movement of Barton W. Stone. Although the resulting association—today called alternately the Stone-Campbell or Restoration Movement—created only a loosely connected church polity with no central church government, this unification is recognized today as the origin of three modern denominations: the Disciples of Christ, the Christian Church and the Church of Christ, and the Churches of Christ.

Wholeheartedly embracing an optimistic millennialism, Campbell worked tirelessly as a speaker and writer to spread the message of the Disciples. Starting in 1810, and following his ordination as a minister, Campbell began making extensive yearly lecture tours: a practice he continued until 1847. By 1820, he began participating in debates with other well-known Christian thinkers and leaders. Ever savvy, and a formidable debater, Campbell made his sole requirement for participation the publication of each debate's transcript. Furthermore, hoping to make the Bible more accessible, Campbell completed a new English vernacular translation of the New Testament. Through the circulation of his debate transcripts and voluminous publications, Campbell gained widespread acclaim as a fierce proponent of both Bible-centred theology and political liberty, including the abolition of slavery.

As part of his democratic principles, Campbell also believed that every citizen of a democratic society had the right to an education. In order to further the educational prospects of the citizens of his home state Virginia, Campbell helped to found two schools, Buffalo Seminary in 1818 and Bethany College in 1840. The following selections are extracted from Campbell's opening address at the first meeting of the college.

Biographical Information: Hiram J. Lester, *American National Biography Online.*

READING XIII

On the Limits of Philosophy[1]

Preamble

Besides a general superintendency of the education and morals of the youth of this institution in the various departments of it, the philosophy of man in its higher and more sublime branches has been made the special duty of the Chair assigned to me. In the discharge of these high and weighty responsibilities, I promise myself, not only much assistance, but much pleasure in the able and faithful co-operation of my fellow-laborers in this great and arduous undertaking. All, I think, who have attentively heard the learned and eloquent addresses of the professors that have preceded me, will doubtless conclude, that I do not promise myself, nor the community, too much from the ability and zeal with which they are entering upon the discharge of their official duties. I have only to regret, on the present occasion, that the protracted indisposition of one Professor present, and the unavoidable absence of another,[2] have deprived us of the pleasure of hearing them also on the subjects of their respective professions.

Anticipated, as I have been, in much that has been submitted to you, gentlemen, in the previous lectures, I do not now arise to address you in a formal introductory lecture on any one branch of science either within or without that extensive range of subjects that come within the proper precincts of my special charge. With some reference, however, to my own department, I will immediately invite your attention to a few fragments of the history of philosophy, and to some fundamental facts and truths in mental and moral science as

---

[1] [Extracted from Alexander Campbell (1841) 'Introductory Lecture', in *Introductory Addresses delivered at the Organization of Bethany College*, Bethany, VA: Alexander Campbell, Electronic Edition (2000), edited with footnotes by Ernie Stefanik, http://www.mun.ca/rels/restmov/texts/acampbell/iabc/IABC04.HTM, accessed October 20, 2011.]

[2] <These are, respectively, Charles Stuart, Professor of Algebra and General Mathematics, and W.W. Eaton, Professor of English Literature. See *Millennial Harbinger* (1841): pp. 377-378, and (1842): pp. 34-36.>

introductory to some notices of that system of education about to be prosecuted in this College.

The philosophy of man, I have said, in its higher and more sublime branches has been made the peculiar subject of my cultivation and didactic labors. The branches of this philosophy are indeed almost as numerous as all the other departments of human science. The reason is that man himself is the philosophy of the planet on which he resides, and perhaps of that solar system of which it is a part. This terraqueous globe with all the appurtenances thereunto belonging, was as evidently created and furnished for man as was the palace of the Thuilleries, for the monarch of France. It is all rational and intelligible to him that contemplates it in this point of view, but to no one else.

Viewed as the predestined nursery, school, and residence of man, as an animal, intellectual and religious being; as prearranged for the development of his person, for the formation and perfection of a character worthy of himself and of his position in the universe, there is the wisdom and the benevolence of an infinite intelligence manifesting themselves in all its parts, in all its modifications and adaptations. Hence all the sciences directly or indirectly terminate on man. Many of them indeed are exclusively devoted to him, and all of them touch some point in his constitution or circumstances that give them all their interest and importance. There is not a single science, taught or studied, but because of its bearings upon man, upon the conditions or contingencies of his present or future existence. The first philosophers were indeed, to a single man, mental and moral philosophers. They speculated upon the mental and moral constitution of man, upon the Divinity that gave him birth and upon his present and future relations to the intellectual and moral universe. And never did they stray away into the other fields of creation but with a reference to some accident or attribute of man.

Mental Philosophy

Few terms have experienced a greater variety of fortunes than the term *philosophy*. Its inventor, the celebrated Pythagoras, some five centuries before the Christian era, while establishing his College at the Italian Crotona, boldly denied to mortals the possession of wisdom, and claimed for the wisest of mankind no higher honor than the mere *desire of it.* This desire of wisdom he called *philosophy,* and modestly enough assumed to himself the title of Philosopher. He was not only the first born of philosophers, but also the founder of the name.

No sooner, however, had Pythagoras discovered the transmigration of souls, and established this new and strange doctrine, than, in the judgment of many, he became a *demon* —a *knowing one,* as some of his successors chose to be designnated. Thus, before the author of the Metempsychosis[3] had himself transmigrated, the *profession* of wisdom, rather than the *desire* of it, began to be regarded as the true definition of the term *philosophy.*

But wisdom itself among the Greeks early began to be distributed into various departments of learning and science, and these were again classified under distinct heads of wisdom and knowledge; and thus in a few years the term *philosophy* was constrained to represent them all.

The versatility of the ancients, as well as their powers of invention, have been fully equalled by the moderns. Hence our acceptance of the term *philosophy* is as equivocal and latitudinarian as theirs. We have not only natural, mental, and moral philosophy; but we have the philosophy of language, as well as the language of philosophy; the philosophy of history, as well as the history of philosophy. We have, indeed, the philosophy of grammar, logic, rhetoric, eloquence, and of theology itself. We have the philosophy of everything, and the philosophy of philosophy into the bargain.

Philosophy, we have said, in the days of her youth was modest and unpretending; but no sooner had she advanced in years and in public admiration, than she assumed a loftier tone and enjoined a more profound homage on the part of her worshippers. Now she speculates with equal confidence on the finite and the infinite—on things celestial and terrestrial. She delights to handle the themes of infinite space and an endless duration. She sports with physics and metaphysics—with abstract natures and the quintessences of all manner of entities—and develops the nature of gods and

---

[3] [The transmigration of the soul, especially after death.]

men. Placing her foot on the summit of all human experience, she rears her aspiring head far beyond the centre of the heavens, and discusses the theogony of its inhabitants, the cosmogony of the universe, and the arcana of eternity. At this giddy height she dares to trace the infinite lines of liberty and necessity, and constructs new measures for ascertaining the root and ramifications of all manner of designs and motives, good and bad, that spread themselves over the illimitable regions of universal being.

But she assumed too much—she soared too high, and could not long retain her hold on human admiration. Finding her impotency by the aid of all manner of hypothesis to unfold the phenomena of nature, she sought to conceal her weakness under the mask of oriental science and scholastic learning. Now she delights in mysteries and mysticism. If she had not the power of bringing light out of darkness, she now displays the no less admirable quality of bringing darkness out of light. She prides herself in cabalistic terms and Eleusinian mysteries. She tells of the *Chronoi* and the *Eons*, of the Demiurgic and Pleromatic beings who partition Divinity and Creation among themselves, and inspire the universe with all the jarring and antagonistic principles with which it abounds.

In one word, the Pythagoreans and Aristotelians, the Platonists and the Gnostics, the Epicureans and the Stoics, the Materialists and the Spiritualists, the Idealists and the Nominalists, filled the human mind with darkness and confusion, and the world with mythology, skepticism, and libertinism; till the very name of philosophy, like that of Gnostic, disgusted every lover of true wisdom and morality. Never were the words *'empty* and *deceitful'* better applied than by Paul to the self-confident and haughty philosophy of his day.[4]

The philosophy, since his day, usually called 'scholastic', was no better than the oriental science of the Gnostics. By its speculations on essences, hypotheses, and predicaments, it sought to explain the whole system of nature, and reveal all its phenomena. During her reign, night, dark night, from her

---

[4] <Colossians 2:8.>

'ebon throne',[5] spread a deep and melancholy gloom over the face of heaven and earth — of things temporal, spiritual, and eternal. Scarce a single discovery aided the progress of civilization during the long and inglorious career of the Aristotelian and Scholastic philosophy. If some advances in true science were made by a few such men as Roger Bacon, Flavio Gioia, Copernicus, Galileo, Kepler, Tycho Brahe, &c. &c., they were all errorists from the false philosophy of the age, and had strayed away into the paths of true science.

But, as Goethe said, it was reserved to Sir Francis Bacon to draw a sponge over the table of human knowledge, and to strike out a new path to science. Bacon substituted facts for hypotheses, observation and comparison for conjecture; induction for imagination, and attributes and properties for the abstract essences of things: and though not the first who reasoned inductively, became the founder of the Inductive Philosophy. Since the publication of his *Novum Organum*, in 1620, within two centuries many more new discoveries, and some of them of the greatest importance, have been vouchsafed to the world, than during the despotic and universal sway of Aristotelianism for almost two thousand years.

No true philosopher — no wise man in the mysteries of nature, providence, or redemption, ever now thinks of discovering the philosopher's stone, the perpetual motion, or the abstract essence of anything; or of looking into the penetralia of nature's sanctuary, or of scanning the hidden ways of God to man. We seek out the laws of nature by her operations, as we seek for the principles of human character in the works of man.

True philosophy blushes not to avow before all the pretended sages and wise men of the world, her ignorance of three chapters in the universe, fraught though they be with sciences of the greatest curiosity and interest to man. These three chapters treat of the *origin* of things, the *nature* of things, and the *end* of things. When interrogated concerning the original commencement of anything, of its abstract nature or essence, or of the final destiny of a single atom of the

---

[5]   [Night, sable goddess! from her ebon throne,
       In rayless majesty, now stretches forth
       Her leaden sceptre o'er a slumb'ring world.
       — Edward Young (1742) 'Night Thoughts'.]

universe, she modestly and candidly lays her hand upon her mouth, and in profound silence intimates her total inability to answer any such questions. Hence the three questions, What am I? Whence came I? Whither do I go? lie wholly beyond all the pretensions of sane philosophy.

After a long and violent controversy between philosophy and Common Sense, they have at length amicably adjusted their differences, and entered into a solemn league and covenant never to be dissolved, of which the following seven items are of superlative importance: —

1. They have mutually pledged themselves always to reason from what they do already know, to what they do not know.

2. That they will always, and only, employ the five senses in ascertaining *sensible* facts; and receive the testimony of any two or more of them as infallible, when it can be shown that they are in good health and in favorable circumstances to ascertain the facts in question.

3. That the internal sense of consciousness will always be regarded as a faithful and competent witness of the mental and moral facts of the inner man, as the five external senses are of the material and external facts and events of the outward man.

4. That they will never form a science or build a system either on hypothesis or *a priori* reasoning.

5. That they will never affirm anything to be a law of nature which has not been ascertained by the observation and classification of facts, and of such a number and character as to leave no doubt of the universality of the facts and of the principles developed in them.

6. That they will always receive the testimony of other persons who simply declare what they have seen, heard, or learned from their own experience, when that testimony is free from suspicion of fraud or fiction.

7. That the assent to every proposition shall always be proportioned to the evidence in favor of its truth and certainty.

Since the ascendancy of the Inductive Philosophy, all men of true sense and true education have acknowledged the several articles of this contract to be just and reasonable; have consequently acquiesced in them, and in every discussion of any question properly scientific, they have pledged themselves to be governed accordingly.

It is nevertheless to be regretted that the inductive mode of reasoning is greatly in advance of the practice, and that it has not found the same popularity in the study of the intellectual as in the analysis of the material system. Hence the sciences usually called Physical, have, within two centuries, progressed in a tenfold ratio, compared with the march of the Mental, the Moral, and the Religious. Whether this fact be owing to the greater interest we take in matter than in mind —in earth than in heaven—in time than in eternity—or to the greater difficulties in the way of psychological and anthropological science, we have not leisure, nor is it important to our present object at this time, to discuss. The fact is public and acknowledged, and we have only to endeavor to correct public sentiment on this most vital department of human education, and to persuade mankind to give that preeminence to mental and moral science which their superior importance demands.

'The proper study of mankind is man';[6] but man is related to everything in the universe, and it is impossible to become profound in the science of man without a general acquaintance with that universe of which he forms so prominent a part. Atoms and elements, principles and laws, scattered over the face of universal nature, or incorporate[d] with any of its organizations, enter into the constitution of man, either as a physical or moral being, and form a component part of his peculiar personality. In sketching out the proper landmarks of human knowledge and the proper subjects of human study, a due regard must then be had to this important fact. Every science in the world affects man in some one point of his nature, because his nature in some one point touches every separate and distinct system in nature. True, indeed, the whole universe comprehends but two grand systems; but these are systems whose component parts are subordinate systems. Our bodies belong to the one, and our spirits to the other. The outward man, all material, directly or indirectly sympathizes with, and is affected by, external and

---

[6] <Know then thyself, presume not God to scan;
The proper study of mankind is man.
—Alexander Pope (1733-4) *Essay on Man*, Epistle II, 1, 2.>

material nature, not only as developed and distributed in the three kingdoms — animal, vegetable, and mineral — but as existing in all the great laws, elements, and cosmical arrangements of the solar system: consequently, high attainments in all these departments of science greatly advance man in the knowledge of his nature.

While we distribute nature into mind and matter, and arrange our sciences accordingly, it must not be presumed that we can either clearly apprehend or define the one or the other. It is, however, I believe, generally conceded amongst the learned that we know about as much of mind as we do of matter. Though ignorant of the essence of either, we know some of the properties and attributes of both. That they are distinct and essentially different, is, however, most evident to those of an unbiassed judgment, and of a sound discriminating intelligence. There are, indeed, some great points of difference between these two creations which are very perceptible, and which ought to be clearly and forcibly propounded to those who are studious to comprehend them. Of these, however, we shall select but one at present; and even this much we should not now attempt, were it not that it comes directly in our path. If fully developed in all its bearings, it is, in our judgment, all-sufficient to establish the essential difference between these two systems. It is this: —

Mind is active — Matter is passive. Philosophers have written so much of the *vis inertiæ*[7] of matter, that some of them have inferred that matter has a *vis* as well us an *inertia*. The *vis*, however, belongs to mind, and the *inertia* to matter. Every atom of matter in the universe is naturally and necessarily passive and quiescent. Motion is no attribute of any material thing. Matter can exist without it. Motion is, therefore, a mere accident of matter.

When, then, we set about proving two systems in one universe, we commence our philosophic proof just at this point. Matter in motion is a sensible demonstration that there is a God — a clear invincible demonstration that there is a Great Spirit and a spiritual system independent of everything we denominate matter; animating, governing, and controlling it in all its movements and changes. This view of the

---

7 ['force of inertia']

universe enables man not merely to perceive, but, to *feel* by his outward senses, and by his internal sense of consciousness, that there is a Spirit in the universe, and a spirit in himself of an unearthly and immaterial mold and temper. Thus, as Paul said to the Athenian, 'We *feel* after God'[8] and find him; for we move and are moved by him, as well as live in him. We also feel a spirit in ourselves. When, then, we attempt to reason on this subject, we commence with something at rest and inquire into the cause of its motion. To exemplify in our persons the fact that the impelling power is not material, we observe that our bones are quiescent till moved by the muscles. These muscles are themselves moved by the nerves; these nerves are moved by the brain, and that brain is moved by a volition from a spirit which is itself both passive and active—passive in sensation, but active in volition. I will to move my hand, and it moves. But the motion of the hand is effected by the intervention of animal machinery, by muscles, by nerves, by brain, by mind. Now whether this volition move ten pounds or ten thousand, depends entirely upon the animal machinery with which the mind is furnished. The volition is the same in the giant and in the dwarf: the machinery is different. The moving power, the force, is exclusively in the will. Hence I affirm the conviction that all power is in the will, and that every motion in the universe, however extended the series of agencies, is to be traced to an intelligent First Cause.

Yonder falls a mountain into the sea. The immediate cause was a torrent; but how came the torrent? In the earth there are certain elements of power, all in a state of perfect quiescence. There lie stores of nitre, sulphur, electricity, hydrogen, water, &c. &c. In the heavens, too, there is a sun, a radiating centre, from which emanate certain undulations or rays, the principles of light and heat. These act upon the atmosphere, and the atmosphere acts upon the earth, pregnant with fire and flood, and tempest. Exhalations rise, imbued with all these hitherto dormant and quiescent principles. They are put in motion. The sulphur, nitre, electricity, water, &c., &c. are on the wing. They meet in the upper regions. A war ensues. The lightnings flash—the thunders roll—the

---

[8] [Acts 17:27.]

clouds assemble—the tempest rises—the torrent breaks upon the mountain's top, at whose base an angry sea has raged for ages. Surge upon surge undermines its broken pillars. It is shaken—it totters—it falls, and is engulfed in the dark deep caverns of the fathomless abyss beneath.

Now when this desolation is surveyed by the enlightened philosopher, and traced through a long series of causes operating as distinct agents; yet, conjointly, he ascertains that the power of every agent was the effect of a cause extrinsic of itself, and that cause was the effect of another, and another, and another, until he reaches the last agent within his vision, and that is resolved into the sovereign will or mandate of the Great Spirit. So that all the laws, impulses, and powers of nature are resolvable only and always into the simple fiat and volition of its Creator.

Man has in himself a consciousness and an evidence of this system of spiritual agency. His body, though composed of organs voluntary, and involuntary as respects the direct and positive influence of his will, is nevertheless subjected to his will: for by means of the voluntary organs he exercises power and dominion over the involuntary. His whole frame is thus subjected to the supremacy of intellect and volition. Thus in tracing the operations of his being, he discovers that in him there is something called spirit that thinks and feels and wills and acts by means of the animal machinery of his system. But this spirit, though *in* this body, is no part of it, but above it, distinct from it, and acting out its volitions through its instrumentality. Thus every man who can look into himself, may feel as well as perceive the supremacy of mind over matter, of spirit over body, and that every action and movement of the whole body is an effect of a simple volition of the mind.

Now it is the same law of motion that pervades the spheres as well as the atoms of creation. The movements of worlds, and the smallest particles of which they are composed are alike the effects of intellect and volition. He that can doubt whether chance or intellect marked out the orbits of all the planets primary and secondary, with all the comets, of seventy-five millions of suns, is not to be reasoned with on any subject whatever. The motion of worlds as well as the actions of men are demonstrably the result of enlightened volition—of volition, guided by wisdom and knowledge.

But we shall no further at present argue the certainty of a spiritual system, but proceed forthwith to that department of philosophy which treats of mind and its peculiar phenomena.

Sciences are sometimes improperly classified into natural, mental, and moral. There is no such contrast in fact. All true sciences are natural. They are all founded in nature and discuss the various phenomena of nature, whether it be material, mental, or moral nature: for nature is just as moral and spiritual as she is material. Now as nature, so far as known, has but two systems, the spiritual and the material, all sciences respect these two. Sciences then are, not properly called natural and mental, inasmuch as mind is just as natural as body, but they are all material or mental. They all respect matter or mind.

Mental philosophy is our special province at present. It is indeed an extensive field, and hitherto very imperfectly cultivated. It comprehends the physiology of the human mind, the phenomena of its moral powers, its social powers and its religious powers. It contemplates all the human faculties, and discusses the duties devolving on man as an individual, domestic, social, and religious being. It, therefore, includes ethics, politics, and theology, according to the dicta of our most distinguished masters, and regards man in all his intellectual, moral, and religious powers, relations, obligations, and susceptibilities.

If indeed such be the immense area of mental science, we need not wonder that it is so far in the background. Besides there are peculiar difficulties at the very threshold of every attempt to form a complete outline of the science of mind. The subject is not only the most recondite and abstract in its nature, but that very subject is the instrument by which we investigate it. Mind is both the agent, the instrument, and the subject of the science. The mind works, and it works by itself, and it works upon itself. If it be difficult for the eye to see itself, for the ear to hear itself, more difficult it is for the mind to see itself, analyze itself, comprehend itself. Yet this is indispensable to a complete and perfect system of mental and moral science. And being so it is not to be regarded as superlatively marvelous that some philosophers have considered the difficulties as insurmountable, and have given up the attempt in despair.

Others, however, of a more sanguine temperament, and of more inductive and speculative habits, have alleged that by observation and reflection properly combined a system of mental science, if not absolutely perfect, yet nearly approximating to it, may be ascertained and established. They allege that as by looking at our own eye in a mirror, by analyzing the living eyes of our neighbors, and by sometimes dissecting the eye of the dead, we can arrive at a correct theory of that admirable and wonderful organ; so may we by taking notice to what passes in ourselves as well as by a minute attention to the developments of mind in others, obtain a very correct view of the mysterious operations and capacities of that most sublime of all earthly creations.

While we should not with the first class fold our hands in despair, and abandon the pursuit of a perfect system as an utopian project; and while we cannot entirely acquiesce with the second class, inasmuch as we cannot apply the dissecting knife to the human mind, dead or alive; we nevertheless must think that a system sufficiently approaching perfection for all useful and practical purposes, may be ascertained, provided only that we are willing to receive a little supernatural assistance, especially in those parts of the system in which human reason feels her own peculiar impotency in the undertaking.

Aristotle, Socrates, Plato, Zeno, Epicurus, Seneca, Cicero, and indeed all the Grecian and Roman schools pre-eminently failed in every attempt at forming a system of mental philosophy and moral science. And when we consider the absolute sway under which the first of these renowned names held the world for 2000 years, we will learn without much surprise that even in Christian nations little or no advance was made in these departments of philosophy till since the revival of literature and the publication of the *Novum Organum*.

The labors of Descartes, Locke, Hutcheson, Adam Smith, Reid, Stewart, Thomas Brown, and many others of these schools contributed much to the advancement of mental philosophy during the last century, not by furnishing a complete or perfect system, but by their analysis of former systems, their expositions of the defects of the ancients, and by their own new theories, collisions and debates. Still, however, as a whole, not one of these systems, can in our opinion, be adopted as a complete and perfect text book in any department of mental science.

As to that branch of mental science usually called 'Moral Philosophy', whose object it is, says Dugald Stewart, to 'ascertain the general rules of a wise and virtuous conduct in life, in so far as these rules may be discovered by the unassisted light of nature, that is by an examination of the principles of the human constitution, and of the circumstances in which man is placed',[9] I have on another occasion, attempted to demonstrate to be a baseless speculation, unworthy of the name of an inductive science.

The late work of George Combe on 'Moral Science'; just now issued from the New York press, based on phrenology, has most signally failed in an attempt to base a perfect system of morals on those views of the human constitution propounded in this new philosophy. That shrewd, profound and distinguished phrenological philosopher, who has so greatly elevated and improved the speculations of Gall and Spurzheim, and given them a more scientific and Baconian form, than any of his predecessors or contemporaries, has nevertheless fully demonstrated that however much the nomenclature of mental science has been improved by himself and his predecessors in their phrenological speculations, the science of morals is as baseless on his hypothesis, as in that of any of the defenders of the old philosophy.

Without discussing either the abstract or comparative merits of phrenology as an inductive science, or as a system of mental philosophy, we may in all truth and candor concede its superior pretensions to an improved nomenclature, and to a more simple, rational and scientific classification of the human faculties, above all its competitors for public favor. That its definitions of the animal instincts, of the perceptive and reflective powers and of the moral sentiment, apart from its theory of cerebral developments, are the best that have yet appeared in any system of mental or moral science, and such as to give it a very strong claim on the att-

---

[9] [Dugald Stewart (1793) *Outlines of Moral Philosophy*, I.1.]

ention of all lovers of true science, will moreover be generally conceded. When, too, we think of the vague generalities and indistinct definitions of sensation, perception, memory, judgment, reason, imagination, and the moral sense, &c., &c., with which our best and most popular systems abound, we cannot but think that the study of mental and moral science, if it have not already been, must eventually be greatly advanced by the learned labors, researches and discoveries of Gall, Spurzheim, and Combe. And although, from the recency of the doctrine of cerebral congeries and developments, some errors and mistakes of its masters and disciples may have subjected the new science to the indignant scoffs of the votaries of more ancient and popular theorists; still there are so many redeeming facts and demonstrations in its history as may well propitiate from all lovers of true science, a more candid, and protracted examination of its various pretensions than some of our more pretending and plausible contemporaries seem disposed to award it.

A degree of obscurity and incertitude in the minds of its most sanguine and able advocates does yet remain on some of its alleged developments and manifestations. Even this, on the admission of its claims to an inductive science, may long, nay, always, continue. Perfection of knowledge in any one science has never yet been the attainment of mortal man. Still less, may it be expected in one of the most mysterious of all the subjects of human consideration.

Alike indifferent to approbation or disapprobation from either school on account of an avowal which a conscientious regard to truth constrains me to make, I must acknowledge the conviction that the old and the new science of mental and moral philosophy are equally at fault in their attempts to deduce from their own premises a system of natural religion and moral philosophy either worthy of God or of man. Paley and Spurzheim, Butler and Combe, Reid, Stewart, and Brown with all the phrenologists are demonstrably equidistant from the equator of truth, when they attempt to make man either religious or moral from any lights contained in, or deducible from, their respective theories, developments and demonstrations. They may expose each other's errors, laugh at each other's follies and wanderings from the path of sober induction and logical conclusion; they may accuse each other of a too refined spiritualism, or of a too gross materialism; but when it comes to the Herculean task of demonstrating from their respective theories, what man ought to be, and what he ought to do, as a rational, voluntary, and responsible agent in the pursuit of the high ends of his destiny, they are equally constrained to exclaim *hic labor hoc opus est*,[10] a labor and a toil to which their powers are wholly inadequate.

I am no special advocate of the old philosophy or of the new. I choose rather, so far as their congruity will admit, to be an eclectic. Still one cannot but smile at the various ingenious missiles by which the rival leaders of the respective systems assail each other. The old school denounces the new as *materialists,* and the new returns the compliment, by denominating them *idealists.* The old say that the new school necessarily tends to infidelity and the subversion of the Bible; the new school reprehends the old as seeking to transmute the laws of nature and to annihilate the essential characteristics of the human constitution through a blind devotion to long consecrated traditions. For my own part, having on a former occasion attempted to shew that moral philosophy on the principles of Paley, Stewart, and Brown is not an inductive science, when called upon, I feel myself under equal obligation on some proper occasion to shew that Mr. Combe's new moral science is as much an assumption, a flight of imagination, as the schemes of those whom he so ably repudiates. This, however, is a task, which I am not now called upon to impose either upon you or myself: Still I ought perhaps to offer a single specification in illustration of my meaning.

---

[10] <*Facilis descensus Averni;*
Noctes atque dies patet atri janua Ditis;
Sed revocare gradum,
superasque evadere ad auras,
Hoc opus, hic labor est.
—*Publius Vergilius Maro*

The descent to Avernus is easy;
Night and day Pluto's gates are open;
But to recall your steps,
and climb to the upper air,
That is the toil, that is the work.
—Virgil, The Aneid, VI, 126–129.>

If prudence be the queen of all the virtues, justice is certainly the basis of them all. The justice of God is indeed the only guarantee of the universe. Now a clear indication of the justice of God is essential to a proper view of justice among men and equally essential to the moral government of ourselves and of the world. Any system, therefore, that either makes no account of the Divine Justice, or propounds an inadequate conception of it as the basis of the social system and the social duties, is not only manifestly inadequate to direct, but wholly impotent to govern the actions of men. This is my first and leading objection to Mr. Combe's system of moral science, as it is to that of Paley, Bishop Butler, and many others of that school.

Butler and Combe are authors of no ordinary stature. Such men are not to be met with in every city or in every state. Their phrenological developments, though I have not seen either of them or their image, give them large causality, but still larger comparison. They are men of gigantic strength of reason, but admirably great in reasoning analogically and by comparison. This needs no other proof than Butler's *Analogy* and Combe's *Constitution of Man*—works indeed of great and lasting merit.

But it must be observed that arguing from analogy, and not only illustrating but sometimes reasoning by comparison, while it is generally more clear, and always more fascinating, than any other style, is nevertheless liable to great abuse, and in the hands of persons constitutionally sophistical, (of which there are never wanting numerous instances) often fatally erroneous and seductive. In this style, indeed, Butler and Combe are generally as fortunate as they are eminent. In reference, however, to the point under consideration, they equally fail in suporting their peculiar systems of moral science.

Butler, indeed, at one time admits the defects of his argument from analogy while writing of this very point before us—the justice of God. He admits that the justice of God is not fully displayed, nor perfectly executed in this world. This admission is fatal to moral philosophy founded on analogical reasonings. Mr. Combe saw this, and made it the occasion of stating his new system. If indeed vice often triumphs here, and virtue goes unrewarded; if the good man is frequently poor, oppressed, and unfortunate, while the wicked man prospers in his way, is independent and happy, where is the proof that God is just. To prove it from the Bible is to give up the cause of the moral science of the schools and to confess that it affords no adequate conception of the Divine justice. Now if it appears from all that is seen in nature and in providence, that God's ways are not equal in the dispensation of justice among men, how can anyone affirm from all that is seen or known that it will be otherwise hereafter in another world! And what on this hypothesis comes of the foundation of natural religion and moral science!

[...]

Both the old philosophy and the new alike fail in animating virtue and restraining vice. They have no consolation for the afflicted, no oil of joy and gladness for the broken and dejected in spirit. They have no bright scenes of future bliss, no heart cheering visions of infinite and eternal good for those who are ready to perish under one or more of the thousand nameless ills and evils of this life. Nor have they arguments or restraints to curb the violence of human passion, to subdue and tame the lions and tigers of the human heart. They fail in furnishing a correct theory of human life, in presenting a perfect standard of human action, as they do in authority, in obligation and in motives adequate to all the demands and conditions of humanity. Hence, no one has been reformed from the waywardness of folly, no one has been reclaimed from the paths of vice and iniquity, and constrained to tread the paths of righteousness and life by all the arguments and inducements of all the systems and schools of moral suasion in all the languages and ages of the world.

These systems and their authors take no account of the catastrophe that has befallen humanity. They assume that man is now in that same state of nature in which God originally made and placed him. They contemplate neither a preternatural nor a supernatural condition of human nature. Their best reasonings are full of doubt on man's origin, nature, relations, and destiny. Concerning moral obligation and the chief good there have been innumerable theories, sects and discords. Even, now, notwithstanding all the plagiarisms of the Bible, and comminglings of revelation and philosophy, the wisest and greatest masters of the Christian schools of moral science, are divided on the very elements of moral obligation, the criterion of virtue, the soul of moral science. The whole body of ethics, whether Christian or heathen ethics, is a dead carcass without a clearly ascertained and fixed moral obligation.

Here we have the celebrated Grotius and Dr. Samuel Clarke and other Rabbis, learnedly descanting upon the '*eternal fitness of things*' from which to abstract the essence of moral obligation. There we have the ingenious Cudworth, Butler, and Price eloquently and plausibly expatiating on the charms and beauties of heaven-born virtue, thence eliciting the remote elements of all voluntary obligation, affirming that a single glimpse of the divine beauties and loveliness of virtue is itself all-sufficient to woo the affections of the human heart and to control the waywardness of human passion.

Lord Shaftesbury and Dr. Hutcheson in another niche in the Pantheon of the virtues, affirm that the roots and grounds of all moral obligation are found in the moral sense itself; and this moral sense, sometimes less learnedly called conscience, is, with those doctors, a sort of instinctive principle which naturally abhors evil and delights in good — others have traced all moral obligation in its ultimate principle to the desire of happiness — others, to the sovereign will of God, and some, with Voltaire, Diderot, and D'Alembert found it all in custom. Their doctrine is, that 'all ideas of justice and injustice, of virtue and vice, of glory and infamy are purely arbitrary and dependent on custom'.

Upon the whole, the provisions of moral philosophy are not adequate to the wants of humanity. We are thus placed under a happy constraint to look for a clearer and more intelligible standard of duty; a higher and a holier authority to enforce, and stronger, more enduring, and more animating motives to impel to action; more vivid, sublime and soul-enrapturing scenes, to inspire our hopes and fears, than philosophy, either mental or moral, knows anything of. The Bible, alone admirably corrects what is erroneous, and supplies what is wanting in every point where human reason and human science fail. The civilized world, if there be such a one, are just but being convinced of the momentous fact, that the most splendid schemes of moral culture, based on moral philosophy, without the teachings and sanctions of the Bible, are but splendid cheats, and sublime abortions. The sons of true science in all Protestant Christendom are but awaking to the all-important fact that the Bible and its evidences, the Bible and its precepts, the Bible and its promises, the Bible and its threatenings, the Bible and its awful, fearful, and glorious sanctions is the only rational, complete, and perfect textbook that can be with perfect safety and with any reasonable ground of hope adopted in any school, high or low, which contemplates a rational and moral system of education.

In strongly affirming this conviction, we do not disparage either mental or moral science. The present crisis demands, and a good education requires, an intimate acquaintance with the best human productions on the animal, intellectual, and moral powers and capacities of man. So far as these productions develop or apply the true principles of mental and moral science, without presuming to originate them, so far they may be used advantageously, in the hands of proper instructors, in accomplishing youth to fill the most useful, responsible and honorable stations in the world.

Even the detection and the exposure of the errors of those systems is an essential part of a good education at the present moment, in advancing the progress of civilization. The correction of a single radical error, for example, in such works as Combe on the *Constitution of Man*; in Watts on the *Improvement of the Mind*; in Butler's *Analogy*; in Lord Brougham's *Natural Theology*; Babbage's ninth *Bridgewater Treatise*; and in various other such works of great literary and scientific merit, would be to every student and lover of true science, a very important and a very acceptable service.

To illustrate this last suggestion by another reference to Combe's *Moral Science* and *Constitution of Man*, I would remark that these works, so far as they respect the physical and intellectual constitution of man, so far as they treat on the constitution of nature, as adopted to that physical condition of man, are, in my judgment, worthy of being read and even studied with considerable advantage to the students and lovers of true science. Now the points on which Mr. Combe, in my judgment, errs, may, even upon the principles suggested in the works themselves, be demonstrated to be aberrations from his own premises and analogies. His capital mistake, as it seems, is that he takes for granted *that man is now, what he always was*—that he has never fallen; and that therefore the disorder and maladaptation of his moral faculties as connected with his animal appetites and propensities, are as much the creation of God now, as the first man was. And yet it would require, methinks, but a moderate effort of his liberal ideality, to find such a perfect head, such an harmonious supremacy of the intellectual and moral faculties, as to have made moral perfection as natural to man as imperfection now seems to be. If idiocy, on his premises, be the result of a falling off in the intellectual development, in the mal-organization of certain portions of the brain, on the same principle then, why may not moral imbecility in the whole species, be resolvable into a similar falling off in the due development of those organs which he has figuratively called the moral powers, but which in fact are but the physical instruments by which the mind operates. If, moreover, a good or a bad organization in the inferior powers be, as he avers, transmissible for many generations, what principle, in his own philosophy, forbids that the same law should not hold good from Adam till now, as respects the superior organs of the human system.

But to return:—if the art of living well cannot be deduced from those sciences, there are at least two arts of great importance which essentially depend upon them, or perhaps rather, are mainly to be deduced from them:—these are the art of teaching and the art of reasoning.

Of the art of reasoning, as dependent on the proper analysis of our powers of acquiring and communicating knowledge, as emanating directly from the science of mental philosophy, we cannot now speak. A few remarks on the art of teaching, as deducible from the premises already before us, must close our present address.

Of the mental and moral philosophers of the last century, none are more deservedly reputable than Stewart and Brown of Edinburgh. According to them, the supreme advantage of mental philosophy is, the aids and facilities which it affords to the projection and establishment of a proper system of education. Hence any important change in the philosophy of human nature has given birth to a corresponding change in the systems of education. An improved philosophy of man, will, of course, introduce an improved system of education. The old and the new school of mental and moral philosophy very remarkably concur in affirming

> the most essential objects of education are the two following: — First, to cultivate all the various principles of our nature, both speculative and active, in such a manner as to bring them to the greatest perfections of which they are susceptible; and secondly, by watching over the impressions and associations which the mind receives in early life, to secure it against the influence of prevailing errors; and, as far as possible, to engage its prepossessions on the side of truth. It is only upon a philosophical analysis of the mind that a systematical plan can be founded for the accomplishment of either of these purposes.[11]

So affirms the most distinguished incumbent of the Chair of mental science in the University of Edinburgh. And yet Stewart farther observes that so late as the close of the last century, he did not know that in any language or country, 'an attempt had been made to analyze and illustrate the principles of human nature, in order to lay a philosophical foundation for the proper culture'. Since the commencement of the present century, however, some such attempts have been made.

Our college has been founded with a special reference to these facts. It is the offspring of a deep and long established conviction that the theory and practice of education are yet greatly behind the onward progress of the age, and that to improve education and to adapt it to the philosophy of human nature, is, of all human means, the most likely to improve and reform the world. We have, therefore, entered upon the arduous task with a firm resolution, to make, as far as ascertained, the true science of human nature in all its powers, speculative and active, not merely the basis, but the rule and measure of that course of instruction which shall be prosecuted in this institution. As light to the eye and music

---

[11] Stewart's *Elements of the Philosophy of the Human Mind*. Vol. 1. page 14. Cambridge Edition — 1833.

to the ear, so should education be adapted to the physical, intellectual and moral powers and susceptibilities of man.

In the present improved state of human knowledge, a better definition of education may, perhaps, be given, than even that of Dugald Stewart. With us the chief object of education is not the acquisition of knowledge. It consists not in mere literature and science. Many of those greatly learned and scientific men of the most distinguished schools were fit neither for the present world, nor for that which is to come. Their great learning disqualified them for heaven or earth.

With us education has primary regard to the formation of habits, more than to the acquisition of knowledge; more in teaching a person the use of himself than in teaching him to use the labors of others. We define education to be *the development and improvement of the physical, intellectual, and moral powers of man, with a reference to his whole destiny in the Universe of God.*

We contemplate man as coming into the world without an idea and without a habit, preadapted for such a world as this, but having everything to learn, and having in his constitution elements and principles that prompt him to look beyond the confines of both time and sense, for the complete development and enjoyment of his own mysterious and wonderful being. Not only the whole constitution, but the whole destiny of man, must therefore be contemplated in every scheme of education adapted to the wants and wishes of humanity. The human constitution must be considered not only in reference to all its parts, but also to their relative importance. His animal constitution must, indeed, be taken into the account, because the *sana mens* is found only in *sano corpore*,[12] but it must be held subordinate to his intellectual, and both of these to his moral nature: for as his moral and social nature is his chief honor and his chief happiness, the expansion and cultivation of these attributes and capacities of his constitution will always command the supreme regard of those competent to the delightful task of instructing and training man in full harmony with his whole destiny in

---

[12] <'*Mens sana in corpore sano.*' 'A sound mind in a sound body.' — Juvenal, *Satires*, X, 356. John Locke, in *Some Thoughts on Education*, § I, writes, 'A sound mind in a sound body, is a short but full description of a happy state of this world'.>

creation. — And when we speak of the whole destiny of man, we comprehend his relations to society, both now and forever; his exact position in that universe of which he is both so humble and so conspicuous a part.

Under the Divine government, which is that of both general and special laws, every defect in education meets with a corresponding chastisement. Is physical instruction and training neglected? Is the child allowed to grow up ignorant of the physical and organic laws of its own being; and allowed to transgress them without admonition? Some fatal functional, or organic derangement, or a premature decay of the whole system, is the immediate penalty. Is the cultivation and training of his intellect neglected? Mental feebleness and general incompetency for the business of life, is the inevitable consequence. But is moral culture neglected? The result is still more fatal, because it involves the whole ruin of man, body, soul, and spirit, and of his whole interests, temporal, spiritual, and eternal.

When according to the best statistics within our reach, we subtract the victims of defective or bad education from the mass of those fashionably called the liberally educated, the proportion lost is of a fearful magnitude, compared with the portion saved to society. Almost three sevenths of that class die under thirty years of age, the prey of disease and physical irregularities, which a few timous[13] lessons might have prevented. Or they fall prey to vicious and licentious habits of life, which soon dispatch them to the grave. Two-sevenths of the remainder, who may live to advanced age, are public nuisances to society, because of the blighting and pestiferous influence of their flagitious example to youth. Of the remaining two-sevenths the more honorable posts of society are filled up; and their duties discharged with more or less honor to themselves and advantage to the community.

Now there is neither physical nor moral necessity for such a state of things. Let education be only in harmony with the present philosophy of human nature; let it be what the most perfect analysis of our constitution says it ought to be; let it embrace the whole man, and the whole range of his powers of doing and enjoying good; let it communicate

---

[13] <According to Samuel Johnson's *Dictionary of the English Language*, 'TIMOUS, *a*. Early; timely; not innate'.>

sound instruction, enforce good examples, and practice moral training by all the appliances of language, science, art, according to the best models, under the supremacy of the moral sentiments and the moral obligations of our nature, and society will be blessed with a superior order of men, with men of a brighter intellectual and moral polish, of greater force and energy of character; of greater power to advance the various interests of the community, to promote the glory of God, and the lasting good and happiness of mankind.

Such is the great and benevolent end proposed in the erection of this new literary and moral institution. For which reason we have selected a rural location, because more favorable to health, to morals, and to study, than the associations of either town or city.

Without going into a specification of a complete course of study, we shall for the present, only say, that it is designed to keep pace with all the improvements of this rapidly progressive age, in every branch of education; and to have to meet and cluster here all the advantages requisite to the full development and improvement of human nature, according to the present advanced state of literature, science, and civilization.

On one point only we shall farther speak with a clear and definite emphasis: It is agreed, almost universally agreed — in Europe and America — that intellectual culture, without moral, is rather a misfortune and a curse than a blessing to every society. We shall therefore place moral worth and moral excellence of character in the highest place, and make everything subordinate, as but a means to that sublime and lofty end. In every department in this institution a supreme and sovereign regard shall be paid to the formation of a pure and irreproachable character.

We are peculiarly favored with means, we humbly hope, adequate to that end. Our trustees in regular attendance, and the faculty of this institution are all of one mind on this subject. They will cordially co-operate in this and every other great object, favorable to the true interest — the improvement, the health and the happiness of all the youth of the college. The young gentlemen now in attendance, so far as good recommendations can assure us, are well disposed to submit to such a course of instruction and training, intellectual and moral, as will further the great objects contemplated in the erection of this seminary. We therefore commence under auspices every way favorable in all these respects. And under that blessing of heaven, without which all human efforts are unavailing, we do hope to achieve for ourselves, our friends, and the community, great and good results to be held in long and grateful remembrance.

But before I sit down, I have a word to say to the students, now in attendance. — Young gentlemen, it has fallen to your lot, I hope it may prove to every one of you one of the most fortunate events of your youth, a subject not only of present but of future congratulation; I say, it has fallen to your lot to become the first fruits of Bethany College. I cannot express to you in ordinary terms the deep solicitude I feel for your individual improvement and for your general advancement in literature, science, and moral excellence. I always knew that I was placing myself in a very responsible attitude to the community, in attempting to establish a new literary and moral institution, adapted to the wants and wishes of this community — to man as an animal, intellectual, moral being; destined to a transient and active life here, and to an endless life hereafter. But deep as this sense and feeling of responsibility was in the commencement and progress of this undertaking, it has become much deeper and more oppressive since, than before your arrival. When I look around me here and see so many young gentlemen convened from North to South, from East to West, sent from their homes, from the immediate personal attention, oversight and guardianship of their parents, and entrusted to our care and protection; having your health, general education, and moral culture entrusted to our direction and management, I feel more than ever penetrated with a profound and unerring sense of my own responsibility, and that of the faculty and trustees of this institution. I feel honored, indeed, with the confidence, your parents and guardians have reposed in myself, as well as my co-adjutors, in confiding your destiny so far into our hands. I can only say that our wishes and intentions to promote your thorough education, in the full import of that term, so far as the time of your continuance here will allow, do not only concur with their views and expectations; but that our best efforts, and most assiduous attentions shall be called forth to promote your thorough and substantial improvement, honor and happiness in every way in our power, so far as a faithful and conscientious regard to the duties of my office can avail to that end.

Much, indeed, will depend on you for the future success of our endeavors. You stand to this institution in the same relation that the first born of a family does to all his junior brothers. The younger members of the family look up to him for a model of what they ought to be. If his example be a good and happy one, the parents will find it, comparatively, an easy task to govern the whole household; but if his be an adverse and unfriendly one, it will increase their troubles an hundred fold. You will then regard yourselves as about to exert a very great influence in forming the character and in giving a favorable turn to the manners of this institution. We shall all feel ourselves greatly indebted to you, should you, as we fondly hope you will, co-operate with us in this most useful, commendable, and noble enterprise. You will also perceive that this very circumstance will exact from the faculty of this institution a very strict attention to the whole details of your behavior in every department of your conduct. They cannot but perceive and feel the responsibility that devolves upon them, in reference to the examples and habits that are to be formed this first year of our existence. They must see to it that good examples are established at the very beginning of our career, and therefore a very strict attention to this part of the duties of their office and to your demeanor is to be expected. We are aware that the too lax discipline of this age, domestic, scholastic, and ecclesiastic, will impose upon us and upon you in the outset a greater degree of vigilance and effort than under more propitious auspices would have been necessary. A due allowance on our part, and on yours, must therefore be made in reference to these circumstances, and in a little time the wheels of our whole literary and moral machinery, well oiled, will perform their regular revolutions without a screak or a jar.

Allow me, young gentlemen, to add that such is my confidence in the good sense, good intentions, and good feelings, as well as in the zeal and abilities of my fellow laborers, to promote your true interests here, and such are my hopes and anticipations of your devotion to your studies and to the formation of good habits, that I do flatter myself that we shall make not only a good and propitious commencement, but that we shall rapidly advance to a high and honorable standing amongst the literary institutions of our country and the age.

In accomplishing all our views and desires, much, very much, I again repeat, must in every view of the case depend upon you. Should this institution speedily become what we desire and intend to make it, it will be eminently through your instrumentality during your collegiate course. And, gentlemen, may I not say in conclusion, and in anticipation of the high destiny of Bethany College, that it would be to you through life and in the zenith of its fame, a pleasing reflection that you helped to lay the foundation of its good fortune and high renown by such a course of study and behavior, as not only secured to yourselves stations of great utility and honor, but which also elevated your *alma mater*[14] to a rank and an influence that made her an honor to the age, and a blessing to the world.

---

[14] <Latin, 'foster mother'; college or university which one has attended.>

Nine

James McCosh (1811–1894)

James McCosh was born into a farming family in 1811, in Ayrshire, Scotland. After first attending Glasgow University, and then Edinburgh University, McCosh earned a degree in theology in 1834. Following graduation, McCosh was called to be a minister in northeast Scotland, where he became deeply involved in the internecine conflicts within the Church of Scotland.

At the time, the chief points of contention between the conservative evangelical party and their opponents, the moderates, concerned the role of the state in the governance of the church, and the importance of Calvinism in the church's theology. McCosh, an evangelical, became a fierce proponent of both Calvinist doctrine and the independence of church polity from the state. Unfortunately for the evangelicals, the moderates managed to block their agenda in the church courts, leading to a schism within the Church of Scotland in 1843. Along with hundreds of other churches and ministers, McCosh therefore left the official state church in order to help form the Free Church of Scotland.

In 1850, McCosh published his first book, *The Method of Divine Governement*. In this work McCosh provided arguments for the existence of God on two fronts: the natural order of the world, and the nature and existence of the human mind. Deftly blending the moderate tradition of Scottish Enlightenment philosophy with explicitly Calvinist theology, McCosh's book was so well received that it led to his appointment to the professorship of logic and metaphysics at Queen's College, Belfast, in 1852. During his tenure at Queen's College, McCosh wrote prolifically, and won wide acclaim for his criticism of utilitarianism and his attempts to reconcile the insights of the Scottish Enlightenment with the idealism of Immanuel Kant.

In 1868, McCosh was invited to become president of the College of New Jersey (now Princeton University). Much like his evangelical Scottish predecessor, John Witherspoon, McCosh was selected in order to heal divisions within American Presbyterianism. Although McCosh was initially seen as sympathetic to the conservative side of American Presbyterianism, his interest in science quickly won him praise from church progressives and criticism from ardent Calvinists. Unlike his fellow Princetonian, the theologian Charles Hodge, McCosh came to see nothing inherently threatening to religious belief in the theory of evolution. Further, breaking from Harvard president Charles W. Eliot and Yale president Noah Porter, McCosh required all undergraduate students of the College of New Jersey to study modern science.

Over the twenty years of his presidency, McCosh oversaw an aggressive building programme on the campus, and secured the college's future by greatly increasing its financial resources and prestige. Additionally, McCosh took an active role in the education of many of the twentieth century's leading men; including future Princeton University and United States president Woodrow Wilson. Until his death, McCosh also exerted significant influence on the intellectual culture of the United States through his many philosophical works. In the selection below, taken from his 1882 book, *Realistic Philosophy Defended*, McCosh argues that it is time for the United States to develop its own distinctive philosophy, using the insights of the Scottish Enlightenment's Common Sense Realism.

Biographical Information: David Hoeveler, *American National Biography Online*.

READING XIV

What an American Philosophy Should Be[1]

America has arrived at a stage at which there is a body of men and women who have leisure and taste to cultivate the liberal arts and advance the higher forms of civilization. She does not claim to have accomplished in a century or two what Europe has done in twice that time. It would not be just to require her, as one country, to be doing as much as all the countries of the Old World are doing. Still, she now ranks with any other one nation in literature, science, and art. She has a literature which promises to rival that of England. Her historians, in respect both of research and style, are equal to those of Europe. She has not yet produced a poem of the highest class, such as the *Illiad*, *Æneid*, the *Inferno*, or *Paradise Lost*, or *Faust*; but some of her poets in this past age may be placed on the same level as any of their contemporaries. She can show statues and paintings (in landscape, for example) full of vigor and freshness. She has humorists, not perhaps of the highest order—they are too much given to startle by exaggeration—but with a manner of their own. Franklin, Thompson (Count Rumford), and Joseph Henry have led the way in original scientific research, and there are professors in our colleges pursuing the most advanced science. In 'practical inventions', called forth by the necessities of the wide country, she is in advance of all other people.

But all enlightened nations have also had a philosophy bent on inquiring into the reasons of things and settling the foundations of knowledge. India and Persia had it in very ancient times in the form of a theosophy. Greece, followed at a distance by Rome, sought to establish the reality and penetrate into the nature of things. France has had a philosophy ever since the days of Descartes, in the seventeenth century, and so has Germany since the time of Leibniz in the following age. The English have had a most influential mental science since the time of Locke, and Scotland has since the

---

[1]   [Extracted from (1877) 'General Introduction', in *Realistic Philosophy Defended in a Philosophic Series*, 2 Volumes, Volume I, New York: Charles Scribner's Sons, pp. 1-26.]

days of Reid. Italy, at this present time, has a promising school.[2] How does America stand?

She has had a considerable number of able philosophic thinkers. It may be doubted whether any country has had a more acute metaphysician than Jonathan Edwards, whose views were restricted, and who was kept from doing more, simply by his want of books, and of collision with other thinkers. The theologians of America have made constant use of philosophic principles in defending their doctrinal positions; but the thinking people have not formed a separate school, as the French, the English, the Scotch, and the Germans have. In the last century and the earlier part of this, they followed Locke or Reid, one or both, always making an independent use of what they adopted — as a rule they took from Locke only what was good, and carefully separated themselves from his sensational tendencies. In this past age our thinking youth have been strongly attracted by Kant and his school, some of them being caught in the toils of Hegel. In the present age a number are following John S. Mill, Bain, and Herbert Spencer. All this, while we never have had a distinctive American philosophy.

The time has come, I believe, for America to declare her independence in philosophy. She will not be disposed to set up a new monarchy, but she may establish a republic confederated like the United States. Certainly she should not shut herself out from intercourse with other countries; on the contrary, she should be open to accessions from all quarters. But she should do with them as with the emigrants who land on her shores, in regard to whom she insists that they speak her language and conform to her laws; so she should require that her philosophy have a character of its own. She had better not engage in constructing new theories of the universe spun out of the brain. The world has got sick of such. Even in Germany, where they summarize, expound, and critically

---

[2] See an account of this school, by Luigi Ferri, in Princeton Review, (55th year). Mamiani, who had so fine a Platonic spirit, is now dead, but it is hoped that *La Filosofia della Scuole Italiane*, of which M. Ferri is now sole editor, will take a lead in this school. I may mention that his book, written in French, *La Psychologie de l'Association*, shows historically and critically that Association of Ideas cannot account for our high intellectual and moral ideas. It is the ablest work on this subject.

examine all forms of speculative thought, they will not listen to any new philosophical systems, and the consequence is that none is now offered — the latest being pessimism, which startled young thinkers by its extravagance, and by its containing an element of truth in bringing into prominence the existence and prevalence of evil which the philosophy of last century had very much overlooked.

But what is to be the nature of the new philosophic republic formed of United States? All national philosophies have to partake of the character of their nation. The philosophy of the East was sultry and dreamy — like the Indian summer. The Greeks used a dialectic, sharp as a knife, and separated things by analysis and combined them by intellectual synthesis. The French thinking excels all others in its mathematical clearness imposed upon it by Descartes. The English philosophy, like Locke, is characterized by profound sense. The Scotch is searching, anxiously careful and resolute in adhering to observation. The German has a most engaging *Schwärmerei*,[3] and is ever mounting into the empyrean, its native sphere, in which it is seeking by criticism to construct boundaries. If a genuine American philosophy arises, it must reflect the genius of the people. Now, Yankees are distinguished from most others by their practical observation and invention. They have a pretty clear notion of what a thing is, and, if it is of value, they take steps to secure it.

It follows that, if there is to be an American philosophy, it must be Realistic. I suspect they will never produce an Idealistic philosophy like that of Plato in ancient times, or speculative systems like those of Spinoza, Leibniz, and Hegel in modern times. The circumstance that Emerson is an American may seem to contradict this, but then Emerson, while he opens interesting glimpses of truth, is not a philosopher; his thoughts are like strung pearls, without system and without connection. On the other hand, the Americans believe that there are things to be known, to be prized and secured, and will never therefore look approvingly on an agnosticism which declares that knowledge is unattainable. The American philosophy will therefore be a Realism, opposed to Idealism on the one hand and to Agnosticism on the other.

---

[3] ['excessive enthusiasm']

REALISM

It holds that there are real things, and that man can so far know them. But if there are things and we know them, we must have a capacity to know them directly, of course having also the power of adding indirectly to our direct knowledge. We cannot by legitimate reasoning infer the existence of mind or matter from a datum or premise which does not contain the existence of mind or matter—the addition or multiplication of 0 can never give us anything but 0. We shall see that Hume made us start with mere impressions or ideas, and thereby, of purpose, landed us in skepticism or what would now be called agnosticism; and that Kant started with phenomena, in the sense of appearances, and tried from these to reach things, but utterly failed to extract reality from what had no reality. If we are ever to get hold of reality, we must seize it at once.

Realism holds that the mind perceives matter. In sense-perception we know things; we know them as external to the perceiving self—as extended and exercising resisting power. We have no need to resort to such theories as those of intermediate ideas or occasional causes coming between the perceiving mind and the perceived object. All of these were brought in to remove supposed difficulties which do not exist, and have only introduced real difficulties.

While we adhere resolutely to the doctrine of natural realism, namely, that the mind knows matter directly, there is room and reason for doubt as to what is the thing perceived directly by the senses generally and by each of the senses. The mature man is apt to think that he knows by directly looking at it the distance of that mountain, and yet it has been shown that all that he knows immediately by the eye is a colored surface, and that he knows the distance of objects by a process of reasoning proceeding on a gathered observation. There is still need to inquire what is the matter we originally perceive, whether it is our bodily frames or objects beyond them. It seems to me that our early perceptions are mainly of our organism; say by taste of our palate, by smell of our nostrils, and by touch proper of our extended frame. I think it probable, however, that by the muscular sense and by the sight of eye, as higher senses, we know objects as external to our body but affecting our body. But there is need of farther experimenting to determine what matter each sense perceives, how far out of or how far in the organism. On this subject, which is a very important one, the experiments and observations of certain German physiologists, such as Lotze, Helmholtz, Wundt, Fechner, also Professor Stanley Hall and Doctor Starr, will throw light. Meanwhile, we must resolutely hold that in the farthest resort the mind perceives matter, whether in the body or out of the body, as external to the mind, extended and resisting energy.

We should hold still more resolutely that we have an immediate knowledge of self in a particular state. By this I do not mean that we know self apart from a mode of self: the self is under a certain sensation, or is remembering, or thinking, or deciding, is in joy or in sorrow. Certainly we do not know the self aloof from the sensation or some other affection, but just as little do we know the sensation except as a sensation of self; nor a sensation without a sensitive object, nor a sensation in general, nor a sensation of another, but a sensation of our own.

Realism farther maintains that in memory we know things as having been before us in time past, and do thus know time as mixed up with the event in time from which it can be separated by an easy process of abstraction. In this we know time to be as real as the event in time.

In contemplating space and time we are led to look on them as without bounds, and thus rise to such an idea as the mind can form of infinity.

In knowing objects we perceive that in the very nature of the things there are relations involved such as that of personal identity, of substance and quality.

We have still higher knowledge. We know certain voluntary acts as being morally good or evil, say as being just or unjust, benevolent or cruel, candid or deceitful. Not that this moral good discerned by us is the same kind of thing as body or mind, or has the same kind of reality. Still it is perceived as a reality in voluntary acts known in consciousness. I am inclined to argue that by the conscience the mind perceives voluntary acts to be free. Philosophy should not attempt to prove this by a process of mediate reasoning. Mind perceives matter at once; but it also perceives benevolence, and perceives it to be good, as clearly as the eye perceives objects to be extended. It is the business of philosophy not to set aside these realities, but to assume them and justify the assumption; and to endeavor—what is often a difficult work—to determine and express their exact nature.

In doing this, philosophy proceeds by observation and according to the method of induction, the observation being made by the consciousness or internal sense. It should decline to proceed in the old Greek method of analysis and synthesis, or of deduction and reasoning. It should refuse with equal decision to proceed in the method of Kant by a criticism, liable itself to be criticized by a farther criticism carried on without end, without a foundation of facts to settle the questions stirred. It is the office of metaphysics to find out what the facts immediately perceived are and enunciate them as first and fundamental truths. Not that it is our observation or induction of them that makes them realities or truths; the correct statement is that philosophy observes them because they are realities.

Obvious objections present themselves to this mode and style of thinking. These can be answered, and they should be answered. First, it should be noticed that our observation does not make the propositions true; we perceive them because they are true. Secondly, we have to call attention to the important distinction between our original and acquired perceptions, and be ready to defend the original ones if assailed; but we are not bound to stand up for all the additions by human thinking. Our intuitive convictions carry with them their own evidence and authority, the others may be examined and criticized, may be proved or disproved. Thirdly, a distinction should be drawn between our sensations proper and our perceptions proper, the former being mere feelings of the organism, which may be misunderstood and misrepresented, the latter only being the cognitions of realities. Fourthly, there is the distinction, often very loosely drawn, between the primary and secondary qualities of matter. The former are energy and extension perceived directly and in all matter, the latter a mere organic feeling or sensation, such as heat as felt, implying an external cause, which is shown to be a molecular motion. Fifthly, there is a distinction between different kinds of realities. There is a certain kind of reality involved in our perception of body as extended and impenetrable. There is also a reality, but of a different kind, in the perceiving of self in a certain mode, say as thinking or willing. The one reality is as certain and definite as the other, but it is of a different kind and is perceived by a different organ, by self-consciousness and not the external senses. There is a third kind of reality in the object perceived by our conscience or moral perception. It is quite as certain that hypocrisy is evil and that truthfulness is a virtue as that body exists or mind exists; but the one is a separate thing known, whereas the other is a quality, a quality of mind, quite as certainly existing as mind itself.

These distinctions are not difficult to comprehend. They are very generally known and acknowledged. But they need to be carefully applied to our cognitions in order to defend first truths and a thorough-going realism.

It will be found that in proceeding on this method we meet with far fewer difficulties than on any other. There is a mode of discovering and testing truth often resorted to, and this successfully in the present day, which I am willing to use in the case before us. Let us begin, it is said, with adopting the doctrine we are seeking to establish as a working hypothesis, and inquire whether it explains all the facts; and if it does, we may regard it as an established law. Let us then adopt realism as a working hypothesis, and inquire how it works, and we shall find that it unravels many perplexities and is encompassed with fewer difficulties than any other doctrine; that by it the real difficulties which present themselves may all, or nearly all, be met and removed, and that realism is consistent with all other truths and throws light upon them. Adopt any other theory, say idealism, and make the mind add to things as it perceives them, or phenomenalism, which makes us know mere appearances, or agnosticism, which makes things unknown, and we shall find ourselves ever knocking against obstacles which cannot be removed, against intuitive convictions which insist on our listening and submitting to them, or against obstinate facts facing us as rocks. Adopt realism, and we shall discover that we have a clear way to walk in. But in order to [do] this our doctrine must be thorough-going. If we resort to compromises, or make weak admissions, we are entangled in difficulties from which we cannot extricate ourselves. If, for instance, we take the position that some of our intuitions or natural perceptions look to realities while others are deceptive or contain only partial truth, our inconsistencies will greatly trouble and weaken us. The sceptic will ask, if one of our primitive perceptions may deceive us, why not all, and we can answer this only on principles which will undermine them all, and leave us in bottomless agnosticism.

It can be shown that the inquiries of the Greek philosopher were after realities; not for the absolute, which is the search of the modern German philosophies of the higher type, but for *to on* or *to einai*,[4] phrases which should not, as they often are, be translated absolute. The Greeks saw that there were appearances without realities, and that appearances were often deceptive. Some of them, such as the Eleatics, came to adopt the maxim that the senses deceive, and appealed from them to the reason, forgetting that the reason has to proceed on the matter given it, and if this is erroneous the reason which rests on it may give erroneous decisions. Aristotle was the first to establish the grand truth that the senses do not deceive, and that the errors arise from the wrong interpretation of the information given by the senses. By the help of the distinctions drawn by him, and since his time by the Scottish school and others, we can stand up for the trustworthiness of the senses, and do not require to call in to our help 'ideas' with Locke, or 'impressions' with Hume, or 'phenomena' with Kant; and we may follow our natural convictions implicitly, and regard the mind as perceiving things immediately, and run no risk of deceptions or contradictions.

IDEALISM

Idealism in thought and in literature is altogether of an ennobling character. But we are to speak of it here as appearing in speculative inquiry. As a philosophic system it holds that the mind out of its own stores always adds to our apprehension of things.

It may be a thorough-going idealism, such as that of Berkeley, who maintained that by the senses we perceive not material things extended and made up of particles but ideas created by the Divine Mind, and that things exist only as

---

[4] ['the being' or 'the essence']

they are perceived. Fichte went to a greater extreme, and held that things are the projections of mind, of the individual mind, or rather of that incomprehensible fiction of the philosopher's brain, the universal ego or consciousness. But by far the greater number of the systems of idealism have been partial and one-sided. Locke was practically a decided realist, believing both in mind and matter; but he holds that mind perceives bodies, not directly, but merely by ideas supposed to be representatives of bodies. Kant speaks of the mind beginning with phenomena, in the sense of appearances, and then tries illogically, I think, to argue the existence of things, which however, he (followed by Herbert Spencer) represents as unknown. Berkeley, coming after Locke, urged that if we can perceive only ideas, we cannot from these argue the existence of material things, the ideas being themselves the things and sufficient. Fichte, coming after Kant, defied anyone to prove from mere appearances the existence of a reality beyond, as this would be putting in the conclusion more than is in the premises. Ever since, the German metaphysicians of the higher sort have been pursuing realities, and in thinking that they have caught them have only embraced a cloud. If we do not start with realities, both in the object perceived and the perceiving mind, we can never reach them by any legitimate logical process.

The half-and-half systems, the ideal-real as they are called, held by so many in the present day in Germany, are in the position of a professedly neutral person between two hostile armies, exposed to the fire of both. On the one hand it is argued that if one part of our native and original perceptions be ideal, why may not the other parts, why may not the whole be so? If the balloon without any weights attached be let loose, it will move as the winds carry it, and cannot be brought down to the solid earth except by a collapse. On the other hand it is argued by the agnostic that if all or so much be created by the imagination we have no warrant for asserting that there is any reality, and we must sink into the slough of nescience and nihilism, which are the same nonentities viewed under different aspects; the one asserting that man has no capacity to know, and the other that there is nothing to know, and both culminating in the absolute blank of agnosticism, which is darkness which cannot be seen, for there is no eye to see it—the darkness of the sepulcher, in which death ends all. But are we in the narrowness of our realism to exclude the ideal? This would be like depriving the flower of its perfume. The imagination is one of the loftiest powers with which our Maker has endowed us. The child with the aid of its doll and other toys weaves its tales of weal or woe and takes a part in them. The mature man has his day-dreams as well as his night-dreams, and in the midst of the hard struggle of life pictures better days to come. The Christian dies gazing into the invisible world as if it were visible. Take away the ideal, and literature would be stripped of half of its charms. Even science cannot do without it. 'The truth is', says D'Alembert, 'to the geometer who invents, imagination is not less essential than to the poet who creates.'[5] In the mind of Newton gravitation was a hypothesis before it became an established law. Philosophy without the ideal would be shorn of the halo which it has in Plato and Leibniz, and could not mount to heaven, which is its sphere. All our higher thought goes out into infinity. The real without the ideal would be like the earth without its air and sky.

Idealism has a wide sphere lawfully allowed it, but it must not be permitted to break out of its orbit. We give it a place, a high place, but we keep it in its place, and we should not allow it to evaporate into nonentity. By all means let us have fancies in our spontaneous thinking. But we are here speaking of philosophy, which is reflective thinking. It is one of the most important offices of philosophy to announce to us the grounds on which we believe in *what is* in opposition to *what is not*, and in doing this it has to define what field the ideal has as distinguished from the real; it has to show us how fancies differ from facts. It will not discourage the soaring into the imaginary, but it requires that all the while we know and acknowledge it to be imaginary. The man who believes in the existence of unreal objects is a madman; the speculation, wild as a romance, but not so attractive, which makes the ideal real is equally lunatic.

[...]

---

[5] [Jean le Rond d'Alembert (1751) 'Preliminary Discourse', *Encyclopaedia or a Systematic Dictionary of the Sciences, Arts and Crafts*.]

AGNOSTICISM

Extremes meet, as the east and west do in lines on our globe. Idealism leads logically and historically to Agnosticism, for, if portions of our original knowledge be ideal, that is imaginary, why may not all be? And if all be so, we are down to Nihilism. Locke's philosophy, partly idealistic, became wholly so in Berkeley, and sunk into nescience in Hume, and continued so in John S. Mill and his school. Kant's phenomenal theory of knowledge, and his forms imposed by the mind on things, are the places of refuge to which Agnosticism retreats when it is pressed.

It should be noticed of Agnosticism that it is seldom or never consistently carried out. Its supporters maintain that we cannot have a knowledge of reality. But they act and speak and write as if there are things. They believe in the existence of some things—they commonly believe in the existence of meat and money. They are convinced of the reality of things that are seen; they begin to doubt and deny only when we press spiritual truth upon them, when we show them that there is an immutable morality, that there is a God, and that this God will call them to account.

The common way of meeting Agnosticism is by showing that it contradicts itself. It is obviously a contradiction to assert that we know that we can know nothing. But when we have proved this, we have only strengthened the opinion we are opposing. One of Hume's strongest skeptical arguments is that our vaunted knowledge is inconsistent, that reason lands us in contradictions. The most effective way of leading us to abandon our assurance of reality is to demonstrate that in pursuing different lines of thought we reach opposite and inconsistent conclusions. The only satisfactory and conclusive way of meeting Agnosticism is to follow the realistic method we are recommending in this paper, and to show that we have a primitive knowledge which we spontaneously proceed upon, and which we ought to assume in philosophy.

In the present day the Americans are still depending on the Europeans, and borrowing from them. The more earnest students go to Deutschland, and are ploughing, as Ulrici used to say, with the German heifer. Others, who are more addicted to the observations of sense and the methods of physical science, are taking what philosophy they have from Professor Bain and Mr. Spencer, and may be called the Modern English School.

THE GERMAN SCHOOL

The American youth of the present day who wishes to carry on research goes for a year or more to a German university. In particular, those of a metaphysical taste do not feel that they have enough to satisfy them at home, and they betake themselves to Berlin or Leipsic to get a full supply of the food for which they crave. On entering the lecture-rooms there they find certain formidable distinctions proceeded on without being explained—such as those between object and subject; *a priori* and *a posteriori*; rational and empirical; real and ideal; phenomenon and noumenon—all of which may involve a concealed error with the truth which they convey, namely, making objective truth subjective, or the creation of the mind. As they go on they find themselves in a labyrinth, with no clue to bring them out into the open air and light.

All these distinctions have had the mark of Kant branded upon them. That powerful thinker has taken possession of the philosophic thought of Germany more effectively than Plato did that of Greece, or Aristotle that of the Middle Ages, or Locke did that of England, or Reid and Hamilton did that of Scotland—he rules over the minds of the Germans as determinedly as Bismarck does over their political action. Some, such as Fichte, Schelling, and Hegel, have been carrying out certain of his principles to greater heights of Idealism. Younger men, feeling dizzy on the elevations to which they have been carried, insist on being carried lower down, and have raised the cry, 'Back to Kant', thinking that they may stop in the descent where he stopped, but find that by the weight upon them they can get no resting-place short of the bogs of agnosticism. All are alike entangled, even Helmholtz and the physicists, in the nets of the critical philosophy from which they cannot extricate themselves.

We have come to a crisis when of all things it is necessary to criticize the critical philosophy. I have been taking exception to certain of the positions of the great German metaphysician. I have all along maintained what Dr. Stirling seems now to be establishing, that Kant did not satisfactorily meet Hume, the sceptic. On the contrary, he yielded to him certain grounds on which he erected a skepticism as deadly as that of the cold Scotchman, but much more alluring. First, he proceeded in a wrong method — in the critical — which has started a series of criticisms with no ultimate ground of fact to rest on, instead of the inductive, which, it should be understood, does not give cogency to first truths, but simply discovers them. Secondly, he started not with facts, but with phenomena, in the sense of appearances, and from these could never logically rise to realities. Hume began with impressions and ideas from which no one could ever draw things; and for these Kant substituted unknown presentations, from which we cannot extract realities any more than we can extract light from cucumbers. He has built a formidable castle in the air, to which agnosticism retreats when it is attacked. Thirdly, he maintains that the mind perceives objects under forms which are not in the things, and has thus created an ideal world, to which poets such as Goethe and Schiller delighted to mount, but which affords no secure abode to those who insist on having on earth a solid domicile in which to dwell.

In the last century Locke was the most influential of all philosophers. It has taken a long time to separate the error from the truth in his system. In order to [do] this it needed the profound examination of Leibniz in the last century, and the brilliant criticism of Cousin in this; it has required, further, the practical sense of Reid and the Scottish school to expose his ideal theory, and the glow of Coleridge to attract the eyes of men to something higher than sensations. Locke's error in supposing that the mind perceives ideas and not things, and in deriving all truth from a limited experience, are clearly seen, and we need now only to accept the great body of truth which he has established forever.

Kant holds in the nineteenth century the place which Locke did in the eighteenth. We need now to have him examined as searchingly as Locke has been. The wave which carried Kant's philosophy to its greatest height crested at his centennial in 1881, and will now fall down to its proper level. His system will be stripped of its fictitious features, that we may receive and welcome the great body of truths which he presents.

For myself, I can scarcely regret the exclusive authority which Aristotle exercised for a thousand years, for he has thereby, through the mediaeval logic, modeled modern notions into their present shape—even as the ocean by its agitations has moulded the pebbles and sands which bound it. But it was necessary for the advancement of thought that the Stagirite should be dethroned from his too exclusive power by such original thinkers as Bacon and Descartes. In like manner the influence of Locke has been for good, but we rejoice that Reid exposed his theory of ideas, and showed that he had overlooked truths of primary reason. So, while we do not grudge to Kant his reign for a hundred years, we may earnestly wish that his whole philosophy be now subjected to a kindly but rigid criticism, in which the true and the good are retained, namely, first truths prior to experience, while the false and evil are cast off, namely, all that is inconsistent with a thorough-going realism.

THE MODERN ENGLISH SCHOOL

It consists of writers who have drawn their philosophy from Locke through Hume. The most eminent representatives of the school are, first, Mr. J.S. Mill, then Mr. Lewes, who brought in an element from Comte, the positivist, and Mr. Herbert Spencer, who has called in the development power, and Professor Bain, who has sought to combine physiology with psychology. The American philosophy must be ready to accept from all these men valuable observations made by them both as to psychical and nerve action—we may borrow from these Egyptians the materials wherewith to build our tabernacle; but we must superadd higher and spiritual truth to give it a form and meaning. The whole school is guilty of great oversights which require to be supplied. They commonly state correctly the physiological facts as made known by the senses and the microscope, but they overlook a great many of the psychological facts quite as clearly revealed by the internal sense or consciousness. They give us the husks, but do not open to us the kernel. We may specify some of their defects, leaving others to carry on the work.

1. There are oversights in their view of the exercises of the senses; not of the bodily organs, but of the mind or intelligence as operating in perception by the senses. They have not seen or acknowledged that in sense-perception there is

knowledge, in fact, our primary knowledge; our knowledge of things as extended, and as having resisting power — the beginning of the idea of power. They have commonly been satisfied with representing the mind as starting with impressions (that vaguest of terms) or sensations from which they can never get the knowledge of things.

2. They have not seen that in consciousness, meaning self-consciousness, they have a knowledge of *self* in some particular act, say perceiving, remembering, judging, or resolving, all of which we know as acts of *ourselves* and not of another. The school speak[s] of the mind as itself unknown, the qualities only being known, whereas the qualities are abstractions from a thing known, known as exercising the qualities. The knowledge of self as conscious, along with the knowledge of a not self as external and extended, is the beginning of all our knowledge. All our other cognition presupposes this and proceeds upon it. This knowledge is of real things, and all knowledge legitimately built upon it is also of realities.

3. The whole school give[s] a defective account of what is involved in the memory. They make it a mere reproduction of the past. There is, first, they say, a perception of an object, say a mountain, and then a reproduction of this perception. But this is not all that is involved in memory. In remembrance there is not only the image of the object, but a recognition of it as having been before the mind in time past. This implies a faith element and the idea or knowledge of time which metaphysicians have had such trouble in dealing with.

4. They do not acknowledge or see what lofty exercises are involved in the imagination, which creates the ideal out of the real, and ever tends toward what it may never be able to reach, the infinite. In these operations the mind rises above the senses into a higher sphere, where the philosophers of the senses do not choose to follow it.

5. They commit a great and fatal error in making the mind perceive only the relations of resemblance and difference, whereas it has the capacity, as Locke and Hume and Brown maintain, of discovering a variety of other relations which penetrate deeply into the nature of things, such as those of space and time, of quantity and active property, all of which the mind can perceive.

6. In particular, they do not take sufficiently deep views of such relations as those of personal identity and causation. In not noticing the knowledge of self in the original perceptions of consciousness, they do not expose to view what is involved in the identity of self in its successive states, which as perceiving we are prepared to believe in its immortality. Again, they represent causation merely as invariable antecedence which may not hold in all times and in all space, whereas it consists in a power in the agents acting as the cause and producing the invariableness, and constraining us to rise from real effects to a real cause supreme in God.

7. Their grand error consists in overlooking what is involved in morality, in our moral perceptions, which discern the good as distinctly as extension is seen by the eye. In not noticing these facts they are missing the very highest qualities in our moral and spiritual nature.

8. Their account of the feelings or emotions is meagre. They are apt to identify them with mere sensations, which again they identify with nervous affections. Herbert Spencer does this. They do not fully apprehend that in all emotion there is an appetence or spring of action, say the love of pleasure, or the love of power, or the love of good, and an idea of the object which calls forth the emotion, as fitted to gratify or disappoint the appetence.

9. They deny that man has free will; they make him the mere evolution and creature of circumstances. The realistic philosophy will require carefully to unfold the nature of free choice as an inalienable prerogative of man.

In all these and in other ways the Modern English School is degrading our nature, and with it all high philosophy — leaving us little but shallows in a waste of weary sand. We are obliged to them for showing wherein man agrees with the brutes, but we must have others to show us wherein man is above the brutes. It must be one of the highest offices of the realistic philosophy to expose the errors and supply the deficiencies of this school.

But it will be urged, that if philosophy is kept within such rigid fences it will lose much of its attractiveness, and metaphysical and dialectic youths will complain — as bitterly as the Indians do when they say they have no room for hunting in these enclosed fields where they must be contented to plough and sow. As the result, there will be no room for speculation such as was indulged in by Plato, by Leibniz and the higher German philosophers.

To this I reply that there will still be a rich possession left to philosophy to cultivate, and one as much more fertile and profitable—above mere guesses—as agriculture instead of hunting will turn out to be to the Indian. By imposing judicious restrictions we do not deny to philosophy any of its prerogatives; we merely prevent it from becoming an arena in which one system lives to fight against another. It will still be allowed to inquire into the opinions of the thinkers of all ages and countries, as Cudworth did in England and Hamilton did in Scotland, and as German scholars are still doing. Not only so, these opinions may be analyzed and criticized, always on the condition that the ultimate test of truth be the facts in our nature. Historical criticism will have a boundless field in determining what were the precise opinions of the eminent thinkers of antiquity, and in settling what truth there is in Plato's ideal theory, in Aristotle's analytic of thought, and in the Stoic and Epicurean discussions as to the relative places of virtue and pleasure. The gold will have to be gathered from the sand in the desert of the Middle Ages. Coming down to modern times it will have to settle what are the limits to the method of induction as expounded by Bacon, and to what fields the combined dogmatic and deductive methods of Descartes and Spinoza are to be confined. It will have to weed out all the idealism and sensationalism in Locke's *Essay*, and so explain the great truths regarding experience which he has expounded so as to keep them from issuing logically in Humism. It will have to take special pains to keep thinking youth from embracing the errors along with the truths of Kant. While standing up resolutely for *a priori* truths such as causation, it will show that these are not forms in the mind imposed on things but realties in the nature of things. It will have to acknowledge that there is such a process as evolution, but it will also prove that this cannot account for the origin or beneficent order of things. I am inclined to go a step farther, and allow full freedom to guesses, queries, speculations, theories, care being taken to represent them as mere hypotheses till they are established as facts by facts.

Is not the world open to our view as it was to that of our forefathers? I am sure that it is as full of wonders as it ever was. The physical investigator does not complain that those who lived in the past have drawn all its wealth from the universe. It is the very fact that so many real discoveries have been made that makes him expect more without limit and without end. The ground that has been so enriched with the deposited vegetation of the past will yield larger and richer vegetation and fruit in the future. I believe that there are as many unexplored regions in the mental as in the physical world. I am sure that all the laws and properties of mind have not yet been discovered. It has secrets alluring us to seek to discover them, and sure to reward us for the labor we devote to the search after them. If the modern cannot go so far and mount as high as the ancient it must be because his mental capacities are not so great, and this he will scarcely be prepared to admit. The world as we look upon it is as boundless as it ever was, and human nature is as full and fresh and inexhaustible as it was seen to be in ages past.

A new region has been opened to the modern. A keen interest within the last age has gathered round the relation of brain and nerves to the operations of the mind, or what is called physiological psychology. It is a difficult subject, but this only makes it more attractive to the adventurous explorer. It is full of the promise of discovery, and youth will rush into it as to a newly discovered mine. We know much now of the laws of the mind, we know something of the physiology of the brain—careful experiments are being performed by competent men in various countries. We seem to have come to a position at which we may unite the two lines of inquiry, and they will be found to throw light on each other. The physiologist in his department will insist on proceeding only in the method of observation; let the psychologist do the same. Let each require of the other that he restrain premature hypotheses. As the result, we shall have an immense accumulation of empirical facts, rising, according to Bacon's recommendation, to 'minor, middle, and major axioms', promising in the end to reach some grand laws which, while insisting that mind and matter are different substances, will realize the sublime conception of Leibniz by uniting them in a pre-established harmony.

They who start this realism are proclaiming a rebellion against all modern schools, *a posteriori* and *a priori*, and if they persevere and succeed are effecting a revolution. In doing so they are not overturning but settling fundamental truth on a surer foundation—as the Reformers in the sixteenth century did not destroy religion, but presented it in a purer form. Fertility will be produced by this new upturning of the soil.

This attempt, if it is noticed at all, will be assailed by the modern systems of Europe. The monarchies of the old world will look with doubt, perhaps with scorn, upon these republics of the new world which acknowledge no king. The Hegelians will not deign to look at us, because we do not proceed by dialectics and put the world into trinities. The materialists will represent us as following illusions, because we claim to be able by internal observation to discover high moral and spiritual truth. But in spite of all efforts to keep it down, realism, which is the obvious and the naturalistic philosophy, will ever, will again and again, come up and assert its claims. Meanwhile we keep our place; we mean to carry on and consolidate our work, and we may in the end secure attention and recognition. Acting on the Monroe principle, permitting no foreign interference, and allowing the old systems to fight their battles with each other, we hold our position and may come to command respect, as the United States have done, after being long contemned by European countries; and they may be induced to seek our established truths—as they do the corn and cattle reared in our virgin territory.

Ten
Charles Sanders Peirce (1839–1914)

Charles Sanders Peirce was born in Cambridge, Massachusetts in 1839; the son of Sarah Hunt Mills and Benjamin Peirce, a mathematics professor at Harvard and one of the founders of the Smithsonian Institution. Reading books on philosophy and conducting scientific experiments beyond his years, Peirce showed a genius for mathematics, logic, and science at an early age. In 1863, Peirce graduated *summa cum laude* from Harvard with a bachelor's degree in chemistry, after which he worked on several research projects in natural science. In 1878, Peirce published his first and only book, *Photometric Research*, based on his research at the Harvard Observatory. On account of this publication, and several smaller papers on mathematics and logic, Peirce was elected to both the American Academy of Sciences and the American Academy of Arts and Sciences in 1877.

As these events attest, Peirce was best known early in his career for his scientific and mathematical achievements. However, alongside these endeavors, Peirce also engaged in philosophical reflection. As early as 1860, Peirce planned to write a book outlining his philosophy of science and epistemology, and delivered draft chapters of this book to the Metaphysical Club at Harvard throughout the 1860s and 1870s. Although Peirce never completed his book, his lectures at the Metaphysical Club contributed to the creation of the philosophical school known today as American Pragmatism in two ways. First, Peirce turned a portion of his lectures into a series of six serial essays, entitled 'Illustrations of the Logic of Science', published in *Popular Science Monthly* (1877–1878). The key insight of these essays is that one did not need to make metaphysical investigations in order to achieve knowledge about concepts. Rather, put simply, one need only know 1) how they are used in speech and language, and 2) what consequences follow from using them in a true proposition. Second, Peirce's lectures also inspired William James's own formulation of pragmatism in the late 1890s and early 1900s.

Although Peirce and James shared much by way of philosophy, they were divided over the exact content of this new American school. Critically, according to Peirce, pragmatism provided a theory of meaning, whereas for James, it provided a theory of truth itself. For Peirce, this latter step was a bridge too far, since it seemed to redefine truth in a way alien to common use. Unfortunately for Peirce, by the 20th century James's brand of pragmatism had become well known, partly on account of James's comparatively lucid prose. Thus rebranding his philosophy 'pragmaticism', Peirce wrote a series of essays for *The Monist*, in which he sought to highlight the salient features of his philosophy and explicate what differentiates it from closely related positions. In the selections below, taken from this series, Peirce explains what makes one aspect of his philosophy, here branded 'Critical Common-sensism', different from the Scottish school of Common Sense.

Biographical Information: Paul Jerome Croce, *American National Biography Online*.

READING XV

Pragmat(ic)ism and Common Sense[1]

Pragmaticism was originally enounced[2] in the form of a maxim, as follows: Consider what effects that might *conceivably* have practical bearings you *conceive* the objects of your *conception* to have. Then, your *conception* of those effects is the whole of your *conception* of the object.

---

[1] [Extracted from Charles Sanders Peirce (1905) 'Issues of Pragmatism', *The Monist*, Volume XV, Number 4, pp. 481–499.]

[2] *Popular Science Monthly*, XII, 293; for Jan. 1878. An introductory article opens the volume, in the number for Nov., 1877.

I will restate this in other words, since ofttimes one can thus eliminate some unsuspected source of perplexity to the reader. This time it shall be in the indicative mood, as follows: The entire intellectual purport of any symbol consists in the total of all general modes of rational conduct which, conditionally upon all the possible different circumstances and desires, would ensue upon the acceptance of the symbol.

Two doctrines that were defended by the writer about nine years before the formulation of pragmaticism may be treated as consequences of the latter belief. One of these may be called Critical Common-sensism. It is a variety of the Philosophy of Common Sense, but is marked by six distinctive characters, which had better be enumerated at once.

Character I. Critical Common-sensism admits that there not only are indubitable propositions but also that there are indubitable inferences.

[...]

According to the maxim of Pragmaticism, to say that determination affects our occult nature is to say that it is capable of affecting deliberate conduct; and since we are conscious of what we do deliberately, we are conscious *habitualiter*[3] of whatever hides in the depths of our nature; and it is presumable (and *only* presumable, although curious instances are on record), that a sufficiently energetic effort of attention would bring it out. Consequently, to say that an operation of the mind is controlled is to say that it is, in a special sense, a conscious operation; and this no doubt is the consciousness of reasoning. For this theory requires that in reasoning we should be conscious, not only of the conclusion, and of our deliberate approval of it, but also of its being the result of the premiss from which it does result, and furthermore that the inference is one of a possible class of inferences which conform to one guiding principle. Now in fact we find a well-

---

[3] ['There are two ways in which a thing may be in the mind, — "*habitualiter*" [habitually] and "*actualiter*" [actually]. A notion is in the mind *actualiter* when it is actually conceived; it is in the mind *habitualiter* when it can directly produce a conception.' C.S. Peirce (1871) 'Fraser's The Works of George Berkeley', *North American Review* 1871, pp. 449-72.]

marked class of mental operations, clearly of a different nature from any others which do possess just these properties. They alone deserve to be called *reasonings;* and if the reasoner is conscious, even vaguely, of what his guiding principle is, his reasoning should be called a *logical argumentation*. There are, however, cases in which we are conscious that a belief has been determined by another given belief, but are not conscious that it proceeds on any general principle. Such is St. Augustine's *'cogito, ergo sum'*.[4] Such a process should be called, not a reasoning but an *acritical inference*. Again, there are cases in which one belief is determined by another, without our being at all aware of it. These should be called *associational suggestions of belief*.

Now the theory of Pragmaticism was originally based, as anybody will see who examines the papers of Nov. 1877 and Jan. 1878, upon a study of that experience of the phenomena of self-control which is common to all grown men and women; and it seems evident that to some extent, at least, it must always be so based. For it is to conceptions of deliberate conduct that Pragmaticism would trace the intellectual purport of symbols; and deliberate conduct is self-controlled conduct. Now control may itself be controlled, criticism itself subjected to criticism; and ideally there is no obvious definite limit to the sequence. But if one seriously inquires whether it is possible that a completed series of actual efforts should have been endless or beginningless, (I will spare the reader the discussion), I think he can only conclude that (with some vagueness as to what constitutes an effort) this must be regarded as impossible. It will be found to follow that there are, besides perceptual judgments, original (i.e. indubitable because uncriticized) beliefs of a general and recurrent kind, as well as indubitable acritical inferences.

It is important for the reader to satisfy himself that genuine doubt always has an external origin, usually from surprise; and that it is as impossible for a man to create in himself a genuine doubt by such an act of the will as would suffice to imagine the condition of a mathematical theorem,

---

[4] [*'Cogito, ergo sum'*, or 'I think, therefore I am', is actually from Descartes (1637) *Discourse on Method*, IV and (1644) *Principles of Philosophy*, I.7. In *De Civitate Dei* XI.xxvi Augustine writes '*Si enim fallor, sum*', or 'Even if I am mistaken, I am'.]

as it would be for him to give himself a genuine surprise by a simple act of the will.

I beg my reader also to believe that it would be impossible for me to put into these articles over two per cent of the pertinent thought which would be necessary in order to present the subject as I have worked it out. I can only make a small selection of what it seems most desirable to submit to his judgment. Not only must all steps be omitted which he can be expected to supply for himself, but unfortunately much more that may cause him difficulty.

Character II. I do not remember that any of the old Scotch philosophers ever undertook to draw up a complete list of the original beliefs, but they certainly thought it a feasible thing, and that the list would hold good for the minds of all men from Adam down. For in those days Adam was an undoubted historical personage. Before any waft of the air of evolution had reached those coasts how could they think otherwise? When I first wrote, we were hardly orientated in the new ideas, and my impression was that the indubitable propositions changed with a thinking man from year to year. I made some studies preparatory to an investigation of the rapidity of these changes, but the matter was neglected, and it has been only during the last two years that I have completed a provisional inquiry which shows me that the changes are so slight from generation to generation, though not imperceptible even in that short period, that I thought to own my adhesion, under inevitable modification, to the opinion of that subtle but well-balanced intellect, Thomas Reid, in the matter of Common Sense (as well as in regard to immediate perception, along with Kant).

Character III. The Scotch philosophers recognized that the original beliefs, and the same thing is at least equally true of the acritical inferences, were of the general nature of instincts. But little as we know about instincts, even now, we are much better acquainted with them than were the men of the eighteenth century. We know, for example, that they can be somewhat modified in a very short time. The great facts have always been known; such as that instinct seldom errs, while reason goes wrong nearly half the time, if not more frequently. But one thing the Scotch failed to recognize is that the original beliefs only remain indubitable in their application to affairs that resemble those of a primitive mode of life. It is, for example, quite open to reasonable doubt whether the motions of electrons are confined to three dimensions, although it is good methodeutic to presume that they are until some evidence to the contrary is forthcoming. On the other hand, as soon as we find that a belief shows symptoms of being instinctive, although it may seem to be dubitable, we must suspect that experiment would show that it is not really so; for in our artificial life, especially in that of a student, no mistake is more likely than that of taking a paper-doubt for the genuine metal. Take, for example, the belief in the criminality of incest. Biology will doubtless testify that the practice is unadvisable; but surely nothing that it has to say could warrant the intensity of our sentiment about it. When, however, we consider the thrill of horror which the idea excites in us, we find reason in that to consider it to be an instinct; and from that we may infer that if some rationalistic brother and sister were to marry, they would find that the conviction of horrible guilt could not be shaken off.

In contrast to this may be placed the belief that suicide is to be classed as murder. There are two pretty sure signs that this is not an instinctive belief. One is that it is substantially confined to the Christian world. The other is that when it comes to the point of actual self-debate, this belief seems to be completely expunged and ex-sponged from the mind. In reply to these powerful arguments, the main points urged are the authority of the fathers of the church and the undoubtedly intense instinctive clinging to life. The latter phenomenon is, however, entirely irrelevant. For though it is a wrench to part with life, which has its charms at the very worst, just as it is to part with a tooth, yet there is no *moral* element in it whatever. As to the Christian tradition, it may be explained by the circumstances of the early Church. For Christianity, the most terribly earnest and most intolerant of religions, — see *The Book of Revelations of St. John the Divine*, — and it remained so until diluted with civilization, — recognized no morality as worthy of an instant's consideration except Christian morality. Now the early Church had need of martyrs, i.e., witnesses, and if any man had done with life, it was abominable infidelity to leave it otherwise than as a witness to its power. This belief, then, should be set down as dubitable; and it will no sooner have been pronounced dubitable, than reason will stamp it as false.

The Scotch School appear to have no such distinction, concerning the limitations of indubitability and the consequent limitations of the jurisdiction of original belief.

Character IV. By all odds, the most distinctive character of the Critical Common-sensist, in contrast to the old Scotch philosopher, lies in his insistence that the acritically indubitable is invariably vague.

Logicians have been at fault in giving vagueness the go-by, so far as not even to analyze it. The present writer has done his best to work out the stechiology (or stoicheiology), critic, and methodeutic[5] of the subject, but can here only give a definition or two with some proposals respecting terminology.

Accurate writers have apparently made a distinction between the *definite* and the *determinate*. A subject is *determinate* in respect to any character which inheres in it or is (universally and affirmatively) predicated of it, as well as in respect to the negative of such character, these being the very same respect. In all other respects it is *indeterminate*. The *definite* shall be defined presently. A sign (under which designation I place every kind of thought, and not alone external signs,) that is in any respect objectively indeterminate (i.e. whose object is undetermined by the sign itself) is objectively *general* in so far as it extends to the interpreter the privilege of carrying its determination further. *Example:* 'Man *is* mortal.' To the question, What man? the reply is that the proposition explicitly leaves it to you to apply its assertion to what man or men you will. A sign that is objectively indeterminate in any respect is objectively *vague* in so far as it reserves further determination to be made in some other conceivable sign, or at least does not appoint the interpreter as its deputy in this office. *Example:* 'A man whom I could mention seems to be a little conceited.' The *suggestion* here is that the man in view is the person addressed; but the utterer does not authorize such an interpretation or *any* other application of what she says. She can still say, if she likes, that she does *not* mean the person addressed. Every utterance naturally leaves the

---

[5] [i.e. what constitutes the proper first principles, principles of logic, and method of enquiry.]

right of further exposition in the utterer; and therefore, in so far as a sign is indeterminate, it is vague, unless it is expressly or by a well-understood convention rendered general. Usually, an affirmative predication covers *generally* every essential character of the predicate, while a negative predication *vaguely* denies some essential character. In another sense, honest people, when not joking, intend to make the meaning of their words determinate, so that there shall be no latitude of interpretation at all. That is to say, the character of their meaning consists in the implications and non-implications of their words; and they intend to fix what is implied and what is not implied. They believe that they succeed in doing so, and if their chat is about the theory of numbers, perhaps they may. But the further their topics are from such préscis, or 'abstract', subjects, the less possibility is there of such precision of speech. In so far as the implication is not determinate, it is usually left vague; but there are cases where an unwillingness to dwell on disagreeable subjects causes the utterer to leave the determination of the implication to the interpreter; as if one says, 'That creature is filthy, in every sense of the term'.

Perhaps a more scientific pair of definitions would be that anything is *general* in so far as the principle of excluded middle does not apply to it and is *vague* in so far as the principle of contradiction does not apply to it. Thus, although it is true that 'Any proposition you please, *once you have determined its identity,* is either true or false'; yet *so long as it remains indeterminate and so without identity,* it need neither be true that any proposition you please is true, nor that any proposition you please is false. So likewise, while it is false that 'A proposition *whose identity I have determined* is both true and false', yet until it is determinate, it may be true that a proposition is true and that a proposition is false.

[...]

The purely formal conception that the three affections of terms, *determination, generality,* and *vagueness* form a group dividing a category of what Kant calls 'functions of judgment' will be passed by as unimportant by those who have yet to learn how important a part purely formal conceptions may play in philosophy. Without stopping to discuss this, it may be pointed out that the 'quantity' of propositions in logic, that is, the distribution of the *first* subject,[6] is either *singular* (that is, determinate, which renders it substantially negligible in formal logic), or *universal* (that is, general), or *particular* (as the mediaeval logicians say, that is, vague or *indefinite*). It is a curious fact that in the logic of relations it is the first and last quantifiers of a proposition that are of chief importance. To affirm of anything that it is a horse is to yield to it *every* essential character of a horse: to deny of anything that it is a horse is vaguely to refuse to it *some* one or more of those essential characters of the horse. There are, however, predicates that are unanalyzable in a given state of intelligence and experience. These are, therefore, determinately affirmed or denied. Thus, this same group of concepts reappears. Affirmation and denial are in themselves unaffected by these concepts, but it is to be remarked that there are cases in which we can have an apparently definite idea of a border line between affirmation and negation. Thus, a point of a surface may be in a region of that surface, or out of it, or on its boundary. This gives us an indirect and vague conception of an intermediary between affirmation and denial in general, and consequently of an intermediate, or nascent state, between determination and indetermination.

[...]

Character V. The Critical Common-sensist will be further distinguished from the old Scotch philosopher by the great value he attaches to doubt, provided only that it be the weighty and noble metal itself, and no counterfeit nor paper substitute. He is not content to ask himself whether he does doubt, but he invents a plan for attaining to doubt, elaborates it in detail, and then puts it into practice, although this may

---

[6] Thus returning to the writer's original nomenclature, in despite of *Monist* VII, 209, where an obviously defective argument was regarded as sufficient to determine a mere matter of terminology. But the Quality of propositions is there regarded from a point of view which seems extrinsic. I have not had time, however, to re-explore all the ramifications of this difficult question by the aid of existential graphs, and the statement in the text about the last quantifier may need modification.

involve a solid month of hard work; and it is only after having gone through such an examination that he will pronounce a belief to be indubitable. Moreover, he fully acknowledges that even then it may be that some of his indubitable beliefs may be proved false.

The Critical Common-sensist holds that there is less danger to heuretic science in believing too little than in believing too much. Yet for all that, the consequences to heuretics of believing too little may be no less than disaster.

Character VI. Critical Common-sensism may fairly lay claim to this title for two sorts of reasons; namely, that on the one hand it subjects four opinions to rigid criticism: its own; that of the Scotch school; that of those who would base logic or metaphysics on psychology or any other special science, the least tenable of all the philosophical opinions that have any vogue; and that of Kant; while on the other hand it has besides some claim to be called Critical from the fact that it is but a modification of Kantism. The present writer was a pure Kantist until he was forced by successive steps into Pragmaticism. The Kantist has only to abjure from the bottom of his heart the proposition that a thing-in-itself can, however indirectly, be conceived; and then correct the details of Kant's doctrine accordingly, and he will find himself to have become a Critical Common-sensist.

Index of Names

Adam, 176, 209
Adams, William, 127n
Addison, Joseph, 103, 104n
Alexander, Archibald, 5, 125–137
Alexander, John K., 56
Apelles of Kos, 74
Aratus, 16–17, 19–25
Aristotle, 80, 89, 160–161, 168, 193, 197, 199, 202

Babbage, Charles, 175
Bacon, Francis, 1, 3, 9, 13, 20, 91–92, 161, 169, 199, 202–203
Bain, Alexander, 187, 197, 199
Baker, Henry, 19n
Bayle, Pierre, 33
Beattie, James, 4
Bentley, Richard, 29
Berkeley, George, 29, 35, 78, 80, 193–194, 196, 207n
Bird, Rachel, 55
Bismarck, Otto von, 6, 197
Bolingbroke, Henry St. John, first Viscount, 69
Bonaparte, Napoleon, 6
Brahe, Tycho, 161
Broadie, Alexander, 8
Brougham, Henry, first Baron Brougham and Vaux, 175

Brown, John, 43
Brown, Thomas, 168, 170–171, 176, 200
Burner, Claude, 29
Butler, Joseph, 52, 170, 172, 174–175

Caesar, Gaius Julius, 69, 109
Calhoon, Robert M., 12
Campbell, Alexander, 5, 155–183
Campbell, Archibald, 48, 106
Campbell, George, 127n
Campbell, Thomas, 155
Channing, William Ellery, 5–6, 138–154
Channing, William, 138
Cicero, Marcus Tullius, 9, 21, 29, 38n, 52, 69, 83, 168
Cincinnatus, Lucius Quinctius, 24
Clarke, Samuel, 37, 38n, 47–48, 117n, 174
Coleridge, Samuel Taylor, 198
Columella, Lucius Junius Moderatus, 9, 21
Combe, George, 169–172, 175–176
Comte, Auguste, 199
Copernicus, Nicolaus, 161

Cousin, Victor, 198
Croce, Paul Jerome, 206
Cudworth, Ralph, 174, 202
Curius, (Manius Curius Dentatus), 24

D'Alembert, Jean le Rond, 174, 195
Descartes, René, 4, 8, 60, 67, 78, 89–90, 168, 186, 188, 199, 202, 208
Diderot, Denis, 174
Douglas, John, 127n

Eaton, W.W., 157n
Edwards, Jonathan, 35, 36n, 48, 117n, 187
Eliot, Charles W., 185
Ellery, William, 138
Emerson, Ralph Waldo, 139, 188
Epicurus, 160, 168, 202
Euridice, 104
Evander, 14, 20, 25–26

Fabius, (Quintus Fabius Maximus Verrucosus Cunctator), 24
Fechner, Gustav Theodor, 190
Ferguson, Adam, 1, 100n, 103
Ferri, Luigi, 187n
Fichte, Johan Gottlieb, 6, 194, 197
Fleishacker, Samuel, 8–9
François, Fenelon, 29, 103
Franklin, Benjamin, 11, 27, 186

Galilei, Galileo, 33, 161
Gall, Franz Joseph, 169, 170
Gilbert, Jeffrey, 86
Gioia, Flavio, 161
Gleig, George, 135n

Goethe, Johann Wolfgang von, 161, 198
Graham, William, 125–126
Grotius, Hugo, 174

Hall, Stanley, 190
Hamilton, William, 197, 202
Hartley, David, 78–79, 177n
Harvey, William, 33
Hegel, G.W.F., 6, 187, 197, 204
Helmoltz, Hermann von, 190, 197
Helvétius, Claude Adrien, 116, 117n, 120
Henry, Joseph, 186
Hobbes, Thomas, 29
Hodge, Charles, 126, 185
Hoeveler, David, 185
Homer, 14, 16
Howe, Daniel Walker, 139
Hume, David, 1–5, 8, 29, 48, 67, 71n, 78, 79n, 80–81, 90, 106, 127–133, 135–137, 189, 193, 196, 198–200
Hutcheson, Francis, 1–2, 34–35, 38n, 41–42, 47–48, 139, 168, 174
Hutchinson, John, 37

James, William, 8, 206
Jay, John, 138
Jefferson, Thomas, 2
Jesus Christ, (or Messiah), 14, 139
St. John, 210
Johnson, Rev. Samuel, 11
Johnson, Samuel, 179n
Juvenal, (Decimus Lunius Luvenalis), 178n

Kames, Henry Home, Lord, 1, 2, 38n, 85n, 116, 117n, 120
Kant, Immanuel, 6, 8, 185,

187, 189, 191, 193–194,
196–199, 202, 209, 212,
214
Kepler, Johannes, 84, 161
Kuklick, Bruce, 9

Lach, Edward L., 94
Leibniz, Gottfried, 177n,
119, 186, 188, 195, 198,
202–203
Lester, Hiram J., 156
Lewes, George Henry, 199
Locke, John, 1, 4, 13, 29, 42,
72n, 78–79, 81–84, 86,
117n, 168, 178n, 186–188,
193–194, 196–200, 202
Longfellow, Henry
Wadsworth, 139
Lotze, Rudolf Hermann,
190
Louis XVI, 3
St. Luke, 154n

Madison, James, 2
Mandeville, Bernard, 38n
St. Mark, 154n
St. Matthew, 154n
May, Henry F., 9
McCosh, James, 7, 184–204
Mill, John S., 187, 196, 199
Mills, Sarah Hunt, 205
Milton, John, 14, 76n, 103
Minucius, (Marcus
Minucius Felix), 24
Monroe, James, 204
Moorhead, James H., 126

Newton, Isaac, 1, 13, 60, 78,
92, 195
Noll, Mark A., 9, 35
Norton, David Fate, 8

Orpheus, 104
Ossian, (James
Macpherson), 107

Ovid, (Publius Ovidius
Naso), 9, 40n

Paine, Thomas, 12
St. Paul, 160, 165
Peirce, Charles Sanders, 8,
205–214
Peirce, Benjamin, 205
Plato, 26, 78, 80, 160, 168,
187–188, 195, 197, 202
Pope, Alexander, 14, 20n,
66n, 69, 106, 163n
Porter, Noah, 185
Porterfield, Thomas, 85n
Price, Richard, 174
Priestley, Joseph, 29, 78–79,
111–112, 116, 117n
Procrustes, 142
Puffendorf, Samuel von,
38n
Pythagoras, 99, 158–160

Racilia, 24
Reid, Thomas, 1, 3–5, 8, 11,
29–30, 32, 35, 56, 61n,
67n, 71n, 73n, 81, 85, 89n,
92n, 100n, 104, 115, 117n,
168, 170, 187, 198–199,
209
Ricalton, Thomas, 37
Robespierre, Maximilien
François Marie Isidore
de, 3
Rousseau, Jean-Jacques, 3
Rush, Benjamin, 1, 27–33,
35

Schelling, Friedrich
Wilhelm Joseph, 197
Schiller, Friedrich, 198
Schopenhauer, Arthur, 6
Seneca, Lucius Annaeus,
the Younger, 168
Shaftesbury, Anton Ashley
Cooper, third Earl of, 29,

38n, 39n, 43, 47, 52–53, 174
Shakespeare, William, 64
Sloan, Douglas, 9
Small, William, 2
Smith, William, 2, 11–26
Smith, Adam, 2–3, 8, 35, 48, 168
Smith, Samuel Stanhope, 4, 9, 11–12, 93–124
Sparks, Jared, 138
Spencer, Herbert, 187, 194, 197, 199, 201
Spinoza, Baruch, 188, 202
Spurzheim, Johann Gaspar, 169–170
Stewart, Dugald, 4, 5, 103, 106, 168–171, 176–178
Stirling, James Hutchison, 197
Stockton, Julia, 27
Stockton, Richard, 27
Stone, Barton W., 156
Stuart, Charles (Bonnie Prince Charlie), 34
Stuart, Charles, 157n
Sullivan, Robert B., 28

Tacitus, Gaius Cornelius, 10, 52n
Terenzio, Count Mamiani della Rovere, 187n
Themistocles, 69
Thomson, James, 104, 107n
Thomson, Benjamin, Count Rumford, 186
Timoleon, 24

Vince, Samuel, 127n
Virgil, (Publius Vergilius Maro), 10, 14, 104, 109, 171n
Voltaire, François-Marie Arouet de, 3, 174

Washington, George, 27, 56, 138
Watts, Isaac, 175
Wilson, James, 1, 28, 55–92
Wilson, Woodrow, 185
Wilson, John, 37
Witherspoon, Ann, 93
Witherspoon, John, 2, 4, 34–54, 93–94, 125–126, 185
Wollaston, William, 38n, 47n
Wolterstorff, Nicholas, 8
Wundt, Wilhelm Maximilian, 190

Young, Edward, 18n, 161n

Zeno, 168

www.ingramcontent.com/pod-product-compliance
Lightning Source LLC
Chambersburg PA
CBHW020946230426
43666CB00005B/198